LARGE
PRINT
EDITION

RANDOM
HOUSE

Another City, Not My Own

DOMINICK DUNNE

A NOVEL IN THE FORM OF A MEMOIR

Published by Random House Large Print
in association with Crown Publishers, Inc.
New York 1997

Portions of this book were previously published in *Vanity Fair.*

Copyright © 1997 by Dominick Dunne

All rights reserved under International and
Pan-American Copyright Conventions.
Published in the United States of America
by Random House Large Print
in association with Crown Publishers, Inc.,
New York, and simultaneously in Canada
by Random House of Canada Limited, Toronto.
Distributed by Random House, Inc., New York.

Library of Congress Cataloging-in-Publication Data

Dunne, Dominick.
Another city, not my own: a novel in the form of
a memoir / Dominick Dunne.
p.   cm.
ISBN 0-679-77448-3
1. Large type books.   I. Title.
[PS3554.U492A8   1997]
813'.54—dc21   97-11736
                                                          CIP

Random House Web Address:
http://www.randomhouse.com/
Printed in the United States of America
FIRST LARGE PRINT EDITION

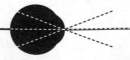

For Griffin, Alex, and Hannah
with love

Another City, Not My Own

1 Yes, yes, it's true. The conscientious reporter sets aside his personal views when reporting events and tries to emulate the detachment of a camera lens, all opinions held in harness, but the man with whom this narrative deals did not adhere to this dictum, at least when it came to the subject of murder, a subject with which he had had a personal involvement in the past. Consequently, his reportage was rebuked in certain quarters of both the journalistic and the legal professions, which was a matter of indifference to him. He never hesitated to speak up and point out, in print or on television, that his reportage on matters of murder was cheered by much larger numbers in other quarters. "Walk down Madison Avenue with me and see for yourself how often I am stopped by total strangers," he said in reply to a hate letter he received from an enraged man who wrote that he had vilified O.J. Simpson "through the pages of your pretentious magazine for two and a half years."

His name, as it appeared in print or when he was introduced on television, was Augustus Bailey, but he was known to his friends, and even to those who disliked him intensely, because of the way he had written about them, as Gus, or Gus Bailey. His name appeared frequently in the newspapers. His lectures were sold out. He was asked to deliver eulogies at important funerals or to introduce speakers at public events in hotel ballrooms. He knew the kind of people who said "We'll send our plane" when they invited him for weekends in distant places.

From the beginning, you have to understand this about Gus Bailey: He knew what was going to happen before it happened. His premonitions had far less to do with fact than with his inner feelings, on which he had learned to rely greatly in the last half dozen years of his life. He said over the telephone to his younger son, Zander, the son who was lost in a mountain-climbing mishap during the double murder trial of Orenthal James Simpson, "I don't know why, but I keep having this feeling that something untoward is going to happen to me."

Certainly, there are enough references to his obliteration in his journal in the months before he was found dead in the media room of his country house in Prud'homme, Connecticut, where he had been watching the miniseries of one of his novels, *A Season in Purgatory*. The book was about a rich young man who got away with murder because of the influence of his prominent and powerful father. Getting away with murder was a relentless theme of Gus Bailey's. He was pitiless in his journalistic and novelistic pursuit of those who did, as well as of those in the legal profession who created the false defenses that often set their clients free. That book, the miniseries of which he was watching, had brought Gus Bailey and the unsolved murder in Greenwich, Connecticut, which, to avoid a libel suit, he had renamed Scarborough Hill, a great deal of notoriety at the time of its publication, resulting in the reopening of the murder case by the police. Gus had fervently believed that the case remained unsolved because the police had been intimidated by the power and wealth of the killer's family, which extended all the way to the highest office in the land.

"It was exactly the same thing in the Woodward case," said Gus, who had written an earlier novel about a famous society shooting in the aristocratic Woodward family on Long Island in the fifties called *The Two Mrs. Grenvilles.* "The police were simply outdazzled by the grandeur of Elsie Woodward, whom I called Alice Grenville, and Ann Woodward got away with shooting her husband."

As always, when Gus's passions were involved in his writing, he ruffled feathers. Powerful families became upset with him. He created enemies.

"You seem to have annoyed a great many very important people," said Gillian Greenwood of the BBC, as a statement not a question, in the living room of Gus Bailey's New York penthouse, where she was interviewing him on camera for a documentary on his life called *The Trials of Augustus Bailey.*

Gus, who was used to being on camera, nodded agreement with her statement. "True," he replied.

"Do people ever dislike you, the way you write

3

about them?" asked Gillian, who was producing and directing the documentary.

"There seems to be a long line," answered Gus.

"Does that bother you?" she asked.

"It's an occupational hazard, I suppose," said Gus.

"Does it bother you?" Gillian repeated.

"Sometimes yes. It depends who, really. Do I care that a killer or a rapist dislikes me? Or the lawyers who get them acquitted? Of course not. Some of those people, like Leslie Abramson, I am proud to be disliked by."

"Yes, yes, Leslie Abramson," said Gillian. "She told us you weren't in her league when we interviewed her for this documentary."

Gus, who was a lapsed Catholic, looked heavenward as he replied, "Thank you, God, that I am not in Leslie Abramson's league."

"What happens when you meet these people you write about? You must run into some of them, the way you go out so much, and the circles you travel in."

"It does happen. It's not uncommon. Mostly, it's very civilized. Averted eyes, that sort of thing. A fashionable lady in New York, Mrs. de la Renta, turned her back on me at dinner one night and spoke not a word in my direction for the hour and a half we were sitting on gold chairs in Chessy Rayner's dining room. I rather enjoyed that. Sometimes it's not quite so civilized, and there have been a few minor skirmishes in public."

"That's what I want to hear about," said Gillian.

Gus laughed. "I seem to have annoyed a rather

4

select number of your countrymen when I wrote in *Vanity Fair* magazine that I believed the British aristocrat Lord Lucan, who murdered his children's nanny in the mistaken belief that she was his wife and then vanished off the face of the earth, was alive and well and being supported in exile by a group of very rich men who enjoyed the sport of harboring a killer from the law. Certain of those men were very annoyed with me."

"Oh, let me guess," said Gillian. "You annoyed the all-powerful James Goldsmith, and he's very litigious."

"Curiously enough, *not* Jimmy Goldsmith, who had every reason to be annoyed," said Gus. "He chose to treat the whole thing as a tremendous joke. 'Gus here thinks Lucky Lucan is hiding out at my place in Mexico,' he said one night at a party at Wendy Stark's in Hollywood, which we both attended, and everyone roared with laughter at such an absurdity."

"Who, then?" persisted Gillian.

"Selim Zilkha, a very rich Iraqi who used to live in London, had dinner with Lucky Lucan the night before the murder, which I wrote about. Now he lives in Bel Air. He made a public fuss about me at the opening night of *Sunset Boulevard* in Los Angeles, when he chastised one of his guests, the Countess of Dudley, who was visiting from London, for greeting me with a kiss on each cheek. He referred to me by a four-letter word beginning with *s* that I can't say on television."

5

"What happened?"

"The countess, who was no stranger to controversy herself, told off Zilkha in no uncertain terms," said Gus. "She said she'd kiss whomever she wanted to kiss and, furthermore, 'Gus Bailey is an old friend of many years.'"

"Tell me more."

"Another Lucan instance happened in your country," said Gus. "Another of the men I mentioned, John Aspinall, a rich guy who owned the gambling club above Annabel's where Lord Lucan was a shill, made a *terrible* fuss at a Rothschild dance in London. He wanted Evelyn to throw me out."

"Were you thrown out?"

"Of course not. The way I look at it is this: If Lucan is dead, as they all claim, why don't they just laugh me off as a quack? Why do I enrage them so?"

Gus always said that the reason he knew so many people was that he had gone out to dinner nearly every night of his adult life. He was a magnet for information. "People tell me things; they always have," said Gus in an interview he did for *Harper's Bazaar* when *A Season in Purgatory* was published. "People tell me things they tell no one else." There had been a time in an earlier career when he was thought to be an unserious person by people who mattered, because of his relentless pursuit of social life. In the overall scheme of things, as Gus came to realize, it was all part of the natural order; the earlier career in film and television had been merely a stepping-stone for the vocation that he was meant to have. It was only the hindsight of years that brought about this realization. He came to understand that the failure and shame with which that earlier career ended were a necessity for him to have experienced in order to fulfill his vocation.

He ran into great numbers of people on his nightly outings. The kind of people he knew, for the most part, were either the possessors of information or friends of the possessors of information. He had an inordinate knack for meeting up with the exact person who could put him in touch with someone who had the piece of the puzzle that he needed right at that moment.

During the several years when the von Bülow case was the most discussed scandal in New York society since the Woodward scandal years before, when Ann Woodward shot and killed her rich young husband as he emerged from the shower, everyone who ever knew Claus or Sunny von Bülow had something to tell Gus about one or the other of them, when he was covering the trial for *Vanity Fair* magazine. "Claus cut Sunny off from all her old friends, Gus," said the social figure Diego del Vayo when they were having lunch at Mortimer's in New York. "The last time I saw Sunny was at Peggy d'Uzes's funeral at St. James. We all wanted to talk to her. None of us had seen her, but Claus kept leading her to the limousine, away from us, so no one was able to speak to her, and as the car pulled away, she waved at me out the window, and our eyes met. She looked so sad. Poor Sunny."

"Newport's split right down the center, Gus, as to whether Claus did or didn't do it," said Kay Kay Somerset at a dinner given by the Countess Lisette de Ramel at her house on Bellevue Avenue. "Most everyone's on the children's side, of course, Ala and Alex, divine kids, but there're a few very powerful ladies who are strongly behind Claus. You simply can't invite Mrs. John Nicholas Brown and Mrs. John Slocum to the same dinners; that's how bitterly the town is divided."

"You know, Gus, if you're interested, I could arrange for you to meet the children of Sunny von Bülow, Ala and Alexander von Auersperg," said Freddie Eberstadt, one of Gus's oldest friends, as the two were chatting in a corner one night at the apartment of Chessy Rayner. "Isabel and I went to Sunny's wedding in Greenwich when she married Alfie von Auersperg. We've known Ala and Alexander all their lives, practically. They're fabulous young people, not at all these druggy spoiled rich kids that Claus and his lady friend, Mrs. Reynolds, are spreading stories about. They've never spoken to anyone in the media, but Pammie Woolworth—I'm sure you know Pammie, Barbara Hutton's cousin—Pammie's one of Sunny's very best friends, and she thinks Ala and Alexander will talk to you, because of Becky, and what happened to you and Peach."

"Gus, would you like to come to Newport and spend the night at Clarendon Court?" asked Prince Alexander von Auersperg, the son of Sunny von Bülow. "I'll show you the closet where we found the bag. You can see for yourself the bedroom where it all happened. Nothing has been moved or changed. It's just the way it was that night. Even Mummy's Christmas presents remain unopened."

"Hello, Gus, this is Andrea Reynolds. Claus and I were wondering if you could come to lunch this Sunday, when we're all back in New York from this ghastly Providence, Rhode Island. It's at one-fifteen. We'll sit down at two. There'll be about sixteen, depending on whether Ormolu and Fran will be in town. Nine Sixty Fifth. Yes, it's the same apartment where Claus and Sunny lived. Now, I have a bone to pick with you, Gus. It is *not* true what you wrote, that I am wearing Sunny's clothes and jewels."

"Come over for lunch today, Gus," said Mollie Wilmot when they ran into each other on the steps of St. Edward's Catholic Church in Palm Beach, Florida, after Sunday Mass. Mollie, who wintered in Palm Beach and summered in Saratoga, had gained a great deal of notoriety when a Russian tanker crashed into the seawall of her property on Ocean Boulevard. "Dimitri of Yugoslavia's coming, and a few others you know."

Gus was then in residence at the Brazilian Court Hotel, while covering the rape trial of William Kennedy Smith for *Vanity Fair.* "Sunday's a writing day for me, Mollie," he answered. "My first article on the trial is due tomorrow, so I'm just going to have lunch in the room at the hotel."

"I live right next door to the Kennedy compound on Ocean Boulevard," said Mollie.

"You do?"

"You're perfectly welcome to stand on a chair next to the wall by my swimming pool, where you can see the whole backyard, where the rape happened, or didn't happen, depending on which side you're on, and everyone in town knows what side *you're* on."

"That is irresistible," said Gus. "Of course I'll come. How much of the Kennedy family's there?"

"Willie's staying there, and all the sisters—Jean, Eunice, and Pat. Ethel comes from time to time," said Mollie. "You must know them, don't you, Gus?"

"I went to Ethel's wedding in Greenwich, when she married Bobby, and Peach and I used to live next to Pat in Santa Monica when she was married to Peter Lawford. I suppose that qualifies as knowing them," said Gus.

"I'd say."

"It would be mortifying if any of them saw me peeking over your wall, but I'll take the chance," said Gus.

"What happens when you see them in court?"

"We pretend we don't see one another."

"Oh, listen, Gus, is it true that Patty whatshername, the so-called rapee—"

"*Alleged* is the word, not *so-called,*" said Gus.

"Alleged. Is it true she called you at the Brazilian Court the other night after you'd gone to bed and wants you to interview her when the trial's over?"

"What time's lunch?"

"Say, Gus," said his friend Anne Siegal one night

during dinner at Mortimer's, just before he left town to cover the Menendez trial in California. "Herb and I have this limousine driver in Los Angeles whom we use every year when we stay at the Bel Air Hotel. Rufus. Can't remember his last name, but Herb will know. Not only is he wonderful, reliable, et cetera, et cetera, *but*—listen to this, Gus—he drove the Menendez brothers when they moved into the Bel Air Hotel a day or so after they murdered their parents. Apparently, those two orphans did quite a bit of partying and not too much grieving. Oh yes. Rufus will tell everything. He has some stories you wouldn't believe about that Dr. Oziel, their psychologist, when the three of them were in the backseat of the limo. Call Herb's office in the morning, and Sarah, Herb's secretary, will fax you a copy of Rufus's card."

"Say, Gus, I know this limousine driver in New Orleans who used to be a photographer in West Hollywood," said Herkie Saybrook during lunch at Herkie's club, the Knickerbocker, which Gus had called the Butterfield in *People Like Us.* "This guy, when he was still a photographer, took some, uh, not exactly nude, but semi-nude, not exactly gay, but semi-gay pictures of Erik Menendez before the murders, when he was still at Beverly Hills High and wanted to be a model. Apparently young Erik wasn't quite as innocent as his lawyer Leslie Abramson would have you believe. Would you like me to put you in touch with him, or him in touch with you?"

Gus always said yes to all the introductions that were offered to him.

2 When Gus was not living in a hotel room somewhere while covering a story for his magazine, he divided his time between a small penthouse that overlooked the East River in the Turtle Bay section of New York and a house in Prud'homme, Connecticut, situated on a cove off the Connecticut River. In New York, he was awakened each morning before six by the sound of the elevator man in his building dropping the four newspapers he always read outside his front door. A few minutes later, the boy from Manny Wolf's delivered his two containers of coffee and a breakfast roll, and he settled into his favorite chintz-slipcovered chair in the living room for an hour of uninterrupted newspaper reading, which he often said was his favorite time of the day. On June 13, 1994, he was riveted by the headlines in all the papers.

Nicole Brown Simpson, the former wife of the great football star Orenthal James Simpson, known to sports fans everywhere as O.J., had been found murdered in the patio of her condominium on Bundy Drive in Brentwood, California, along with a young man named Ronald Goldman, who had come to the condo to return a pair of glasses to Nicole Simpson that her mother had left behind earlier when the family dined at the restaurant where he was a waiter. Gus was mesmerized by the newspaper accounts and at seven turned on *Good Morning America* to watch the television accounts. A few hours later, calls started coming in from reporter friends in California with whom he had covered the Menendez trial.

"Did you ever know O.J., Gus?" asked Shoreen Maghame of *City News,* who had sat next to Gus during the Menendez trial.

"I didn't, no."

"I thought you knew everyone, Gus," said Shoreen.

"That's just a myth," said Gus. "I used to see him at the Daisy years ago, but I never knew him. The Daisy was a big nightclub in Beverly Hills for years. Peach and I were charter members."

"I was sure you'd known him."

"I was never big with the sports crowd when I lived out there," said Gus.

"Can you remember anything about him?"

"Not much. I remember him as being rather charismatic, a good-looking guy. People always stared at him and said, 'There's O.J.,' but I was more interested in looking at the movie stars than at the sports stars."

"The Daisy was where he met Nicole. She worked there," said Shoreen.

"Lucky for him he was in Chicago when it happened," said Gus.

The next night, Gus sat next to Fernanda Niven at Patricia Patterson's dinner party at Mortimer's. Mortimer's was a sleek watering hole on the fashionable Upper East Side of New York, which Gus had called Clarence's in his society novel *People Like Us,* the book that had so offended the social figure Annette de la Renta and Jerome R. Zipkin, whom Gus had portrayed as Loelia Manchester and Ezzie Fenwick. At the time of the turmoil that Gus's book had caused in New York society, Fernanda Niven had publicly stuck up for him when he was being denounced by Zipkin and others.

By the night of Pat Patterson's dinner, O.J. Simpson had returned from Chicago, had been briefly handcuffed on the grounds of his Brentwood estate, and had hired the famed defense attorney Howard Weitzman, who had come to national attention several years earlier when, against all odds, he won an acquittal for the flamboyant automobile designer John DeLorean on what seemed to be irrefutable drug charges.

"Gus, I've been dying to tell you this. I sat next to O.J. at dinner just a week or so before the murders," said Fernanda Niven.

"I knew this was going to be a good seat as soon as I looked at your place card," said Gus. "Tell me everything."

"You know Louis Marx, don't you? Louis and Noonie Marx? O.J. was on the board of Louis's company, the Forschner Group, which imports the Swiss Army Knife, among other things. O.J. and

Louis are great golfing buddies, or were until this. Louis says there's no way that O.J. is guilty of these crimes. Anyway, after the board meeting, which had taken place that day, Louis and Noonie had a party at their apartment up on Fifth, and O.J. was there, and I sat next to him. He *couldn't* have been nicer, and of course he was devastatingly attractive. He talked about Nicole. He said how upset he was that they couldn't work out their problems, but it didn't mean so much to me then as it does now."

"Interesting," said Gus. "Keep going. I'm riveted."

"*Then* let me tell you what happened. On his other side was this heavenly little blond girl who was a friend of one of Louis and Noonie's daughters—I can't remember her name—and O.J. said to me, 'I'm going to hit on her,' or something like that, and it sounded innocent and cute. But he started coming on to her. I mean, she was only just past being a kid, and she didn't know how to act, and he got very raunchy in his talk. He rolled up his tie over and over until it got up to the knot at his throat, and he dropped it, and as it unrolled, he said to her, 'That's what my tongue's going to do to you.'"

"That's class," said Gus.

"The poor thing left the table and never returned, and I can't say I blame her. I mean, it was unacceptable, what he did, but no one said anything, until later, after he was gone. You know how it is with stars."

"I never realized that O.J. Simpson was as famous as he seems to be," said Gus.

Gus had a friend named Lucianne Goldberg, whom he referred to as his "telephone friend." They saw each other only a couple of times a year, but they talked every day, usually after they had read all the morning papers, and hashed over the news. Like Gus, Lucianne was a newspaper junkie. Like Gus, she had contacts in high places. Like Gus, she was a font of daily information. They had met in Providence, Rhode Island, at the second of Claus von Bülow's trials for the attempted murder of his wife, Sunny. They saw things the same way, although she had considerably less tolerance for President Clinton than Gus did. They both thought Claus von Bülow was guilty. They both thought William Kennedy Smith was guilty. They both knew the Menendez brothers were guilty.

"What do you think?" asked Gus, after the murders of Nicole Brown Simpson and Ronald Goldman.

"He did it," said Lucianne.

"Fuckin' A," replied Gus.

The next day, Gus was having lunch at the Four Seasons with Betty Prashker, his book editor, to discuss the progress he was making on his novel about the trial of the Menendez brothers, *The Sins of the Sons.*

"I've brought along the chapter where one of the aunts of the Menendez brothers met with me in secret one Sunday night at Zev Braun's house high up in the hills of Beverly Hills to tell me the name of the book the boys read in jail, where they got all the information about sexual abuse they said their father did to them," said Gus. "It's an interesting scene, I think."

"That sounds good," said Betty.

"All that crap that Erik said about his father sticking tacks in his ass for sexual gratification, it's all in this book they read," said Gus.

"I wonder how they got that book in jail," said Betty.

"They probably had it mailed from Book Soup on Sunset Boulevard," replied Gus.

Just then, Louise Grunwald, a prominent figure in New York society who was married to Henry Grunwald, the former editor of *Time,* stopped by Gus's table on her way out of the restaurant. Gus introduced her to Betty.

"There's something I've got to tell you, Gus," said Louise. "You know Louis Marx, don't you? Louis and Noonie?"

"Kind of, not really," said Gus. "They're friends of Fernanda Niven's. Friends of O.J.'s, too, I gather."

"You knew that O.J. was on the board of Louis's company, the Forschner Group?" asked Louise.

"I just heard that from Fernanda last night," said Gus.

"And you know that the Forschner Group makes Swiss Army Knives?"

"I do."

"Did you know that at the end of the meeting all the board members could take any of the products they wanted to?"

"No."

"And do you know what O.J. took?"

"No, but I want to know."

"He took a bagful of knives," said Louise.

"My God," said Gus. "This is fascinating."

Gus felt the quickening beat of his heart. It was a feeling he sometimes experienced when he heard the sort of story that aroused his interest. But he had a book to write about the Menendez brothers and shook the thought from his head.

That night at dinner at Elaine's, the famed restaurant on the Upper East Side of Manhattan that was a gathering place for the literary set, Gus repeated the stories he had just heard about O.J. Simpson. He rolled his tie up to the knot and let it drop the way Fernanda Niven told him Simpson had done to the pretty young girl at the party and repeated his line, "That's what my tongue's going to do to you." He told his companions about the Forschner Group and the bag of knives.

"But there's more," said Elaine Kaufman, the proprietor, who had come to sit at Gus's table. "I heard that when O.J. left the board meeting in Shelton, Connecticut, where the firm is, he was picked up by a chauffeur who drove him out to Long Island to play golf with some guy in the garment industry."

"Apparently he's an avid golfer," said Gus. "Go on."

"The chauffeur says that O.J. waved one of the knives around in the back of the limousine and said, 'You could hurt someone with this. You could even kill someone with this.'"

"That would be a good scene in a book, wouldn't it?" said Gus. "The football star. The chauffeur. The bag of knives. It's called establishing the murder weapon early on in the story. Where did you hear all this, Elaine?"

"You hear things here, Gus," said Elaine.

Two days later, Gus flew to Las Vegas, where he was to accept an award from the American Academy of Achievement. He was sitting in his suite at the Mirage Hotel in Las Vegas, halfway dressed for the evening ahead. His dinner shirt and trousers were on. His blue enamel cuff links and studs were in place. His black tie was hanging untied around his neck. His just-pressed dinner jacket was still on the valet's hanger. He was shortly to receive a golden plate from the Academy, along with an impressive array of Americans distinguished in the fields of the arts, business, public affairs, and science, but he was mesmerized by what he was watching on television, and it took precedence over the award he was about to receive.

Sitting in another chair in the room, equally engrossed, was June Anderson, the opera star, whom he had sat next to on the plane from New York that day. Gus rarely got into conversations with people he sat next to on planes, but she had been frightened during a long period of turbulence, and he had spoken to her to distract her from her fear. They discovered they were both heading for the Mirage Hotel and the American Academy of Achievement awards ceremony.

"What is this award we're getting?" asked June Anderson.

"I haven't a clue. It's very mysterious," said Gus.

From then on until they landed in Las Vegas, they talked without stopping. He told her he was writing a book on the Menendez case. She told him she was going to sing Desdemona to Plácido Domingo's Otello at the Los Angeles Music Center at the opening of the next season.

"Will you be in L.A. then?" she asked.

"Oh God, no," replied Gus. "L.A.'s always been a complicated place for me to be. Good times. Bad times. The bad times were badder than the good times were good, if you get the drift. These days, I keep my distance from the place."

The front pages of the *New York Times*, the *New York Daily News*, and the *New York Post*, all of which Gus was holding in his lap, were full of the news of the murders in Brentwood.

"Don't you think it's strange that Nicole was laid out in an open casket at the wake, considering that she was nearly beheaded?" asked Gus, pointing to a picture in the *Post*. "The head was supposed to be hanging on by a piece of skin."

June shuddered. "I'm sure they put her in a high-necked blouse," she said.

"Well, I should hope *so*," said Gus.

He kept looking at the pictures of the wake. "Look at all these young, blond, pretty women; they're all wearing very short black dresses and very big dark glasses," said Gus. "They look like actresses going to a premiere and having their pictures taken, instead of a wake. Turn this way. Turn that way. They're showing Jackie Kennedy–type stoic grief on their faces, just the right amount, and turning for their best angle to the photographers. I'm sure they're saying things like 'I loved Nicole. She was my best friend.'" They laughed. "Now look at this one. What do we think about her? Is she Polynesian, maybe? Something exotic."

The woman Gus was pointing to in the newspaper was called Faye Resnick. She was just out of a drug rehab—for problems with cocaine—for the funeral. She had talked with Nicole on the telephone shortly before the murder. Nicole had said to Faye on many occasions, as she had to almost everyone she knew, "O. J.'s going to kill me, and he's going to get away with it because he's O. J. Simpson."

June pointed to a photograph of O. J. Simpson at the wake.

"I wonder what was going through that man's mind when he looked at Nicole lying in the casket," she said.

"'I won, you fucking bitch,'" said Gus.

"Gus!" said June. There was shock in her voice.

"I know, that sounds awful, doesn't it? But all the same, it's the thought that went through my mind, and you can't censor your thoughts," said Gus. "I happen to know a great deal about men who beat women, and I'll bet you any amount of money that is going to turn out to be the case here, you wait and see. Guys like that want to be the one to do the leaving in a relationship. Guys like that can't handle being left. Even if they don't want her anymore, they don't want anyone else to have her."

"Whatever happened to 'innocent until proven guilty'?" asked June.

"That sounds good in court, but it has nothing to do with what your initial instinct is. I'm willing to have my mind changed, but I bet I turn out to be right. I have an instinct about these things."

What engrossed Gus so completely on the television set in his suite at the Mirage Hotel was a freeway chase going on in Los Angeles at that very moment. A. C. Cowlings was driving his friend O.J. Simpson, the former football star now wanted by the Los Angeles Police Department for the double murders of his former wife and her friend, in the direction of Mexico, after Simpson had failed to turn himself over to the authorities, in a deal arranged by his lawyer, Robert Shapiro. Gus, enthralled, moved off the chair and onto the floor and walked on his knees to be closer to the screen. His mouth was hanging open in shock at what he was watching. A man in a white Bronco with a gun held to his head. On the lam from two murders. People on the side of the freeway holding placards that said GO, JUICE, GO, cheering on a fugitive.

He turned to June Anderson and said for the first time words he would repeat in various ways over and over again in the year that followed: "Dear God, what is happening to us in our country when people cheer for a man to get away, to beat the law, to escape, when he's wanted by the police for double murder?"

"We better go down, Gus. The dinner will be starting," said June Anderson, who was dressed and ready to go. She rose from her seat and picked up her gold-and-diamond minaudière and a long chiffon scarf the same color as her dress. She threw the scarf around her neck with an operatic gesture that was not lost on Gus, who liked people who could carry off grand gestures, despite his total concentration on the television set.

"You go ahead, June. I have to see this. Tell them I'll be down shortly," replied Gus, not taking his eyes off the screen. "I want to see Al Cowlings drive the white Bronco through the gates at the house on Rockingham and let O.J. out."

"It'll be on the news later," said June.

"I want to watch it live," he said. "I want to see it happen while it's happening. I'm having the same feeling I had when I watched Jack Ruby shoot Lee Harvey Oswald live on-camera after Jack Kennedy was assassinated."

When Gus was tying his black tie in the mirrored bathroom, he looked himself squarely in the eye and knew with total certainty that fate would take him back to Los Angeles, a city he had once said he hoped never to return to again. It was there that Peach had asked him for a divorce. It was there he had had his descent into failure and oblivion. It was there that Becky had been strangled by Lefty Flynn. It was there that Lefty Flynn had received a slap on the wrist as punishment for the murder and was now out and about in a new life, as if he had atoned.

Whenever Gus was interviewed, either in print or on television, about a new book or a new article he had written, he was invariably asked about Becky's murder. He understood that interviewers always saved their most personal questions for last, and he could pinpoint when the time was nigh for the questions to be asked.

"What happened to that guy?" the interviewer would usually ask, meaning Lefty Flynn, the killer.

And Gus usually answered, "I don't have any idea where he is, and I don't want to know. For a while, after he was released, I hired a private investigator named Anthony Pellicano to follow him, but I stopped that. I didn't want to live a life of revenge. I believe in ultimate justice. I believe that life will take care of what the courts don't succeed in doing."

He took the elevator down to the ballroom floor for the cocktail party that preceded the dinner and awards ceremony. He was the last of the recipients to enter the room. His mind was still on the bewildering

24

scene he had just watched on television upstairs. Academy staff members, nervous because of his lateness, rushed to greet him and pin on his name tag. The cocktail party was well under way; there were indications that it was time to begin the move to the ballroom for the dinner and speeches. As Gus looked around at the others, he realized he knew most of the Hollywood and media people who were also being honored.

Leslie Stahl of *60 Minutes* greeted Gus by saying, "Did you watch? This story's right up your alley, Gus." Gus didn't have to say, "What story?" The freeway chase was already the main topic of conversation. Many of the Hollywood people knew O.J. Simpson. Whoopi Goldberg said to Gus when he kissed her on the cheek in greeting, "Gus, this is awful about O.J. I can't stop thinking about it." She shook her head in sadness. Harrison Ford, who before he became a star had once done construction work on the house that Gus's brother Malachy and his wife, Edwina, rebuilt in Malibu, said he knew Simpson. "I mean, I met him a couple of times, at closed-circuit games and boxing matches, stuff like that. I didn't really know him." Robert De Niro and Francis Ford Coppola were telling stories about O.J. Simpson. Michael Eisner, the C.E.O. of Disney, said, "O.J. just did a television pilot called *Frogman* for NBC. I wonder what's going to happen to that now." Eisner had once been unhappy with Gus for writing that he shook hands with people he was being introduced to without bothering to look at them, but that night they shook hands and all was forgiven, as they exchanged information about the freeway chase. Steve Wynn, who owned the Mirage Hotel and was himself a past recipient of the golden plate, said, "Yeah, I know O.J. I can tell you about O.J."

"Hi, Augustus, I'm Sam Lefrak." Sam Lefrak, the New York real-estate tycoon, flew to the American Academy of Achievement awards every year, wherever it was held. "We were in Jackson Hole last year, and we're going to be in Colonial Williamsburg next year. I hope you'll come back. Barry Diller over there got his golden plate five years ago, and he comes back every year. We're glad you could come, Augustus. My wife's a big fan of yours. She reads all your books. We really enjoyed your articles on the Menendez case. My wife didn't believe that sexual-abuse stuff for a minute, and you didn't either, did you? What we want to know is, Edith and I, will you be writing about the O.J. Simpson case? Wasn't that freeway chase the damnedest thing you ever saw? We also wanted to offer you a ride back to New York on our jet. We have a good chef on board. Oh, Kary, come over here a minute. Gus, I want you to meet Dr. Kary Mullis, another of the honorees. Kary's a leading authority on DNA. You know about DNA, don't you? Better than fingerprints. *And* he received the Nobel Prize for science."

Gus and Mullis shook hands. Dr. Kary Mullis didn't look like scientists usually look. He was handsome, deeply tanned, lived on the beach, and talked about surfing, which was his passion. There was about him a sense of the stardom that accompanies fame. Fame was a subject that fascinated Gus. That night, Gus did not know that he and Dr. Mullis would meet up again at the Simpson trial in Los Angeles, where Mullis would be an expert DNA witness for the defense.

"Fame is at the root of this whole story," said Gus. "I'm talking about celebrity type of fame. It fascinates people."

3

Since the murders of Nicole Brown Simpson and Ronald Goldman, the name of the famed lawyer F. Lee Bailey was very much in the news again, after having been dormant for some time. The lead attorney for O.J. Simpson, Robert Shapiro, who was gaining in national name recognition every day, had brought Bailey on as part of his defense team. No one could say that Shapiro's choices for his team were not of the highest caliber. Even before the freeway chase, Shapiro had brought Dr. Michael Baden, the former chief medical examiner of New York City, and Dr. Henry Lee, the foremost forensic scientist in the United States, onto his team.

Gus's friend Karen Lerner, a television and film executive, said to him one night at dinner, "You'll never guess who I'm having dinner with tomorrow. F. Lee Bailey!"

"I didn't know you knew F. Lee Bailey," said Gus.

"I haven't seen him in a long time, and he called me up and said he was going to be in town."

"He's flying high these days," said Gus. "O.J.'s put him back in the news again."

"He's got some Mafia client who's up on a big drug charge. I don't know the details," said Karen.

"Where's he taking you to dinner?" asked Gus.

"Lespinasse, in the St. Regis. It's free. Lee's client is putting him up at the St. Regis. Everything's free for him, as long as it's in the St. Regis."

They both laughed. They were old friends who had known each other for years.

"Now listen, honey," said Gus, warming up.

"You don't even have to ask, Gus," said Karen, anticipating what he was going to say. "I'll ask him to meet you. I'm sure he'll want to meet you, too."

"Thanks, Karen."

"Send me over the articles you wrote in *Vanity Fair* about the Menendez case, so I can show them to Lee before you meet."

A few days before he left for Los Angeles, Gus Bailey took F. Lee Bailey to "21" for dinner. Bailey, who was best known as the defender of Dr. Sam Sheppard and the Boston Strangler, was in town from Palm Beach, where he lived, for meetings with a client of his. Walter Weis, the maître d' at "21" for forty years, made a tremendous fuss over the lawyer and the writer as he led them to the corner table to the left, considered the best in the house, which, he informed them, had just been vacated by the ambassador to France, Pamela Harriman, and the business tycoon Linda Wachner. People at banquettes and other tables turned to look at F. Lee Bailey. His new association with O. J. Simpson had increased his celebrity. Bailey, in turn, seemed pleased with the attention he was receiving. It was the first time that Gus saw the cat-that-ate-the-canary expression on his face. The two men quickly established that, although they shared the same last name, there was no family connection between them.

"We do share something in common, though," said Bailey.

"What's that?" asked Gus.

"Neither one of us seems to like Leslie Abramson very much."

Gus laughed. He was pleased that Bailey had taken the time to read his articles on the Menendez case.

"Do you know Leslie?" asked Gus.

"About as much as I want to. She contacted O.J.'s mother, Eunice Simpson, and tried to take the case away from us. She told Eunice we had the wrong defense and she guaranteed that she could get him an acquittal. Eunice called Shapiro and told him, and that was the end of it."

They ordered dinner. They chatted amiably. They talked about the William Kennedy Smith trial in Palm Beach. Bailey had done television commentary on the trial for Court TV, as Gus had for *Good Morning America,* but they had not met there.

"Moira Lasch was no match for Roy Black," said Bailey. Lasch had been the prosecutor and Black the defense attorney at the trial.

"The prosecution was pathetic," agreed Gus. "Do you know yet what kind of defense you're going to come up with at the Simpson trial?"

"In the first place, O.J. Simpson is innocent," said Bailey with firmness. "He didn't do it. The police arrested the wrong guy. Talk about a rush to judgment! It is simply not possible in the time frame that he could have done it."

Gus remained noncommittal. "Who, then?" he asked.

"Very simple. It's not nice to speak ill of the dead, but the truth is that O.J.'s wife was deep into drugs, and she was talking too much about her sources. She was killed by a Colombian drug gang. It was a hit."

"I feel like you're talking to me as if I were a juror, and you have a very persuasive manner, but really, you can't think anybody's going to fall for that Colombian-drug-gang stuff," said Gus.

"It's the truth. It's the absolute truth," replied Bailey sharply, his tone indicating a certain dislike that his version of the murders was being doubted. "Her slashed voice box is the clue. When people talk too much in the drug trade, that's how they end up. Those guys cut her voice box."

Gus knew when not to persevere, and he went on to other things. "You've known Shapiro for some time, haven't you? I think I read that."

"Yeah, a long time. I'm godfather to one of his kids."

"He represented you on a drunk-driving charge in San Francisco, didn't he?"

"An acquittal."

"Wasn't it supposed to be the longest drunk-driving trial in the American court system?" asked Gus.

"Eleven days. Some cop tried to set me up because I'm famous, but he got his. Do you know Shapiro?"

"No. I never met him, but I was in the courtroom during the Cotton Club murder case when he represented Bob Evans, who used to be the head of Paramount, and who produced the movie *The Cotton Club*," replied Gus. "When I was still in the picture business, I produced an Elizabeth Taylor film for Evans. It was a flop, my swan song in show business."

Evans's onetime partner on *The Cotton Club* was a controversial fellow named Roy Radin, who had been murdered gangland-style by the two hired guns who were on trial.

"Evans took the Fifth at the trial, with Shapiro standing next to him. That was the first time I ever saw Shapiro. I have a deep prejudice against people who take the Fifth."

"They're great friends, Shapiro and Evans," said F. Lee Bailey. "I just went to a party out there in Beverly Hills that Evans gave in his pool house for Shapiro. Warren Beatty, Jack Nicholson, you name 'em, they were all there."

"I know Shapiro did the plea bargain for Christian Brando, Marlon's son, after he killed his half sister Cheyenne's boyfriend, and I know also that he was the first lawyer the Menendez brothers had, before Leslie Abramson, but I've never met him."

Bailey smiled and shook his head. "Shapiro asked me to come aboard with him on the Menendez case, but I said no way, I wouldn't touch that one with a ten-foot pole. I always knew those two little shits were as guilty as hell. So did Bob, that's why he quit the case."

"You think the Menendez brothers are guilty, but you don't think O.J. Simpson's guilty?" asked Gus.

Bailey shrugged. "I *know* he's not."

"You ought to tell Shapiro, if he's your friend, that he should stop signing autographs and waving to the crowds, like he's Brad Pitt going to a premiere. He's acting as if he had won the case, and the trial hasn't even started yet."

Bailey smiled. "Let me tell you about Bob, Gus," he said. "He's a crackerjack lawyer, but he's never *really* made it into the big time until now. He's always been near the limelight but never in it, and that's what he's always wanted. Now he's up there. He's as big as me, Dershowitz, Roy Black, Gerry Spence, Tom Puccio, any of them."

"I know Roy Black and Tom Puccio," said Gus, "and neither one of them would wave to the crowds and sign autographs. It's called class. You've either got it or you haven't got it."

Bailey smiled. "Bob'll calm down when he gets used to being in the spotlight. Fame is a heady experience at first."

When they were parting in the lobby of "21," Gus said to Bailey, "I'm sure it's no surprise to you to know that I believe O.J. *is* guilty of the murders."

33

"Yeah, I kinda figured that out myself, Gus," said Bailey wryly, and they both laughed.

"People can have different opinions and still be friendly to each other," said Gus.

"Absolutely," answered Bailey.

"Karen told me you'll probably be doing the cross-examination of Detective Mark Fuhrman?"

"Oh, I hope so," replied Bailey in a tone of voice that suggested he was salivating in anticipation. "Any lawyer in his right mind who would not be looking forward to cross-examining Mark Fuhrman is an idiot."

His eyes looked off for a second, as if visualizing the scene in the courtroom on national television between him and Detective Mark Fuhrman, who had found the famous bloody leather glove on the grounds of Simpson's estate, which matched the leather glove at the scene of the crime. Since *The New Yorker* had published an article revealing troubling information about the detective's past, a word-of-mouth campaign was underway to establish Detective Fuhrman as a racist cop, who had moved the glove from Bundy to Rockingham in order to frame O.J. Simpson.

In his journal the following morning, Gus wrote: "Interesting evening with F. Lee Bailey. He *almost* had me believing he thought O. J. didn't do it. Watching him visualize the cross-examination of Mark Fuhrman, I think he saw what ecstasy was for him. Why do I think that by the end of the trial we won't be speaking?"

4 "You really ought to get to know Gil Garcetti before the Simpson trial starts," said Suzanne Childs, the Los Angeles district attorney's media-relations adviser, when she called Gus at his house in Prud'homme, Connecticut, a few weeks before he was to leave for Los Angeles. He was at the time working on his novel about the Menendez brothers, called *The Sins of the Sons,* in which he had created a main character named Valerie Sabbath, who was based on the defense attorney Leslie Abramson, about whom he had written critically in his magazine pieces during the trial. "Gil's going to be in New York next week, and I wonder if we could arrange something."

"I'd like to know Gil," said Gus. "I wanted to meet him during the Menendez trial, but he only came to court a couple of times and stayed very briefly."

"It's time the two of you met," said Suzanne.

"It just happens that I'm going to be at the apartment in New York all next week. Give me a date."

"He's only got breakfast Wednesday or dinner Friday open on the calendar I'm looking at," said Suzanne.

"Friday's out," replied Gus, who never stayed in

the city on weekends. "I will have gone back to the country, but Wednesday breakfast is fine."

"Now, the problem is where. He'll be staying at a hotel called the Wales, way up on Madison Avenue somewhere, in the nineties, I think—I never heard of it before—and right after breakfast he has to be at the *New York Times* on West Forty-third Street for an interview with the staff before the trial starts. Can you think of anywhere between those two places? Preferably, he doesn't want to be anywhere where he's going to be recognized. He's been on TV so much since the freeway chase and the arrest and everything. Wherever he goes, people are always yelling questions at him about the case."

"It's called the problem of instant fame," said Gus.

"I never saw anything like it," said Suzanne. "You're the New Yorker. Think of something."

"I have the perfect solution. I belong to this stuffy men's club at Sixty-ninth Street and Park Avenue," said Gus. "We could meet there. I can assure you, just as I can assure you that today is Monday, that not one member who happens to be having breakfast there next Wednesday is going to know who the hell Gil Garcetti is, much less yell any questions at him or ask for his autograph."

"Can't wait, Gus. See you Wednesday."

The three of them met on the Wednesday morning at Gus's club in New York. "This is sort of embarrass-

36

ing, Gil, but you can't bring your briefcase into the dining room. You'll have to leave it here in the cloakroom. Club rules. No business is ever done in a gentlemen's club, that kind of stuff," said Gus in an apologetic tone. He led them up the marble stairway to the elevator on the main floor, which they entered and ascended to the third. He walked on ahead of Gil and Suzanne.

"Beautiful library," said Suzanne, stopping to look in at the huge paneled room with its thousands of books in shelves up to the double-height ceiling and its well-worn green leather chairs, on which several members were reading the *New York Times.*

"They have all of my brother Malachy's books, but only one of mine," said Gus as they entered the dining room. "That's always sort of pissed me off. Good morning, Ramon. Do you think we could have that table way over in the corner, away from everybody?"

"What sort of people belong here?" asked Gil.

"Look around you. It's pretty much of an inbred fraternity of WASPs, like in a Louis Auchincloss novel. I've never quite understood what I was doing here; my family were the rich micks in a WASP town," said Gus. "When I was asked to join, I was put up by the then ambassador to France and seconded by someone equally swell, and then I was blackballed. It takes only one member to blackball you, and no explanations have to be given. They never tell you who blackballs you, but I'm not an investigative reporter for nothing. It didn't take me long to discover it was Claus von Bülow, about whom I had had much to say at the time of his trial for the attempted murder of his wife."

"Fascinating, Gus," said Suzanne. "What happened?"

"I wrote a letter to the president of this club and said that if I had known Claus von Bülow was a member, I would never have allowed my name to be put up for membership. I also said that I continued to believe he was guilty of the crime of which he had been acquitted."

"What happened?"

"For the first time in the history of the club, they overruled a blackball. I was in, and a short time later Claus resigned," said Gus. "I saw him here once before he resigned. We passed on those marble stairs. I could literally feel his hatred as we passed."

"Does that sort of thing happen often?" asked Suzanne.

"My work is constantly overlapping into my life," said Gus. "I'm not really a club type, but it's nice to have, like now, when I can have breakfast in peace with the district attorney of the city of Los Angeles without getting mobbed by the unruly hordes."

Gil and Suzanne laughed. They ordered: juice, coffee, eggs, bacon. Suzanne had French toast. Before they got around to talking about O.J. Simpson, they talked about the Menendez verdict.

"The two hung juries of the first Menendez trial have to be considered a victory for Leslie Abramson," said Garcetti.

"Don't you think it's odd, though, that none of the other three defense attorneys from her team is going to join her for the second trial?" asked Gus.

"There's no Menendez money left, apparently," said Suzanne. "Lyle is going to have a public defender this time."

"I hear Leslie's going to shoot a pilot to host a television series," said Gus. "We are living in the age of the defense attorney as superstar."

The name of David Conn came up. Garcetti had assigned him to be the new prosecutor in the second trial of the Menendez brothers.

"He's great," said Garcetti.

"I saw him in action at the Cotton Club trial," said Gus. "He's got a real sense of drama in the courtroom. Women jurors like him, and he's not going to take any bullshit from Leslie Abramson."

"Hear, hear," said Suzanne.

"When I saw David Conn on TV, standing next to Marcia Clark at the podium at the press conference after the freeway chase and arrest, I thought you were going to take him off the Menendez trial and put him on the Simpson trial."

"No," said Garcetti. "Marcia had just separated from her husband four days before the murders, and he was a friend. I think it could turn out to be a rough divorce. There're two little kids, four and two, both boys, or five and three, something like that."

"It couldn't have come along at a worse time," said Suzanne.

"Bill Hodgman's very strong. Hodgman and

Marcia are like two halves of a whole. They'll be a good team," said Garcetti.

"I wish you weren't having the trial in downtown Los Angeles, Gil. I wish you were having it in Santa Monica, where it should be," said Gus. "I always thought that from Beverly Hills west, murder trials were usually held in Santa Monica. This is a major error."

"No, no, no, it is *not* an error," said Garcetti. "I'm beginning to hear this all the time. In the first place, you probably don't know much about the Santa Monica courthouse, Gus."

"Actually, I know a great deal about the Santa Monica courthouse," replied Gus. "I once spent nine weeks there, during the trial of a man named Lefty Flynn, who strangled a young actress named Becky Bailey, who happened to be my daughter. It was held in the courtroom of a Judge Burton Katz. The trial got quite a lot of press at the time—nothing like the press Simpson's getting, of course—but I got to know that place very well."

"The Santa Monica courthouse is simply not equipped for a trial of the magnitude of the Simpson trial, I'm telling you," said Garcetti firmly. "There is not enough room for the media. There is not enough room for the parking. There are security problems. And there is still earthquake damage from two years ago that hasn't been repaired yet."

Pouring another cup of coffee, Gus said, "I heard from someone I trust that the reason you decided against going after the death penalty for Simpson, and the reason that the trial is in downtown Los Angeles rather than in Santa Monica, is that everyone's terrified of another riot if a white jury finds Simpson guilty."

"That is simply not true," said Garcetti.

"I've got an awfully good source," said Gus. "The same person told me the thinking was that if a predominantly black jury found him guilty, there probably wouldn't be a riot. Personally, I don't believe a black jury is ever going to convict a black hero, no matter what he's done. I keep remembering those people on the freeway cheering for him to get away."

"Not true," said Garcetti.

"Wouldn't a black juror who helped to convict O.J. Simpson have a hard time returning to the old neighborhood after the trial?" asked Gus.

"If the jury takes a look at all of the evidence, and then accepts the law, as they must, there is only one conclusion they can reach," said Garcetti.

"You have to be at the *Times* on West Forty-third Street in about twenty-two minutes," said Suzanne. "We won't have trouble getting a taxi on Park Avenue, will we, Gus?"

Before Gus left to cover the Simpson trial for *Vanity Fair,* he had lunch in the executive dining room at CBS in New York with several producers and executives from the news department. The subject of the luncheon was the television coverage of the upcoming Simpson trial.

"The interest in this trial is overwhelming," said one of the producers of the evening news. "This is the longest-running news story since the Kennedy assassination. People cannot seem to get enough of it. The plan would be for you to do a segment with Dan Rather every Friday, with you in L.A. and Dan here in New York."

"The only thing that is making me hesitate," said Gus, "is that I am not a lawyer, and there will be specifics of the law that I won't know."

"Don't worry about that. That's not what we want from you. We have Bill Whitaker for that. From what we gather, in all probability you're going to get a seat in the courtroom. What we want from you is the color, what's going on in the courtroom that we aren't seeing on-camera, your impressions of Judge Ito, the lawyers, and particularly the families."

"I have a tendency to get too personally involved in these trials I cover, even emotionally involved at times," said Gus. "That works in a magazine. I don't know how it's going to go over on television."

"Didn't you get friendly with one of the aunts of the Menendez brothers when you were covering that trial? I remember reading that in one of your pieces."

"That's right," said Gus. "She told me the name of the book where Erik and Lyle got all the sexual-abuse stuff they said their father did to them. The father was a prick, but he never buggered those boys."

"The personal touch. That's what we're looking for, Gus."

42

"It sounds good to me," said Gus. "I have to make it clear, though, so there's no misunderstanding, that I don't have a doubt in the world that O.J. is the killer."

"We'd like to take you in to meet Dan Rather."

On the night before Gus left New York, he went to a cocktail party given by fashion designer Calvin Klein and his wife, Kelly, at the Royalton Hotel on West Forty-fourth Street in New York, to celebrate the publication of the author Fran Lebowitz's children's book.

The Royalton, known to be a mecca for celebrities, was jam-packed that evening with what the columnist Richard Johnson, who covered the party for Page Six of the *New York Post,* called "an amalgam of the literary crowd, the magazine crowd, and the fashion crowd." As Gus maneuvered his way through the throng, he stopped to chat with his friend Tina Brown, the editor of *The New Yorker.* It was she who had first brought Gus into magazine writing.

"Good luck out there in L.A., Gus," said Tina. "It's going to be a long haul."

"Tell me about this guy Jeffrey Toobin you're sending out to cover the trial for *The New Yorker,*" said Gus.

"You're going to like Jeffrey, Gus. He's very smart. Very nice," said Tina.

"I *hated* the article he wrote about Detective Mark Fuhrman," said Gus. "I thought that was irresponsible. I bet it was that publicity hound Shapiro who fed Toobin all that shit. Oops, I shouldn't get into this."

"Trust me, Gus, you're going to like Jeffrey," said Tina.

"We'll see."

"I'll be going out there myself; I can't remember exactly when," she said. "Harry's publishing Gore Vidal's memoirs, and we're going to give a party for Gore at L'Orangerie. You know Gore, don't you?"

"Do I know Gore? When I was twenty years old, I met Anaïs Nin at Gore's house in Guatemala, and she took me away with her to Acapulco. Top that!" said Gus.

Tina laughed. "I'll see you out there."

Gus moved on into the room. He shook hands with Liz Tilberis, the editor of *Harper's Bazaar.* He hugged his friend Jesse Kornbluth, the writer, on whom he had based the character of Bernie Slatkin, who married and then divorced the richest girl in New York in his book *People Like Us.* He posed for a picture for his friend Heather Cohane, who was the editor of *Quest.* He kissed Fran Lebowitz, the honoree, on both cheeks, complimented her on her tuxedo, and got her to sign his book.

His friend Susan Magrino, who had been the publicist on all his books, whispered in his ear, "Malachy and Edwina are here, in case you want to avoid them. They're over on the other side of the room."

Malachy Bailey and Edwina Calder were writers

of note, as well as Gus's brother and sister-in-law. The brothers, whose relationship had always been shaky, had not spoken since Malachy dedicated his last book to Leslie Abramson, at a time when Gus was referred to in the media as her archnemesis. Gus interpreted the dedication as a slap at him rather than as an homage to Leslie Abramson.

"I'm only staying for a second. I'm in and out," replied Gus. "I'm leaving for Los Angeles tomorrow."

"Gus, I hear you're going to L.A. for the Simpson trial," called out Paul Morrissey, the avant-garde film director, who had let it be known to one and all of his group that he was obsessed with the murders of Nicole Brown Simpson and Ron Goldman. He moved away from Jed Johnson, Bob Colacello, and Brigid Berlin, with whom he had been discussing the lawsuit brought by Ed Hayes against the trustees of the Andy Warhol estate, and made a beeline for Gus.

"I am," said Gus. "I'm leaving tomorrow."

"The guy's guilty as hell. You know that, don't you?" said Morrissey excitedly. In the mid-seventies, Paul had directed a movie for Andy Warhol in Italy at the same time Gus was producing a movie there with Elizabeth Taylor and Henry Ford called *Ash Wednesday.* They became friends. Years later, when they met at parties in New York, they usually talked about those days. Gus loved to talk about old times. "Do you remember that night in Rome when Elizabeth got so furious at Andy when she discovered he had a tape recorder hidden under her mink coat on the banquette and was recording

45

every word she said?" Or, "Do you remember that lunch that Franco Zeffirelli gave at his house on the Via Appia Antica, and Hiram Keller shocked all the titles when he jumped in the pool nude?" But these days, the O. J. Simpson case superseded all else in conversation.

"I certainly believe that he's guilty," replied Gus. "But, as they say in my business, we must keep an open mind, ha ha ha. That's like innocent until proven guilty. The other night at dinner, F. Lee Bailey tried to convince me that Nicole and Ron were killed by Colombian drug dealers. I felt like he was trying out his argument on me."

"F. Lee Bailey!" screamed Paul, so loudly that people turned to look. Gus smiled. He liked it when Paul got wound up on a subject. "Have you ever gotten Patty Hearst going on the subject of Mr. F. Lee Bailey? One of the richest girls in the country, right? She's kidnapped. She's raped. She's locked in a closet, and she goes to *prison,* for God sake. So she picked up a machine gun and robbed a bank. *So what?* Wouldn't you? Wouldn't anybody? It's called self-preservation. A *public defender* could have gotten Patty off, and F. Lee Bailey lost the case. Get Randy Hearst going on the subject of F. Lee Bailey. And now he's saying it's Colombian drug dealers who killed Nicole and Ron? Yeah, sure, F. Lee."

"The thing is, Paul, I believe that Lee Bailey believes it," said Gus. "He looked me right in the eye when he told me Nicole was killed by a Colombian drug gang, and I could see that he was daring me to disbelieve him. I think he creates the plot, and that becomes his reality. That becomes the way it happened, and nothing ever will deter him from that version of events."

"The defense doesn't have a chance in this case," said Paul.

"Hold it a minute. F. Lee's got this guy who works for him, a private investigator named Pat McKenna. I met Pat in Palm Beach. The Kennedys hired him for Roy Black's team at Willie Smith's trial. The odd thing is, Pat McKenna's a nice guy—you can have a good time with him, a lot of laughs—but he's the kind of private investigator who could dig up dirt on Mother Teresa. Give Pat two weeks, and he's going to know about every drug, every dick, and every nude photograph that Nicole Brown Simpson ever came into contact with. Don't think for a minute that this trial is going to be a cakewalk for the prosecution, no matter how much overwhelming evidence they have."

"O.J. used to beat the shit out of Nicole. You know that, don't you?" said Morrissey.

"I heard the 911," said Gus. "She sure sounded scared of him to me, and he sure sounded terrifying, but you'll find that there will be a logical explanation for everything."

"He stalked her. You know that, too, don't you? It sounds like that guy who killed your daughter—whatwashisname?" said Paul.

Gus, stunned, did not reply.

Paul, embarrassed, hurried on. "Do you remember an actress named Jennifer Lee?"

"Of course I remember Jennifer. I haven't seen her in years. She wrote a wonderful book about Hollywood."

"*Tarnished Angel.* Call her when you get there. She lives with Richard Pryor."

"I thought she divorced Richard Pryor."

"She did, but they're back together, kind of. He's got multiple sclerosis, and she's taking care of him. She and Richard and O.J. and Nicole used to hang out together. Two black stars and their beautiful white wives. Jennifer's got some stories about O.J. that will knock your hat off."

"Thanks, Paul."

"Where are you staying out there?"

"Chateau Marmont."

5

In his monthly "Letter from Los Angeles" in *Vanity Fair,* Gus wrote:

When I returned to New York last February, after seven months here covering the first Menendez trial, it never occurred to me that another cataclysmic event, another double homicide in high circles, would bring this city to a halt again so soon. But it has, and I'm back, and there's quite a lot going on even though the trial hasn't started yet.

The Menendez brothers, Lyle and Erik, who held the city of Los Angeles in their thrall for four years, have ceased to fascinate the town, so overwhelming is the interest in O. J. Simpson. Simpson is the most famous American to be charged with a violent crime since Fatty Arbuckle was tried for manslaughter back in the twenties, amid rumors that he had inserted a Coca-Cola bottle into a young woman's vagina during an orgy at the St. Francis Hotel in San Francisco, thereby causing her death. Arbuckle was acquitted after four trials, but his reputation and career were ruined. In the wake of the killings of Nicole Brown Simp-

son and Ronald Goldman last June, O.J. Simpson has superseded all others in history as the town's top topic, a topic that will continue to captivate until the jury arrives at a verdict, if it does arrive at a verdict. The cynicism of the citizenry about the possibility of a conviction, after the two non-verdicts in the Menendez trial, makes hung jury *and* acquittal *the most often-repeated words in the community.*

When Gus Bailey was nine years old and growing up in Hartford, Connecticut, a city that he knew from the age of four would not be the city of his life, his aunt Harriet, a maiden lady who had once been a Catholic nun but quit the convent—a subject that fascinated him, although it was a subject that was never discussed in his family—took him out West on a summer trip. The first stop was Los Angeles. For Gus, it was a breathtaking experience. He loved every second that he was there. On the tour bus that took them to look at movie stars' homes, he sat next to the tour guide so that he wouldn't miss anything. For years afterward, he remembered that Shirley Temple had lived on Rockingham Drive in Brentwood, the same street that O.J. Simpson lived on years later, and Deanna Durbin had lived on Amalfi Drive, in the same house that the television mogul Steve Bochco now inhabited, and Clark Gable and Carole Lombard had lived in a house in the flats in Beverly Hills, where Gus had lived when he was married to Peach and where they raised their three children.

On that trip, he and his aunt went to the Coconut Grove in the Ambassador Hotel to hear Eddy Duchin and his orchestra and the next day to Schwab's drugstore on the Sunset Strip. The tour guide pointed out the soda fountain and told Gus that was where Mervyn LeRoy had discovered Lana Turner. "And now she's one of the biggest stars at MGM," the guide said.

Gus believed everything. He couldn't get enough information. Outside Schwab's, Gus pointed to a châteaulike building, towering high over Sunset Boulevard. "What's that?" he asked.

"That's the Chateau Marmont," said the guide. "That's where Greta Garbo lives."

Gus stared, captivated. He had fallen in love with a city. What he knew with total certainty at age nine was that at some time in his future, Los Angeles was going to play an important part. He knew that it would become his city. He knew that he would be walking in the front doors of the houses that he had stared at from the tour bus. It wouldn't matter when he found out later that Mervyn LeRoy had *not* discovered Lana Turner at the soda fountain of Schwab's drugstore on the Sunset Strip, or that Greta Garbo had *never* lived at the Chateau Marmont. It was where he wanted to be.

When Gus checked into the Chateau Marmont on Sunset Boulevard for the long stay ahead, he was delighted to see that paperback copies of one of his earlier novels, *An Inconvenient Woman,* were on display and for sale in a vitrine near the front desk in the lobby. *An Inconvenient Woman* was about the murder of the mistress of Jules Mendelson, the billionaire friend of the President of the United States. It had caused a furor in Los Angeles social circles at the time of its publication, as well as a public snubbing of Gus in some quarters.

"How could he?" asked people about Gus at the time. "He knows us all. He's been to her house for dinner, for God sake." Jerome R. Zipkin, a dilettante of consequence in social life, on whom Gus had based the character of the social fool Ezzie Fenwick in *People Like Us,* reported to one and all that his great great friend on whom the vile Gus Bailey had based the character of Pauline Mendelson in *An Inconvenient Woman* was devastated, simply devastated, and would never, ever, ever speak to Mr. Bailey again, thank you very much, and no one else should, either.

"I'm back," said Gus, staring into the vitrine.

The book was on display in the vitrine because the narrator, an investigative reporter named Philip Quennell, whom Gus had based on himself, at a younger age, had lived at the Chateau Marmont in the novel, and a crucial scene had taken place in Suite #48. As a consequence of the recognition, the Marmont's owner, Andre Balazs, invited Gus to stay at the Chateau Marmont for the length of the trial, in Suite #48, which was a living room, bedroom, kitchen, dining area, and a balcony that looked out on a pink Georgian mansion, far too large for the lot on which it sat. The empty house fascinated Gus. It had been built on speculation during the 1980s and had never sold. Every day the lawn sprinklers went on, and every night the house was all lit up, both inside and out, as if a wonderful party were going on. "I have to fit that house into my novel," said Gus late one night, sitting on the balcony.

Gus loved the old hotel. He called it his home away from home. There were friends everywhere. He ran into the great photographer Helmut Newton there, with whom he had done many stories, including the Claus von Bülow trial, and his wife, June. He ran into Warren Beatty in the garage, who told him that his house on Mulholland had been wrecked in the earthquake and that Annette was having another baby. He ran into writer friends there, out from New York on assignment, and he never tired of looking at the rock stars and movie stars who frequented the Chateau. "Courtney Love has the room across the hall from me," he told his son Grafton on the telephone, "and Keanu Reeves has the room next to me."

Within days of his arrival, Gus's telephone started to ring.

"You get more calls than anyone in the hotel," said Mario Maldonado as he handed Gus a fistful of messages at the front desk.

Mary Jane Stevenson of Court TV and Shoreen

Maghame of *City News*. Reunion of the Menendez reporters at Orso on Third Street Friday night. Mrs. Marvin Davis, dinner for Plácido Domingo. Linda Deutsch of Associated Press, lunch at the Beverly Hills Hotel on Sunday with Elaine Young, the Beverly Hills realtor, and Theo Wilson, the great crime reporter. Janet DeCordova, dinner at Chasen's Sunday night. The Billy Wilders would be coming. Mart Crowley, dinner at Orso. Martin Manulis, dinner at Morton's. Tita Cahn, dinner at her home.

In the years between Gus's flight from Los Angeles in 1979 and his return in 1994, the circumstances of his life had changed considerably. He had left as a failed film producer with a drinking problem, in bankruptcy, who was no longer invited anywhere, and he returned as a best-selling author, with four novels and four miniseries based on his novels to his credit. In the circles in which he had once moved, success is the most valued of all commodities, and Gus was seized upon. People who had once written him off as a failure now said, "You know, Gus, I always knew this was going to happen to you." His old friend the playwright Mart Crowley, who wrote *The Boys in the Band,* the movie of which Gus had produced during his show-business career, said to him, "I don't know how you could go to their house for dinner, after the way they treated you when you were down-and-out," when he heard Gus accept a dinner-party invitation from a very swell couple who had done just what he said. Gus didn't see it that way. He was open to all the experiences. He replied, "This is what I write about. This is how they live."

Gus went out to dinner every night. Since he never made a secret of exactly how he stood on the guilt of O.J. Simpson, he invariably met someone, often in the most unlikely houses, who either gave him information or offered to introduce him to someone who would be willing to give him information relevant to the case.

"I can introduce you to the technical adviser who taught O.J. how to use a knife to slit a throat on the *Frogman* pilot," said a customer who recognized Gus having dinner at the Book Soup Bistro.

The actress Polly Bergen said to Gus one night at Drai's, the restaurant of the moment with the movie and media crowd, after hearing him refer to Simpson as the killer, "You should remember that O.J. is innocent until proven guilty."

"Oh bullshit, Polly," replied Gus. "While we're supposed to be saying O.J. is innocent until proven guilty, his lawyers are sitting around a table in Bob Shapiro's office creating a scenario that a Colombian drug cartel is responsible for the murders committed by their client."

"Don't mind Polly, Gus," said Jolene Schlatter, the wife of the television producer. "She's a great friend of Bob and Linell Shapiro's. They fed her that line."

Before the trial started, Gus met several of the principal players who would dominate the news in the months to come. At the billionaire Marvin Davis's Carousel of Hope Ball, he saw Robert Shapiro. Marvin Davis and his wife, Barbara, had become the top hosts in Hollywood society, entertaining in a lavish style that recalled an earlier era. Shapiro was at the time riding high, the master of his universe, signing autographs, waving to the crowds, being interviewed on television, being invited to the best parties. The stigma of being associated with O.J. Simpson, which would come in time, was still a long way off.

That night, Shapiro was one of the most photographed superstars of the Davises' party, in the heady company of Hillary Clinton, Barbra Streisand, Warren Beatty and Annette Bening, Dustin Hoffman, Goldie Hawn and Kurt Russell, Arnold Schwarzenegger and Maria Shriver, Tom Hanks and Rita Wilson, and Fergie, the Duchess of York.

Gus, fascinated by him, could not stop looking at Shapiro as he walked through the crowd with a beatific smile on his face, a man content with his role in life. He was in the world he wanted to be in, a part of it, a member of the elite and privileged. He was one of them. The defense attorney as celebrity had begun to eclipse the movie star as celebrity. Leslie Abramson had become a national figure for her emotional defense of the young parent-killing Menendez brothers, Lyle and Erik. Now Robert Shapiro was becoming a national figure as the defender of O.J.

Simpson, and the town was paying deference to his position of importance.

He turned and saw Gus staring at him. Each held the look. They had never met, but each knew who the other was. Gus walked across the room to where Shapiro was standing and put out his hand.

"Mr. Shapiro, I'm Gus Bailey."

"I know who you are," replied Shapiro, smiling. Once he had written a guide to show defense attorneys how to deal with the media. Charm played a large part.

"I hear the biggest draw in the silent auction is lunch with Robert Shapiro at the Grill in Beverly Hills," said Gus.

"But not until after the trial is over," said Shapiro.

"You're getting more attention tonight than the Duchess of York," said Gus.

Shapiro smiled.

"I hear you're out here to crucify me, like you crucified Leslie Abramson at the Menendez trial," said Shapiro, smiling and full of self-confidence, as they shook hands.

"What do you mean, I crucified her? I made her famous, that's what I did," said Gus. "She was just local stuff until I started writing about her."

They both laughed. Shapiro reminded Gus of an agent he used to have when he was still in the picture business.

"Now, who could have told you such a thing?" asked Gus.

"I've already heard about your dinner at 'Twenty-one' with my friend Lee Bailey," said Shapiro. "He tells me you think I shouldn't sign autographs."

"Lee's a good reporter," said Gus.

"We should have lunch one day," said Shapiro.

"I'd really like that," replied Gus. "I hear you go to the Grill every Friday."

"You know everything, and you just got to town," said Shapiro.

"The story of my life," said Gus. They shook hands and went back to the ballroom.

Later, after Plácido Domingo sang and Kenny G played, Jay Leno, the master of ceremonies, openly mocked the glove that was then being touted as having been moved by Detective Mark Fuhrman from Nicole's condo on Bundy to O.J. Simpson's estate on Rockingham, as part of a police conspiracy to blame Simpson for the murders. A spotlight found Shapiro at his table, and the entire ballroom watched his nonreaction to Jay Leno's jokes. Later, when people talked about the night of the Davises' ball, several hostesses in the town claimed that that moment, watching Shapiro fail to laugh at Leno's joke about Johnnie Cochran and the glove, made them realize for the first time that they wouldn't be able to ask him and Linell to dinner much longer. Feelings were beginning to heat up.

"Shapiro was at Jackie Collins's house for dinner the other night," said Wendy Stark. "Thank God she didn't seat me next to him."

6 In his "Letter from Los Angeles," Gus wrote:

In the circles in which I travel, Marcia Clark is perhaps the most admired member of the legal teams, but her role in this case is a difficult one, made even more difficult by the fact that Gordon Clark, her estranged husband, is seeking primary custody of their two sons, claiming that his wife is never home during this single-most-important moment of her career. I have found in covering trials that juries tend to dislike female prosecutors, especially if the defendant is male, goodlooking, rich, famous, or young, all of which categories Orenthal James Simpson falls into except the last. They have little sympathy for a woman who is trying so hard to send a man to prison, perhaps for life. Sexist? Yes, of course. The jury disliked Moira Lasch, the prosecutor in the Palm Beach rape trial of Willie Smith. The jury disliked Pamela Bozanich in the Van Nuys murder trial of the Menendez brothers. The dislike is unrelated to intelligence or ability; it is simply the nature of the beast. Conversely, the female defense attorney does not have this problem, even though she may be trying to win an acquittal for a guilty defendant. Very often, she comes off as a lioness trying to protect her cub.

The day after the Marvin Davises' ball, Wendy Stark, who was both the daughter and granddaughter of eminent show-business figures, which qualified her for the status of Hollywood royalty, called Gus at the Chateau Marmont. He was settling into his suite for the long stay of the upcoming Simpson trial. Gus was a meticulous organizer. For him, everything had to have a proper place, a trait that drove his former wife, Peach, to distraction at times. That day, he had purchased pens, pencils, pencil sharpener, paper clips, pushpins, pink Hi-Liters, spiral pads, Scotch tape, file folders, videotapes to record the news on television, and audiotapes for interviews and monitoring telephone calls. "I can't work if there's disorder around me," he wrote over and over again in his journal. He had brought his laptop computer with him from Prud'homme, and Mario Maldonado, who worked at the front desk in the hotel, was supervising the installation of both a fax machine and a LaserJet printer for him. The television set was on to Channel 5, in case of any late-breaking news on the Simpson case.

"My father wants to know if you can come for

dinner on Tuesday," said Wendy Stark. "He's having a small group, and he's running the new Brad Pitt movie, *Legends of the Fall,* after dinner, only no one's supposed to know he's running it, because the producer hasn't shown it to the studio yet, so don't say anything about it to anyone."

Wendy had a way of running all her sentences into one when she spoke. Although there was a considerable difference in their ages, Wendy and Gus were old friends. Sometimes he teasingly referred to her as "my friend the Hollywood heiress" when he introduced her to people. She had stuck by him during the years of his downfall, one of not many who had, and Gus felt a great affection for her. He had a long history with the Stark family and had even used them as characters of wealth and power in his early novel about Hollywood, *The Winners.*

"Ray's starting to entertain again, on a small scale," said Wendy. From the age of fifteen, Wendy had begun calling her father Ray rather than Dad. Her mother, Fran, an important figure in the town's social life, had died a year earlier.

"Damn it, I can't go, Wendy," said Gus.

"Why?" asked Wendy.

"I'm having dinner Tuesday with this spy I have in the L.A. county jail who gives me all the jailhouse gossip on the Menendez brothers and O.J. Simpson. He knows great stuff," said Gus.

"Oh," she replied. Her voice implied that she didn't think his engagement for the evening was in the same league with the one she was offering.

Gus, excited by the information provided by his source, went on. "Did you know that O.J. and Erik Menendez were in adjoining cells at the county jail for a bit?"

"David Geffen's coming," replied Wendy, in answer to Gus's enthusiasm, as a lure to entice him. David Geffen was one of the two or three most important moguls in the film business, as well as the most publicized. The word *billionaire* usually preceded his name in gossip columns.

"Oh, it's a big-time evening, huh?" said Gus. "I wish I could go, but I've already canceled this guy once, and I don't want to lose him as a source. Who else do you know who has a mole in the county jail?"

"Marcia Clark's coming," said Wendy in a casual, throwaway voice. "But that's a *big* secret no one's supposed to know, and I *promised* Ray I wouldn't tell."

Suddenly, Gus gave Wendy his full attention as the importance of his jailhouse spy's information began to diminish in the face of the presence of Marcia Clark at Ray Stark's house for dinner on Tuesday night. "Let me get this straight," said Gus. "Marcia Clark is going to your father's house for dinner and a movie on Tuesday? Did I hear that correctly?"

"That's what I said," replied Wendy, sounding like her father when he outpowered a difficult film star or director in a contract dispute.

"How did that come about, for God's sake? How do you get Marcia Clark to dinner at this juncture of her life? She's the lead prosecutor in what they are saying is going to be the most famous murder trial of the century. I would think she'd have her hands full these days, and nights."

"Oh, you know Ray," said Wendy. "He has a friend in the D.A.'s office, Suzanne Childs, and that's how it got arranged. Ray thinks Marcia ought to know that everyone in the film industry is behind her and rooting for her."

"I'm all for that," said Gus.

"So Suzanne's bringing her. You must know Suzanne. Used to be married to Michael Crichton? Divorced him before he became famous. Went to law school. Does media relations for Gil Garcetti?"

"Sure, I know Suzanne," said Gus. "I had breakfast with Suzanne and Gil Garcetti in New York."

"She's also supervising Marcia's makeover before the trial starts. She's the one who suggested Allen Edwards to do the new hairstyle, get rid of the tight curls, give her kind of a Diane Sawyer look. Allen does Farrah Fawcett and Candy Bergen. I forget who's going to do her clothes, somebody I never heard of before, medium-priced working-girl clothes, that kind of thing. Suzanne wanted Armani, which would have been *perfect* on Marcia, but he's expensive, and they're afraid it might turn off the women in the jury if her clothes are too expensive."

"You're a fund of information, Wendy. I'm going to make some notes. What's that hairdresser's name? I might give him a call."

Thoughts began racing through Gus's head. How could he tell his jailhouse spy that he had to cancel him for the second time and still not lose him as a source, a source introduced to him by Bruce Nelson, a famed real-estate broker, about whom Gus had once written in an article for his magazine on the mansion-building sprees of the new rich in the eighties. "You've made me a star," Nelson wrote to Gus after the article appeared. "If there's anything I can ever do for you, etc." Nelson was a man who was true to his word. When Gus had wanted to get inside the Menendez house in Beverly Hills shortly after the brothers had shotgunned their parents to death, Nelson passed him off as a rich client from New York who wanted a pied-à-terre in Beverly Hills, and Gus was able to spend time in the room where the murders had occurred. Recently, Nelson had put Gus in touch with a friend of his in the county jail.

There were many things Gus wanted to find out about O.J. Simpson in jail. He wanted to know if it was true that Simpson was allowed to have a treadmill outside his cell so that he could work out. He wanted to know if it was true that Simpson was permitted to receive his visitors in a private room with no guard present, only a lawyer from Johnnie Cochran's office named Nicole Pulvers. He wanted to know if it was true that sounds of partylike hilarity were often heard in Simpson's visiting room. He wanted to know if it was true that Simpson had shouted out a confession to the murders to the Reverend Roosevelt Grier, which was overheard by a guard in the jail. He wanted to know if it was true that O. J.'s exact words were "All right, goddamit. I did it. I killed them both."

"Listen, Wendy, I've been thinking. I just decided to cancel my spy from the jailhouse for the second time. 'Sorry, fella. A better offer came along,' I'll tell him," joked Gus.

Wendy laughed with delight. "I knew I'd get you," she said. "I know my old friend Gussie. Besides, you can always see your spy some other time."

"Tell Ray I'd love to come. I have been *dying* to meet Marcia Clark before the trial begins."

"There's a catch," said Wendy.

"What's that?"

"You can't ask her anything about the case. No one can. Suzanne told Ray Marcia's not going to know anyone there, she doesn't want to be the center of attention, and she can't talk about the case anyway. Ray's going to tell everyone that before she comes."

"I still want to meet her before the trial starts," said Gus.

For the occasion at hand, a small dinner to meet Marcia Clark, the gates of Ray Stark's estate in Holmby Hills were open as Gus drove through. There were green hedges, white flowers, and the occasional piece of sculpture on either side of the long drive. He had been there before, many times, in years gone by. He'd been there even before the Starks bought the house, when the previous owners, the film stars Humphrey Bogart and Lauren Bacall, had lived there with their two small children. "That was a long time ago," Gus said to himself. He drove up to the guest parking area in front of the beautiful white brick mansion. There, parked in place, was the police car that Stark always kept in the driveway, on view from the street outside the gates, as a message to the unsavory that they were unwelcome in these environs. The police car was a prop from a television cop series, given to Ray as a Christmas gift by Aaron Spelling, the television mogul and friend, who lived nearby in an even larger mansion. "You can't be too safe these days," said Spelling, who had two bodyguards.

Ever since the riots three years earlier in the area of Los Angeles known as South Central—during which much of that part of the city burned—after the acquittal of the police officers who were caught on videotape beating Rodney King with clubs, people who lived in the fashionable areas on the other side of town were in a state of constant apprehension. Security was a prime topic of conversation. At the grandest houses and the residences of the celebrated, gates and guards had become necessities. Marlene Schlessinger, the wife of Irv Schlessinger, the television producer, said to Gus at Drai's one evening at dinner, "I never drive my Rolls anymore, except from the house in Beverly Hills to the house in Malibu and from Malibu back to Beverly Hills. I'm afraid to. The less attention you draw to yourself these days, the better. Let me give you some advice,

Gus. If someone hits you from behind when you're driving, just keep moving. Don't stop, whatever you do. That's when they get you. You heard what happened to Craig Johnson, didn't you?"

The apprehension in the area increased tenfold after the murders of Nicole Brown Simpson and Ronald Goldman. They had, after all, taken place in Brentwood, so nearby, where so many people lived whom everyone knew. At dinner parties in the area, people said things like "Next time, they're not going to burn down their own part of town again. They're going to come *here*." No one had to be told who the "they" of the sentence were, as they looked at one another nervously across the table. Invariably, to ease the tension, someone told the joke about the Beverly Hills matron who said to her maid, Bertha, who had been with her for many years, "Bertha, if a riot comes, you wouldn't kill me, would you?" To which Bertha answered, "Oh, no, ma'am. I wouldn't kill you, but the maid next door might." There was always laughter, and then they returned to other matters of less immediate interest, like the unpleasant situation between Jeffrey Katzenberg and Michael Eisner of Disney. "That's going to be a dirty fight," people said.

"Is it okay to park here?" Gus called out the window of his rented car to Ray Stark's uniformed guard, who was holding a rottweiler on a leash.

"That's saved for the guest of honor," said the guard. "Pull up behind Mr. Geffen's car. Now, you are?" He had a list of the guests on a clipboard.

"Bailey. Gus Bailey."

"Yes, go right in, Mr. Bailey."

Gus got out of his car and began to walk to the black-lacquered front door, but the rottweiler, still on a leash, pushed against his legs.

"Listen, can you pull your rottweiler back a little bit, please? I don't like him smelling me like this," said Gus, who had always had problems with dogs.

"You got nothing to worry about, Mr. Bailey. Frenchy there wouldn't hurt a guy like you," said the guard.

"But Frenchy might give a guy like me a heart attack," said Gus. "Pull him back."

As he walked up the steps to the front door, it was opened by Wilbur, the Starks' butler, who had been with the family for years.

"Hi, Wilbur," said Gus, holding out his hand.

"It's been a long time, Mr. Bailey," said Wilbur. "Wendy tells me you're doing real good these days in New York."

"A lot better than I was when I left this town," answered Gus with a smile.

"I'm happy for you. Are you still drinking Diet Cokes, Mr. Bailey?" asked Wilbur.

"Cut the Mr. Bailey crap, Wilbur. It's Gus, the way it's always been, and I've been drinking Diet Cokes for fourteen years now."

"Good for you, Gus. They're all in the living room or the library. You know where to go. They're all talking about O.J. Simpson. That's all anyone talks about these days. At least they're talking about O.J. Simpson until Miss Marcia Clark arrives. You want to know something, Gus? They all stop talking when I come in to pass a drink. That's what it's like now. Everyone still says 'Hello, Wilbur' or 'Good to see you, Wilbur' when they come in, but when I walk into the room and they're talking about O.J. Simpson, somebody nudges somebody, and they all stop. Sometimes, like a week ago or so, when Mr. Stark was running the new Schwarzenegger movie—I forget the name—David Begelman, who's been coming to this house for thirty years, says to me at the dinner table when I'm passing around a tray of lamb chops, 'What do *you* think, Wilbur? Do you think O.J. is guilty? Do you think he killed Nicole?' Everyone at the table stopped talking and looked at me. They all really wanted to know what I thought, because I'm the closest most of them ever came to knowing a black man."

"What did you answer?" asked Gus.

"I said, light-hearted-like, 'Oh, I'm not getting into this one,' or something like that, and walked off into the kitchen. Mae heard it. She took the tray from me and passed around the rest of the lamb chops."

"Any repercussions?"

"Just from myself, for myself. I hated it that I copped out. You see, Gus, I don't think the Juice did it, but I keep my mouth shut. I've been with the family a long time, and I don't want to cause any problems."

69

"Wilbur, I can't give you any crap. I do think he did it," said Gus. "I think he's guilty as sin. That's what I've come out here to write about."

"But you don't know, Gus."

"You're right, I don't know, but he's never for a second acted like an innocent man since it happened. Look at the videotape when the cop put the handcuffs on him, after he got back from Chicago. An innocent man would be screaming, 'How fucking dare you put these on me? Why aren't you out looking for the real killer?' But he didn't. An innocent man wouldn't have tried to run away in the white Bronco."

"He wasn't running away, Gus. He was on his way to the cemetery to visit Nicole's grave," said Wilbur.

"He had long passed the exit for the cemetery, Wilbur. He was heading for Mexico."

Wendy Stark raced into the hallway from the living room, adjusting an earring and heading for the dining room. "Hi, darling," she said, kissing Gus on both cheeks. "I have to put the place cards on the table for Ray." As she went into the dining room, her father entered the hall.

"Gus, what are you doing out here in the hall for so long? Come on in," said Ray Stark.

"Good to see you, Ray," replied Gus. "Wilbur and I were just catching up." He put out his hand.

"So, the writer has returned," said Ray while shaking hands. He spoke to Gus in a slightly teasing tone. "Wendy tells me you're here for the trial."

"I am. Staying at the Chateau Marmont for the duration. Is this new?" asked Gus, pointing to a black marble sculpture of a reclining female nude with upturned breasts. "It's beautiful."

"Mr. Stark's always buying some new piece of sculpture," said Wilbur as he headed for the bar.

"Maillol," said Ray. For a moment, Ray and Gus stared at the exquisite object with pleasure.

"Really beautiful," repeated Gus as he ran his hand across the smooth surface of her stomach. Gus had portrayed Ray Stark as a studio head named Marty Lesky in *The Winners,* which he had written in rage in a cabin in Oregon after his failure and retreat from Hollywood fifteen years earlier. The plot was partially based on the forgery scandal involving studio head David Begelman, the Academy Award–winning actor Cliff Robertson, and Columbia Pictures, which had been the main topic of gossip and conversation at every dinner table in Hollywood. The scandal had rocked the town. Gus, who was on his uppers at the time, knew every person involved in the case—and their wives—and he helped two reporters from the *Washington Post* break the story, which the *Los Angeles Times* wouldn't touch. It was Gus's first foray into investigative reporting, and he felt a thrill that he had long since failed to feel in the film business. Neither Ray nor his late wife, Fran, had ever acknowledged that they were the characters in Gus's book, but their daughter, Wendy, recognized herself as Cecilia Lesky, the Hollywood heiress, and didn't care.

"Did Wendy tell you no questions to Marcia Clark about the case when she comes?" asked Ray.

"She did, and I won't ask any," said Gus.

"She doesn't want to be the center of attention," said Ray.

"Even though she will be," replied Gus. "I wouldn't by any chance be sitting next to her at dinner, would I?"

"Will you listen to this guy?" asked Ray, pointing his thumb at Gus. "Now he wants the seat next to the guest of honor."

Gus was one of those people who could survey a room in an instant. He was interested in seeing what sort of group Ray had put together to meet Marcia Clark, who was the name on every lip in Los Angeles, and the trial hadn't even started. There were fourteen for dinner. An eclectic mixture, Gus thought. A little of the new power of the industry—David Geffen and Ron Meyer. A little of the oldtime Hollywood glamour—Kirk Douglas. A little Los Angeles society—Betsy Bloomingdale. Gus knew everyone except a young man who was staring intently at Monet's painting of the water lilies at Giverny, one of the treasures of the Stark collection.

"Who's the Latino staring at your father's Monet?" asked Gus.

"Some trick Skip Hartley brought," replied Wendy. "Wouldn't you know my father would seat me next to him at dinner? I wanted to sit next to you."

"What's his name?"

"He told me about three times, and I forgot it three times," said Wendy. "He said he went to Bishop's School in La Jolla."

"That's where Peach went," said Gus. "He doesn't look like the Bishop's type. What did his place card say?"

"The calligrapher only used first names. Andrew. Andrew somebody. Cooney. Cunihan. Cunanan. Something like that."

"He certainly likes your father's pictures," said Gus. "He's moved on to a Picasso."

"The kid's got taste," replied Ray, walking up. "Gus, you know Betsy Bloomingdale, don't you?"

Betsy and Gus looked at each other. "I was a character in one of his books," said Betsy. "Not to mention his miniseries of the same name, which, thank heavens, I never saw."

"God, I forgot," said Ray. "What do you mean, you were a character in his book? You were the plot."

"This is my least favorite conversation," said Gus, blushing. "It's time for you to appear, Marcia Clark, and get me out of this."

Kirk and Anne Douglas joined them. "This is going to be some trial, Gus. Did you ever see anything like this guy Shapiro? He thinks he's a movie star, for God sakes. My son Michael—you know Michael, of course you know Michael—saw him at the fights in Vegas last week, and he got a standing ovation."

"What is this telling us?" replied Gus.

"Anne and I were at the same party O.J. was at the night before the murders, a charity thing at some guy's house in Bel Air," said Kirk Douglas. "I had a talk with him. What can I tell you? The guy was charming."

"When we read about the murders two days later, we couldn't believe it," said Anne Douglas.

"He was with Paula Barbieri," said Kirk. "She's gorgeous."

"Paula used to go out with Bob Evans," said Wendy. "Remember, Ray? Evans brought her here one night to see a picture."

Ron Meyer joined the group to get into the conversation about O.J. Simpson before Marcia Clark arrived. As Gus moved around the room saying hello, everyone told him something about O.J. Simpson, or something that related to him.

"Has anyone ever told you the story about O.J. being at the Daisy on the night his daughter drowned in the pool?" . . . "Paula Barbieri was with Michael Bolton at the Mirage Hotel in Las Vegas on the night of the murders." . . . "Gus, did you ever hear what Bill Bixby said about Al Cowlings before he died?" . . . "Bob Shapiro was Tina Sinatra's lawyer in her stalking case against Jimmy Farentino." . . . "Rosa Lopez used to work for some close friends of mine before she worked in the house next door to O.J., and I know for a fact they'd be happy to talk to you about Rosa." . . . "Shapiro got Marlon Brando's kid a plea bargain when he killed his sister's boyfriend."

"Marcia Clark just arrived, Ray," said Wendy.

"Remember, no questions about the trial," said Ray to the room.

Everyone turned to the entrance of the living room, where Marcia Clark was standing, to look at her as she stared back at them. Her face had become instantly recognizable, with the kind of fame usually reserved for film stars. Ray and Wendy hurried forward to greet her. Everyone had watched her on television at the preliminary hearings, and the consensus was that she had acquitted herself magnificently. They believed in her. They felt confidence in her. They wanted her to convict O.J. Simpson, whom they all felt was guilty of the murders with which he was charged. Stark's guests, all famous themselves, moved in to meet her, in the way they do at the great houses of Hollywood when stars like Barbra Streisand come to dinner. They crowded around her, eager to talk to her, eager to listen to her, biting their tongues to keep them from uttering the questions they longed to ask her.

Gus waited before he went up to speak to her. He wanted to be alone.

"Marcia, I'm Gus Bailey," he said.

She turned to him, smiled, and gave him her full attention. "So you're Gus Bailey. I read all your coverage of the Menendez brothers' trial," said Marcia. "Is Leslie Abramson giving you a big welcome to L.A. party?"

They both laughed.

"David Conn told me you were coming out for

75

the trial. He's going to be the prosecutor in the second Menendez trial."

"Sure, I know David," said Gus. "I saw him in action at the Cotton Club trial. He's great. I hope he can take on Leslie Abramson."

"Oh, he can, believe me," said Marcia.

"I know we're not supposed to talk about the case tonight, and I won't—I don't want to get on Ray's bad side, or yours, either—but I'm sure it's okay to tell you you've been great in the hearings."

"Thanks, Gus."

Then he added quickly, "And I wish the trial wasn't being held in downtown Los Angeles instead of Santa Monica. Gil Garcetti's going to rue the day he made that decision."

"No comment," she replied, smiling.

"Do you like being so famous?"

"I don't think so," she said with a shudder. "This has never happened to me before. I can't go to the supermarket anymore. People crowd around me, and it's bewildering for my little boys."

"We're going into dinner, Ms. Clark and Gus," said Wilbur.

"I hope I'm sitting next to you, Gus," said Marcia.

"You're not. I already checked. You've got the big guns on either side of you. Not what anyone in his right mind in this town would call a bad seat."

"Oh my," said Marcia.

"But remember this, you're the power in this house tonight. They're more interested in you than you are in them, and that doesn't happen very often in this crowd."

Ray Stark was a stickler for time. There was never lingering over drinks at the Starks'. Ray liked the movie to start promptly at nine o'clock. Movie people got to the studios early, he often said. Immediately following the crème brûlée, he led his guests from the dining room into the library, which had been transformed during dinner so that all the seats faced toward a cinema screen that had been lowered from the ceiling. There were plates of candy and chocolate pretzels on every table. Wilbur was serving coffee and drinks at the bar. The Picasso paintings on the wall opposite the screen rose at the push of a button, revealing the windows of the projection room behind.

"Now, everybody, keep quiet about seeing this picture," said Ray as a warning to his guests. "The studio hasn't seen it yet, and even the producer doesn't know I have it."

Gus sat on a chair by the wall. He watched Marcia Clark chat with Betsy Bloomingdale as they were taking their demitasse cups to their seats. Marcia seated herself on a sofa and sipped her coffee as she glanced at one of the art books on the table in front of her. Suddenly, she looked up and saw Gus looking at her. She smiled at him, tapped the seat next to her, and signaled to him with her head to come and sit by her.

"Is this your kind of life, Gus?" she asked him in a low voice, indicating with a hand gesture the transformation of the library into the screening room. "You act like you're used to all this."

"I suppose you could say it's one aspect of my life, not all of it," replied Gus.

"Pretty ritzy, Gus," she said in a teasing voice. "You don't seem intimidated by any of these movie moguls."

"I don't need anything from any of them anymore, that's why," said Gus. "I left the business and went into other fields, like covering trials for *Vanity Fair,* or I'd probably be over there at the bar right now sucking up to David Geffen or Ron Meyer, like I used to when I was still in the picture business."

They both laughed.

"This is all new to me, people like this, houses like this, showing movies after dinner. For years, I've been reading about Betsy Bloomingdale in the society pages and fashion magazines, and here I am talking to her about the clothes I'm going to wear at the trial, as if I knew something about fashion, which I don't."

Gus laughed. "You're holding your own," he said. "I was watching you across the table during dinner. You had the moguls enthralled."

"You say all the right things, Gus," said Marcia. "Is that why everyone talks to you?"

"Maybe one of these days you'll talk to me, Marcia," said Gus. "I'd really like to write about you."

She smiled and changed the subject. "Didn't I read a book you once wrote about Betsy Bloomingdale?"

"Yeah, probably."

"And she speaks to you?"

"She's a classy lady."

"So this is society, huh?"

Just then the movie started.

7

In his "Letter from Los Angeles," Gus wrote:

The Simpson case is like a great trash novel come to life. It's a mammoth fireworks display of love, lust, lies, hate, fame, wealth, beauty, obsession, spousal abuse, stalking, brokenhearted children, interracial marriage, the bloodiest of bloody knife-slashing homicides, and all the justice that money can buy.

With Kato Kaelin, Al Cowlings, Faye Resnick, Denise Brown, and Detective Mark Fuhrman in key supporting roles, there's not a vanilla character in the whole story. Even the lawyers on both sides are bigger than life. By now, who doesn't know who Robert Shapiro and Johnnie Cochran are? Or Marcia Clark? At dinner parties and in restaurants, whole evenings are spent discussing the case. Everyone has a tidbit of information. Everyone has a theory about what happened. Even those people who affect weariness with the subject, who say things like "I'm sick, sick, sick to death of O.J.," lean in and listen intently when a new nugget is brought forth. A great many people I have en-countered were friends, or friends of friends, of O.J.'s and Nicole's before the knifings. Everyone has a topper to everyone else's piece of informa-tion. "I saw Nicole jogging in Brentwood just the day before," said a man at a screening, to which another man immediately replied, "Craig Baum-garten played golf at Riviera with O.J. on the morning of the murders."

Gus became a regular at the best restaurants in town. All the maître d's soon knew his name and always found him a good table on the right side of the room, even when he called at the last minute from the court-house or the greenroom of the Larry King show to say he was coming by in half an hour and he needed a table for two, or three, or four. He had known for a long time that people who had things to tell him relaxed and talked more when they were sitting on a velvet banquette perusing a pricey menu.

"Gus, do you have any interest in meeting O.J.'s caddy at the Riviera Country Club? He was caddy-ing for O.J. when he played with Alan Austin and Craig Baumgarten on the morning of the murders. Apparently, O.J. became enraged at his friend Craig Baumgarten because he talked while O.J. was teeing off. The caddy says he never saw O.J. lose it like that, all the times he's ever caddied for him. He said O.J.'s rage at Craig was out of all proportion to what

8 1

Craig had done. He'd be happy to talk to you, Gus. I could set it up for you to meet him. He said he'd be happy to go to the Chateau after court one day."

"You have to look at it this way, Gus. Nicole knew how to push O.J.'s buttons," said Jennifer Lee during lunch at Le Dome on the Sunset Strip. They had already talked about their mutual friend Paul Morrissey; about Jennifer's book, which Gus had liked; about Gus's book, which Jennifer had liked; and about Whoopi Goldberg's wedding, which Jennifer and her former husband, Richard Pryor, who were together again, had attended.

"You would have loved it, Gus. Whoopi had FUCK YOU painted on the roof of the house to keep the reporters in the helicopters away," said Jennifer. "Remember how the helicopters ruined the whole thing when Madonna and Sean Penn got married?"

"I saw Whoopi in Las Vegas awhile back," said Gus. "It was the night of the freeway chase, and she was terribly upset about O.J."

"That's all anyone talked about at the wedding. O.J., O.J., O.J.," said Jennifer.

"It's become the prime subject of conversation in Los Angeles," said Gus.

"When Nicole didn't save a seat for O.J. at little Sydney's dance recital that last afternoon, she knew what she was doing," said Jennifer. "She knew perfectly well how crazy that was going to make him, having to walk up and down the aisle looking for a place to sit. That's not a good look for a guy with an ego like O.J. Simpson's. Nicole knew that was the equivalent of giving him the middle finger in front of her family."

"The beginning of his rage," said Gus, making a mental note. He was beginning to see how he was going to write in his novel about the buildup of Simpson's rage on the day of the murders. The early-morning rage at Craig Baumgarten on the golf course. The reignited rage at his daughter's dance recital.

"Have I lost you, Gus?"

"No, no. Go on, Jennifer."

"And then she didn't ask him to join his kids and her parents and her sister Denise for dinner at Mez-zaluna," said Jennifer. "He's standing there with egg on his face. She's embarrassed him in front of her family."

"The rage builds," said Gus.

"You see, once Nicole found out he was still seeing Paula Barbieri on the side, after she and O.J. were supposed to be reconciling, she said, *Over, out!* Fuck you, Charlie. I think what he realized was that she really meant it. It was over. It was over for good this time."

"Guys like O.J. do the leaving. They don't like to get left," said Gus. He was thinking of Lefty Flynn. Becky had broken it off, moved back to Peach's house in Beverly Hills, and he had stalked her and killed her. "Explain something to me, Jennifer: Why did Nicole keep going back to O.J. when he had beaten her and would certainly beat her again?"

"Blame it on the way she was brought up, Gus. She'd gotten used to having her laundry done. After the divorce, she was pushing the grocery cart up and down the aisles of the supermarket, just like any other mom. She wasn't special anymore. She'd lost her cachet," replied Jennifer.

"That's what I don't miss about living out here," said Gus. "This is the only divorce I ever heard of where the husband keeps the mansion and the maids in a divorce, and the wife and kids move downscale to a condo on the wrong side of Sunset," said Gus.

Jennifer opened her gold-chained Chanel bag and fished out a package of cigarettes. "This is one of the few restaurants in town where you can still smoke. Are you going to have a fit if I smoke, Gus? I bet you don't smoke."

"I don't, but I don't mind if you do," replied Gus, not wanting her to stop talking.

"Really, you're sure?"

"I recognize an addict when I see one," said Gus.

"Oh, are you right. Richard *haaates* it if I smoke. He used to smoke like a chimney, but ever since he practically burned himself to death in that accident he was in, he won't let anybody smoke in his house. He makes me go outside, for God sake."

"How is Richard?" asked Gus.

"Did I tell you what he said to me this morning, about an hour or so ago? He said, 'Where are you going all dressed up like that?' And I said, 'I'm going to have lunch at Le Dome,' and he said, 'Who with?' and I said, 'My old friend Gus Bailey,' and he said, pointing a finger to emphasize each word, 'Don't you dare talk about O. J. Simpson with Gus Bailey, do you hear?' And he meant business. That's the way it is these days in the interracial set, Gus."

"Go on," said Gus.

"Richard is a lot like O. J. It's always *his* way. Controlling, always in control."

"Why did I think you and Richard got divorced after you wrote that book about him?" asked Gus.

"Richard and I *are* divorced, but I'm back with him. He's sick. He's got multiple sclerosis. Terrible disease."

"I know all about MS. That's what Peach has," said Gus. "My sons have been pushing her wheelchair for years."

"You're sure you don't mind? I'll blow the smoke in the other direction, toward Wendy Stark's table. Hi, Wendy," called out Jennifer.

"Honey, you can smoke the whole pack, and I'll keep lighting them for you, but, puleese, go on with your story," said Gus, striking a match to light her cigarette.

"You see, Nicole stayed too long at the fair. You're supposed to get *out* of an abusive relationship, not stay in it. Even after they were divorced and she moved out of the house, they were still involved. Nicole was a provocateur. I'm probably not pronouncing that right, but you know what I mean. She knew he was going to kill her, and she never stopped doing the one thing that she knew was going to drive him to do it."

"I could never understand Nicole giving that guy Keith Zlomsowitch a blow job in the living room of her rented house on Gretna Green, with the candles lit and the curtains open, when she knew O.J. was stalking her," said Gus.

"Well, now you do," replied Jennifer. "That's the game. Do you know what happens when you don't get out? It becomes a dance of death. That's what Nicole and O.J. were in, Gus, a dance of death. You won't quote me, will you, Gus? I mean, you can tell the story, but don't attach my name to it. Is that a deal?"

"I won't use it in the magazine. I'll save it for the novel, which I'm going to write when the trial's all over. But I don't understand why so many of you who know things never want to have your names used. There're two people dead here."

"Suppose he's acquitted, Gus. That's why. Richard and I move in the same circles."

"He can't be acquitted, Jennifer. There's no way," said Gus. "From what I hear, the evidence the prosecution has against him is overwhelming."

"Oh, get real, Gus," said Jennifer, giving him a pitying look for his lack of understanding. "None of you gets it, what's going to happen. This is O.J. Simpson. Don't ever forget that."

She was right. Gus didn't get it. He thought the DNA evidence was going to cinch it for the prosecution.

Gus liked to have dinner with the reporters so that they could spend the whole time talking about the case. David Margolick of the *New York Times* and he went to Cicada. Shirley Perlman of *Newsday* and he went to Morton's. Harvey Levin of KCBS and Pat Lalama of *Hard Copy* went to Eclipse. That night, he went to dinner at Drai's with Dan Abrams, the young commentator on the Simpson trial for Court TV. Dan, a lawyer himself, was the son of the famed constitutional lawyer Floyd Abrams. Gus was impressed with Dan's grasp of the most minute legal points and his ability to translate them almost instantly on-camera, making the information totally understandable to the television audience.

"I'm good with the people part of the trial," said Gus. "I'm not so good with the legal part, so I crib from your reports when I watch you on Court TV at night, and my editor at *Vanity Fair* thinks I'm smart as hell that I know so much about the law."

Dan laughed. "Shapiro says that you know more about the story than anyone else except him and Johnnie Cochran, because you stand out there in the corridor and everyone comes up and tells you things," said Dan.

Gus laughed. "That's true," he said. "Including him. He's told me a couple of amazing things. You know, I've sort of gotten to like Shapiro, and I didn't think I was going to like him at all when the trial started and he was playing Brad Pitt at the premiere. I saw him here at Drai's the other night. He was having dinner alone with Linell. I stopped by his table on the way to the men's room, and he introduced me to Linell. At first, she was a little cool to me. Shapiro said, 'I see you're with the big guns over there.' I was with Lew and Edie Wasserman, about whom it's always said or written that he's the most powerful man in Hollywood. Shapiro's really a part of the show-business community, and he was impressed with the Wassermans. Then Linell said the damnedest thing to me. She said, 'This whole thing has been awful for us, Gus. Everyone we know thinks O.J. is guilty, and friends we've had for years don't see us anymore because they don't want to be seen with us. Bob likes to go out nights and see people, but we can't anymore. It's become a nightmare for us. We hardly ever go to restaurants, because people come up to our table and say terrible things to Bob because he's representing O.J. "How could you represent that killer?" Things like that. I thought that was what you were going to do when you came up to the table.' I'd never really thought of it from her point of view before. I bet Shapiro wishes he'd never come near this case. Except for Cochran, I think every one of O.J.'s lawyers is going to be damaged by their association with him."

"How do you remember conversations like that? What Linell said to you?" asked Dan.

"I just told you that I was on my way to the men's room when I stopped to speak to them, and I took out this little green leather notebook I always carry and wrote it down," said Gus.

During their conversation, people came up to the table and greeted Gus. Everyone had something to say to him about O. J. Simpson.

"Hi, Ed," said Gus to Ed Limato, a famous actors' agent, as he passed the table with a beautiful film star. Gus popped to his feet and kissed the lady on both cheeks. During their thirty-second conversation, the star said she enjoyed reading his commentary on the trial in *Vanity Fair,* and Gus told her he was thrilled she was going to play Evita. They both mentioned Gus's son Grafton.

"Oh, excuse me, this is Dan Abrams, who's covering the trial for Court TV," said Gus.

"Yes, I've seen you," she said, and then moved on.

"Gus, that was Madonna, for Christ sake. You just introduced me to Madonna," said Dan, who was ecstatic. "How do you know her?"

"My son Grafton was in a picture with her once," said Gus.

"Who was the guy she was with?"

"He's her agent, Ed Limato. Ed handles every big star you ever heard of. And he gives the best Academy Awards party each year."

"How come you know all these movie people?" asked Dan.

"I used to be in the picture business. For many years, as a matter of fact."

"I didn't know that. Director?"

"Producer. That was a long time ago."

"Did you produce any pictures I might have heard of?"

"Probably."

"Which ones?"

"Let's not talk about my film career now. It's all blessedly behind me."

"What's it like for you coming back here again?"

"Strange, quite strange. I have mixed feelings. Some terrible things happened to me here, to me and to people I loved. My career in films ended out here because I fucked things up for myself. Failure is the one unforgivable sin here, and I failed."

"Really?" asked Dan.

"There's a line in one of my books about it. It goes something like this: 'Hollywood is very unforgiving of failure. It will forgive you, even overlook, your forgeries, your embezzlements, and, occasionally, your murders, but it will never forgive you your failure.'"

"But all these people seem thrilled to see you," replied Dan.

"Oh, yes. It's as if it never happened. Writing a couple of best-sellers changes a lot of people's minds about you, even the kind of people who have categorized you as a failure in the past."

"Are you bitter?"

"Not in the least. That's the way of the world, at least the world I've always lived in," said Gus.

"Do you produce the miniseries they make from your books?"

"No. I'm sometimes offered that, but it's not what I want to do anymore," said Gus.

"You like this career better than the movie career?"

"Hell yes. I was faking it then. I'm not faking it anymore."

8

In his "Letter from Los Angeles," Gus wrote:

O. J. Simpson, whatever his private torments may be, puts on a front that is as audacious as his absolutely 100-percent-not-guilty reply to the guilty-or-not-guilty query of Judge Ito. He enters the courtroom each time looking like a star in a courtroom drama. Robert Shapiro and Johnnie Cochran often precede him out the door of the holding room, where Simpson's manacles have been removed from his wrists and feet by Deputy Jex and he changes from his jailhouse blues into his own beautifully cut suits, which his friend Robert Kardashian takes to get cleaned and altered at a tailor shop in Brentwood. They often enter laughing, as if they had just heard a wonderful joke. Shapiro sometimes turns back to Simpson to whisper some final thing. They are all aware that the camera is on them, and behave accordingly. In showbiz, where I once toiled, it's called making an entrance.

The leading players in the story are beginning to find the camera intoxicating. They have

92

learned to know exactly when the camera is on them without having to look into the lens, and they assume their attitudes as it pans past them. They are aware when the lens zooms in for a close-up and act accordingly. Simpson is particularly good at it. So is Shapiro. No one loves it more than Judge Ito, although he pretends to despise it. He is said to be delighted with the success of the Dancing Itos on the Jay Leno show, and people claim that he shows videos of the Dancing Itos to some celebrity visitors in his chambers.

"You know why Ito got the job, don't you?" asked Mavis Jordache, a reporter friend of Gus's from several previous trials, with whom he was having lunch in the cafeteria of the Criminal Courts Building in Los Angeles, where the trial was taking place. Between trials, they kept in touch by telephone.

"I don't, no," replied Gus. "I'd never heard of Judge Ito before."

Mavis looked in both directions to make sure no one was watching her and then pulled the skin by the side of each of her eyes sideways, turning herself into an Oriental.

"May I quote you?" asked Gus.

"But it's true," insisted Mavis. "If they had a white judge, it would be said that he was favoring the prosecution, and if they had a black judge, it would be said that he was favoring O.J., and neither side wanted a Hispanic, because Hispanics don't like blacks, and blacks don't like Hispanics. So who's left? No one's going to admit that's true, Gus, but I happen to know."

"What's Ito like?" asked Gus.

"Hates the media. Calls us 'jackals.' Secretly, he loves getting famous, though. I know one of the law clerks. He tells me stuff. Writes fan letters, I hear. And Ito's wife, you know about his wife, don't you?"

"I know she's the highest-ranking woman in the Los Angeles Police Department. Is there more than that?"

"Captain Peggy York by name. She's involved in this story, too, far more than she wants anyone to know," said Mavis.

"Tell me everything," said Gus.

"She has a past history with Detective Mark Fuhrman, which ought to disqualify Ito from sitting on this case. They had some serious problems together, and a big dislike exists. What I hear is, Peggy Policewoman is going to deny she knew Fuhrman, or say she can't remember him. She doesn't want her Lance to lose the biggest gig of his career at the trial of the century."

"A novelist couldn't make up a cast list like this," said Gus.

"And Cochran knows the facts, but he doesn't want to lose Ito. This way, he's got a hold over him. Cochran's going to run that courtroom, not Ito," said Mavis.

"Other than looking Oriental, hating the media, and being married to a cop with a secret, what are his qualifications for the job? What kind of a judge is Ito supposed to be?" asked Gus.

"His only other big case was the Charles Keating trial," replied Mavis.

"That's a good sign," said Gus. "How many years did Keating get?"

On the day Jerrianne Hayslett, who was in charge of media relations for Judge Lance Ito, posted the seating arrangement for the media in the courtroom, there were screams of disappointment from those who had to share seats, or did not get seated at all in the courtroom. To Gus's astonishment, he received a permanent seat in the front row that he did not have to share for alternate periods with other reporters. Gus could feel that there was a great deal of resentment toward him because of his privileged appointment.

An article appeared on the front page of the *Los Angeles Times* in which he was sneeringly referred to as a "celebrity author," who had been given preferential treatment by the judge, and, more mockingly, as "Judith Krantz in pants," which an unpleasant fellow from the Copley News Service was quoted as saying. No one enjoyed the Judith Krantz appellation more than Leslie Abramson, with whom Gus had crossed swords in print in the past, who found it hilarious to refer to Gus thereafter as Judy and to his books as "jumped-up romance" novels.

Abramson's husband, less celebrated than she, was a reporter for the *Los Angeles Times,* assigned to cover the Simpson trial as part of their team, and Abramson herself had become a legal commentator on the Simpson trial for the ABC network.

Judge Burton Katz, who had presided at the trial of the man who had killed Gus's daughter fifteen years earlier, showed up in the media pool one day at the Simpson trial as a legal correspondent for a tabloid television show, with press credentials from the *Malibu Times*. Katz was no longer a judge. An article that Gus had written years before, about the mockery of justice that the trial had been, had always been rumored as having had something to do with that, but the fact was that Katz had retired from the bench with a disability pension and was in the process of developing a new career as a television commentator. He looked familiar to Gus on the morning of his first day, while the reporters were waiting in line for their daily press badges, but he did not immediately recognize him after so many years.

"Yeah, I'm the guy you keep taking potshots at," said Katz, a hint of self-pity in his voice. He was sitting on a bench in the corridor outside the courtroom. Several reporters turned to watch.

Then Gus remembered who he was. Vile feelings erupted within him as memories of their bitter exchange on the final day of the trial returned to him. The cockiness and the swagger that Gus remembered so vividly were no longer apparent, but his eyes had not lost their hardness as they locked for an instant with Gus's eyes.

In that instant, Gus sensed again the rage he had

felt on the day of the verdict, when Judge Katz thanked the jury on behalf of the families for the verdict that would release Lefty Flynn from prison in two and a half years. Outraged at the affront by a judge he had grown to disrespect and then dislike during the trial, Gus stood up in the courtroom and yelled out, "Don't thank the jury on behalf of *my* family, Judge Katz." As he continued his harangue, two deputies carried him out of the courtroom.

Seeing Katz again, Gus relived that moment. He made a sound of disgust and turned away. Their unpleasant encounter was reported in *USA Today.*

"Judge Ito would like to see you in chambers," said Deputy Jex to Gus a few days later, in the snarling tone of voice he used when speaking to members of the media. From the beginning, Gus had not been able to abide Deputy Jex, whose face was perpetually scowling. Gus might not have minded Jex's unpleasantness quite so much if he had been equally unpleasant to the defendant on trial for double murder. Instead, he addressed him in the fawning manner of a fan at a Buffalo Bills game.

It was the first time that Gus had met Judge Ito, who had sprung to national prominence since his appointment as judge in the Simpson trial. There were those in the media who had taken an early dislike to him because of the contemptuous manner with which he treated them.

Judge Ito, who was smaller than Gus expected

him to be, was in his shirtsleeves, sitting at his desk when Gus entered.

"Sit down, sit down, Mr. Bailey," he said, motioning Gus to a sofa opposite his desk. Behind the sofa, at the end of the room, several law clerks were busily at work. Gus wondered which one was Mavis's friend.

"I've read some of your coverage from the Menendez trial," said the judge. "You certainly take a very definite stand. There's no mistaking how you feel about those young men."

"I'm lucky to write for a magazine that lets me take a stand, Your Honor," replied Gus.

"It's come to my attention that there are some people who are giving you a hard time because of your seat in the courtroom," he said.

"I can handle that, Your Honor," said Gus.

"You must understand, they're giving me a hard time as well, because of your seat in the courtroom," said Judge Ito.

"Oh?" For a minute Gus thought that the judge was going to take the seat away from him.

"I would like you to know that *I* assigned you that seat. That seat is yours for the length of this trial," he said.

"Thank you, Your Honor," said Gus. "I am very grateful."

Ito stood up, indicating that the meeting was over. He walked with Gus to the door of the chambers. As they stood by the door, he asked, "Have you ever seen anything like this, Mr. Bailey?"

Gus didn't have to be told that the judge was referring to the media event that the trial was becoming.

"I haven't, Your Honor," he replied, "and I've covered a lot of high-profile cases. Sometimes it's scary outside the building, with all those people yelling. I often have the feeling that the slightest spark could ignite something very ugly."

Ito looked Gus squarely in the eye. "You see, I felt very safe in giving you a seat next to either the Brown or the Goldman family," he said. "I knew that you would know how to deal with the families, that you wouldn't intrude on them or ask questions."

Gus, understanding, met the judge's look. He knew that Judge Ito, without saying the words, was referring to the murder of his daughter, Becky. He knew that the judge realized that he, like Louis Brown, the father of Nicole, and Fred Goldman, the father of Ron, was the father of a murdered child.

"Thank you, Your Honor," he said again as he went out the door.

"I don't know Faye Resnick. I've never met her. She came into Nicole's life in the last couple of years," said a lady who was also named Nicole. She called Gus at the Chateau Marmont from the car phone in her Ferrari. She didn't want to give her last name. "I work at Van Cleef and Arpels in Beverly Hills, and I just can't get involved in this thing, but I loved Nicole. She was my friend. We went to high school together. We were both blond. We were both named Nicole. We both had daughters the same age. We both drove Ferraris. We were both in abusive marriages. Only I got out of mine. Nicole's mother always wanted those girls to connect with rich men. Nicole was with O.J. from the time she was about seventeen. Faye Resnick covered it all in her book. She got it right. The Browns may not like the book, but the way Faye wrote it is the way it was. What she wrote is heartbreakingly true. I could have done without the blow-job story—some day the kids are going to read that—but it was her life. Nicole was a woman with her own life."

"I want to meet Faye Resnick," said Gus to Michael Viner. Viner was the publisher of Faye's best-selling book, *Nicole Brown Simpson: The Private Diary of a Life Interrupted*. "I had her all wrong. I thought she was some bimbo who was capitalizing on her friend's murder, but I saw her interview with Connie Chung last night, and I changed my mind. She's a gutsy lady, and she makes no bones about how she feels about O.J.'s guilt. Can you set it up for me, Michael?"

On the night of the murders, Faye Resnick, Nicole's close friend, was in a drug rehab center, for problems with cocaine. As far as was known, she had been the last person to speak on the telephone to Nicole before she was murdered. Their conversations were intimate. She told Faye private things—it was only afterward, when it was too late, that all her friends began to compare notes.

Faye was an unknown at the time of the murders, except in her own immediate circle, which in no way overlapped with any of the Los Angeles circles in which Gus Bailey moved. But, with the publication of her book, which documented her friendship with Nicole, the spotlight of fame began to shine on her, and the name Faye Resnick became known to everyone who followed the trial. No publicist or rave review could have done a better job of making her book known throughout the land than Judge Ito, who, miscalculating his newfound importance, asked the networks not to interview her on the debut of the book. His ill-advised interference caused people to rush to their bookstores and guaranteed weeks and then months on the *New York Times* best-seller list.

Faye's book showed a world of fast-living, drug-taking, promiscuous B-crowd people with money, and Ferraris, and Rolex watches, on their way to nowhere. It was a group that Gus was aware of but had never interacted with in the years he had lived in Los Angeles. "This is not what I would call a productive crowd," said Gus to Viner. "All the women seem to do is jog on San Vicente, drink coffee at Starbucks, go to the gym, dance the night away at clubs, and suck the dicks of strangers. I found her book fascinating but eerie. That kind of life is a blueprint for disaster."

From the minute they met, Gus and Faye were an unlikely duo, but they got on well and became friends.

"O.J. couldn't look me in the eye at the funeral," said Faye to Gus one night at Drai's, when Viner arranged for them to meet. "He knows how much I know. He wants me dead, Gus. I know too much about this guy. It wasn't just what Nicole told me; I saw it with my own eyes. I know all about his drug use. I've done cocaine with him. And he's saying now that he didn't do drugs. Bullshit!"

"Does it worry you that so many people think he didn't do it?" asked Gus.

"Get real, Gus. The kind of people who think O.J. didn't do it are not the kind of people he's interested in," said Faye. "If they release him, they're releasing a dangerous man. He's not sorry for what he did. He's sorry he got caught."

"Hear, hear," said Gus. "You're getting famous, Faye. Every time you sound off on *Larry King* the way you do, you sell another ten thousand books."

"I'm so tired of people going on television and talking about me," said Faye. "I'm getting attacked by people I don't even know, who say they know me. Some guy said on TV he had nude pictures of me. There are no nude pictures of me. They're talking about a different person. It's not me. People I don't know say they did drugs with me."

"The 'fallout from fame,' it's called," said Gus. "Everyone wants to be in on the act in this case. Do

you think the defense will put you on the stand?"
asked Gus.

"I doubt it. I'm too full of ammunition on O.J. I
know too much, and I'm one of the very few people
who isn't intimidated by him," said Faye. "Chris
Darden thinks they'll rip me apart without calling
me. He thinks they're afraid of what I might say up
there."

9

In his "Letter from Los Angeles," Gus wrote:

The loyalty of the Simpson family toward the defendant on trial is extraordinarily touching. His mother, daughter, son, nieces, a brother no one knew about, his brother-in-law, his first wife and her current husband, and others have attended the trial, but none have been as stalwart in their attendance and devotion as his two sisters, Shirley Baker and Carmelita Durio. Both San Franciscans, they and Shirley's husband, Benny, are staying at Simpson's heavily guarded house on Rockingham Avenue. Most nights, they visit him in jail. Carmelita attends the trial Monday through Thursday and then goes to San Francisco on a three-day weekend. Shirley attends Tuesday through Friday and then goes to San Francisco to be with her daughters and grandchildren, so one or the other or both are always in the courtroom as supportive presences for their brother. "I go back up to San Francisco to make sure my job is still there, and my husband is still there, and my child is still there," Carmelita told me.

For reasons he had not yet discovered, Gus's fascination with the case exceeded by far the normal fascination that a journalist or novelist feels for a good story in the making. One of the many curiosities of Gus's life during that period was that he became friends with O.J. Simpson's sisters and brother-in-law, even though he firmly believed that Simpson was guilty of the murders with which he was charged. Benny Baker, who was married to Simpson's sister Shirley, said to him in the corridor outside the courtroom, "Did it ever occur to you, Gus, how similar this case is to your own?"

It was a thought that was waiting to happen for Gus, and Benny, without knowing it, brought it to fruition. He had just read Gus's article, called "Justice," from fourteen years before, about the trial of the man who had killed Gus's daughter. Gus thought that what Benny was referring to were the beatings, the bruises, the stalking, the abject fear that characterized both Nicole Brown Simpson and Becky Bailey in the days before their deaths.

The two men looked at each other for an instant and then quickly looked away. They had never discussed the heart of the matter, the crux of what had brought them together on a daily basis: the dreadful bloody murders of Nicole and Ron. Nor had they discussed the defendant on trial, about whom they had very different opinions as to his guilt or innocence.

"What happened to that guy, Gus?" asked Benny.

"He did two and a half and got out," replied Gus.

"Where is he now?"

"I don't know."

"Don't know? Really?"

"We let go after awhile, my sons and I. I hired a private detective to follow him right after he got out, a guy by the name of Pellicano, Anthony Pellicano— you probably read about him during the Michael Jackson case with the little boy—but I didn't want that to become what my life was about, trailing a killer. You can't let your life be about revenge, Benny. I don't know where he is. I don't want to know where he is. He's out of my life, never to be heard from again, I hope," said Gus.

Gus had not set out to make friends with the family of O.J. Simpson with the ulterior motive of gleaning information out of them about life at Rock-ingham, where they were living in Simpson's house during the trial. The friendship between them developed over a period of time and a succession of minor events. In every courtroom in which he had sat since the death of Becky, watching rich-people justice, which was his specialty, he was more interested in the people in the case than in the legalities. He was particularly interested in the defendant's family, individuals who had had nothing to do with the murders but whose lives were changed forever because of them. In the first weeks of the trial, he had stared at the

Simpson family and was struck by both their loyalty and their dignity. Back then, they spoke to almost no one, except one another. They were there every day, always on time, always smiling warmly at their brother each time he entered the courtroom from the holding room in the company of his lawyers.

"What's this like for you to be going through?" he asked Carmelita one day during a bomb scare, when the courthouse was evacuated. They had taken refuge from the blazing sun in the television trailer of Channel 9, after the ninth floor of the courthouse, where the trial was being held, had been cleared. There were twenty television monitors in the trailer, and O.J. Simpson's face was on every one. He was the biggest story in the country.

Carmelita stared up at her brother on the monitors and for more than a minute didn't reply to Gus's question. Gus wondered if he had been pushy and had offended her, but then she started to talk, very quietly, without turning to look at him. "It's like living in someone else's nightmare, Gus, a nightmare that's never going to end. There's no way anyone can know what it's like."

"I know," said Gus.

"Not from our side you don't," said Carmelita, still staring at the monitors.

"I used to watch the mother of the man who killed my daughter in the courtroom during that trial. My feeling was that she was a good woman, who'd worked hard all her life, and she was sitting in a courtroom, being loyal to her son, who had strangled a girl. No one ever spoke to her. Her son never even waved at her. I hated her son. They'd dressed him up like a sacristan in a Catholic seminary, and he always read the Bible with a beatific expression on his face. That was his act to fool the jury, and the assholes fell for it. But I felt sorry for his mother. Siobhan, her name was. She had red hands and carried a cheap suitcase, but there was a quiet dignity about her. She didn't do anything wrong. That's how I know what it's like from your side."

Carmelita turned around to face Gus. Before she could speak, David Goldstein, the commentator for Channel 9 on the Simpson case, came on the monitor to say that the pipe bomb had been detonated by the bomb squad and that it was safe to return to the courtroom.

Not long after that, Carmelita said to Gus one day, "Truman's coming to court tomorrow."

"Who's Truman?" asked Gus.

"Our brother," she replied.

"O.J. has a brother? I didn't know that," said Gus in a tone of voice that registered surprise.

"We all have a brother, Gus," replied Shirley.

"Of course. I'm sorry, Shirley. He is brother to all of you."

Until then, almost no one seemed to know that Truman even existed. He came to court the next day in the company of two friends, and Shirley Baker introduced him to Gus in the corridor outside the courtroom. "This is our brother Truman," she said quietly.

"Hello," said Gus, turning to Truman and putting out his hand.

"Gus Bailey is the one who wrote those books that Benny is reading back at the house," said Shirley.

Truman smiled and shook hands with Gus, nodding his head to acknowledge that he knew who Gus was from family conversations. There was indeed a strong family resemblance, Gus noticed, but the looks that worked so perfectly on the face of O.J. Simpson did not work as well on the face of his brother. Gus noted also that there was a vacant look in his eyes.

"And these are Truman's friends, Billy Maple and Conrad, uh, forgive me, I forgot your last name, Conrad," said Shirley.

"Oxnard."

"Oh, right, Conrad Oxnard, Gus Bailey," said Shirley.

Gus shook hands again. "All of you down from San Francisco?" he asked, making small talk. Gus was good at small talk when the situation warranted, and he kept up a running commentary for the trio on the personalities of the trial, as they arrived for the morning session, at the same time that he was observing Truman Simpson.

"Too bad you guys weren't here yesterday," he said. "A man wearing a dress, earrings, and pearls caused a disruption in the courtroom and was dragged out by a couple of deputies, and then Barbara Walters came to court and, naturally, Judge Ito took her back into chambers for a chat while we cooled our heels out here. Every time a celebrity comes to court, which is practically every day these days, the trial stops while the judge has a backstage chat. Let me see now. There was James Woods, the movie star, who's an O.J. addict, as is Mark Hamill of *Star Wars,* and Larry King, Katie Couric, Diane Sawyer—on and on. It's the new status symbol in L.A., getting a seat at the Simpson trial. Oh, look, guys, there's Marcia Clark coming in, in the beige suit with the very short skirt." They chatted until Deputy Jex opened the door and allowed the Simpson family members and guests to go into the courtroom and take their seats for the morning session.

Gus had noticed that no one else was introduced to Truman. Having had a personal drug involvement in his long-ago past, it occurred to him that the mystery brother in the Simpson family might be similarly inclined. "It's a look in the eyes," Gus said later. It had also occurred to him that the two friends of Truman were probably keepers hired by the family to hold him in check in the event of untoward behavior. After the lunch break, Truman and his friends did not return to court for the afternoon session.

That evening, after taping a segment for *Rivera Live,* Gus was in his suite at the Chateau Marmont dressing to go out to a dinner party at Betsy Bloomingdale's. "Gus, can I get you for dinner on Tuesday, dressy, not black tie? The Annenbergs will be here, and they're *dying* to hear about the trial, and you'll know everyone," Betsy had said when she invited him. "Can you come?" asked Betsy. "Hell yes," replied Gus. It was to be his first visit back to that house. He called down to the garage for his car to be ready. As he was leaving the room, the telephone rang.

"Hello?" He answered in a tone of voice that suggested he was rushed and late for where he was supposed to be at that time.

"Mr. Bailey?"

"Yes? Who is it?"

"Conrad."

"Who?"

"Conrad Oxnard. I met you in court today. I was there with Truman Simpson."

"Oh, of course, Conrad, forgive me. What can I do for you?"

"I've got quite a story to tell, Mr. Bailey—you know, for the right price, I mean. I could tell by the look on your face today that you got the picture."

"The picture?"

"The family secret. You knew the minute you looked at Truman what the story was," said Conrad.

"Put it this way, Conrad, it takes one to know one. I had my own troubles in that department years ago," said Gus.

"That's why we didn't come back after lunch," said Conrad. "Did you notice the family didn't introduce him to anyone? Did you notice none of O.J.'s lawyers even looked in his direction? Did you notice O.J. didn't even nod to his own brother? They want anything about drugs to stay as far away as possible from this trial, especially drugs in the Simpson family."

"Why did they let him come to court, then?"

"He insisted, and they couldn't stop him. He said everyone in the country's talking about this trial, and he wanted to see it, because it's his own brother. Are you interested in getting together? I could tell you some stuff Truman told me about the family that would knock you on your ass."

Gus was not alone in believing that O.J. Simpson had been high on drugs when he killed Nicole and Ron. A drug dealer named Ron X, who had come to see Gus at his hotel, had taken and passed a lie-detector test after claiming that he had sold crystal meth, the highest form of speed, to O.J. and Kato Kaelin in the parking lot of a Burger King franchise in the Brentwood area on the night of the murders. But there was no proof, and both the defense and the prosecution seemed to want to avoid the topic of drugs in the murder trial.

"Listen, Conrad, I don't pay for news, and my magazine doesn't pay for news, either. What you're selling about O.J.'s brother has nothing to do with the trial or the murders. I'm sorry. I'm not interested. Listen, I have to go. I was due somewhere for dinner half an hour ago."

On the Sunday and Monday evenings before the Tuesday that Gus was due for dinner at Betsy Bloomingdale's, the ABC network had substituted its regular program at the last minute with a rerun of the four-year-old miniseries of *An Inconvenient Woman*. Gus had no inkling of the change in programming until O.J. Simpson's niece, Terri Baker, the daughter of Shirley and Benny Baker, told him she couldn't wait to see it on Sunday and Monday nights, as she had just finished reading the novel. "Dear God," said Gus, joyless at the news of his good fortune. He considered calling Betsy and backing out of her dinner, so as not to cause her any further embarrassment, but he kept postponing making the call, and didn't. All day at the trial, people had told him they had seen it.

Always late for parties, he was the last to arrive at Betsy's house. As the butler handed him the small white envelope with the number of the table at which he was to sit at dinner, Gus was reminded of the similarity to the scene in his book when the character of Philip Quennell, which was based on himself, had arrived late on his first visit to the magnificent art-filled house, where the Mendelsons' party was already under way.

The butler, whose name was Dudley, had also been a character in Gus's book, and Gus could tell from his greeting that he had seen the miniseries the night before in which he had been portrayed.

"Hello, Dudley," said Gus.

"Mr. Bailey," replied Dudley. "The guests are having cocktails in the pool house."

"Do you think I should have canceled, Dudley?" asked Gus.

The butler smiled. "From what I gather, more

people saw the rerun the last two nights than they did when your miniseries first came out."

"The entire city seems to have seen it," said Gus. "Why am I not exulting at the ratings?"

"At least it took their minds off O.J. Simpson," said Dudley.

"There's that to be said."

"We watch you on *Larry King* and Dan Rather. Just one thing?"

"What?"

"Do you think O.J. will walk?"

"Oh, no, I don't think he'll walk, but they won't be able to convict him, either. Not with that jury. One of them was carrying a black-power paperback book in court today. Hung jury is what I think it's going to be," said Gus. "Well, here I go into the fray."

He walked out through the atrium, where the tables were set for dinner, and across the lawn, past the pool, to where the guests were gathered in the pool pavilion. Everyone was in the appropriate attire of summer, the ladies in chiffon dresses, wearing pearl necklaces and diamond pins, and the men in blue blazers and white linen trousers. Gus was aware as he walked toward the pavilion that he was being looked at and talked about. There was a time when he had been persona non grata with this very group, after the publication of the book that had been on television the night before. Then he saw Betsy detach herself from her guests and walk out onto the lawn to greet him with a kiss on each cheek, in full view of all as he came down the lawn.

"I'm sorry to be so late, Betsy," said Gus, reciprocating the society kiss.

"I was sure you had to be on *Larry King,* or *Geraldo,* or that other one—whatshisname?" replied Betsy. "Dudley tells me. He watches you religiously."

"None of the above, actually. I had the most extraordinary telephone call from a keeper of O.J.'s mystery brother, wanting to sell me a story about him. Everyone's trying to make a buck off poor Nicole and Ron."

"Denise Hale called earlier tonight from San Francisco," said Betsy. "I told her you were coming to dinner. She said, 'Gus Bailey leads the most interesting life of any of us.'"

"I just hang out with more killers than you guys do," said Gus.

"Everyone wants to sit next to you."

"O.J. Simpson has improved my social position," said Gus. "The other night, I had a better seat at the Marvin Davis dinner than Kevin Costner did."

"Wouldn't O.J. love to hear that?" replied Betsy.

"Listen, Betsy, thanks for coming out here and greeting me like this in front of everybody. Now all your guests know it's okay to speak to me. Believe me, I didn't know they were going to run the miniseries again."

They turned to walk toward the guests in the pavilion. "Did you get paid again for the rerun?" asked Betsy.

"Ouch," replied Gus.

When Charles Wick, who had been part of the

kitchen cabinet during a previous presidential administration, rose from his seat and tapped his dessert fork against his champagne glass for silence, Gus knew that he was going to be asked to speak. It was the sort of thing that had started to happen to him almost nightly, at whatever house he was dining. To his amazement, he had grown to enjoy giving his capsule version of the events of the day in the courtroom. Charlie, who understood protocol, gave thanks first to Betsy for the beautiful party they were attending; then he said, "Gus Bailey here has been entertaining us at our table with some stories from the courtroom, and I was wondering, Gus, if you'd care to stand up and share some of them with Betsy's guests, or answer some of their questions?"

"Oh, of course, Charlie, sure, just for a minute or so," said Gus, rising. "One of the things that is so surprising about being in the courtroom every day is to watch the relationship and interplay between Nicole's family and O.J.'s family. They have, of course, been interrelated for seventeen years, but when you consider that the son of one family is on trial for murdering the daughter of the other, it seems quite unusual that they should greet one another each day as warmly as they do. Just today, Nicole's mother, Juditha, was showing pictures of little Justin's seventh-birthday party to Eunice Simpson, O.J.'s mother. At one point, Juditha said about Justin, 'He has the most beautiful eyes.' The friendliness won't last, of course. By the end of the trial, they won't be speaking."

"This was a wonderful evening, Betsy," said Gus when he was making an early exit. "I'm going to be on *Good Morning America,* and we go on the air at four A.M., so I have to get back to the hotel and get some sleep. It was a terrific party."

"Oh, thank you, Gus," replied Betsy. "You bring out the Emerald Cunard in me." They both laughed. "I hear you go out to dinner every night."

"I'm finding all this dining out very Proustian," said Gus. "Swann, who was socially controversial, went out to dinner every night. Whether he was at the Guermantes or the Verdurins or wherever, every-one talked about the Dreyfus case. Out here, I go out to dinner every night, and everyone talks about the O.J. Simpson case. Only here, at least in the houses where I have dinner, nobody is divided in their opin-ion about the guilt of Mr. O.J. Simpson, the way they were about Dreyfus at those Parisian dinners Swann went to."

"I hope you didn't mind when Charlie asked you to speak."

"Oh, no. It's become a nightly occurrence on the social circuit. I call myself 'the floor show,'" said Gus.

"That was a nice story you told about the two grandmothers, looking at their little grandson's pic tures. It's heart-wrenching, really."

"By the end of the trial, they'll never speak to each other again. Whether the jury finds Simpson guilty or innocent, either way, one side's going to win and the other is going to lose, and the damage between the families will be irreparable. Listen, Betsy, before I go, there's something I want to say to you. I know I hurt your feelings when I wrote that and I know I hurt your kids' feelings, and it's always bothered me. That was never my intent."

"Oh, Gus, let's not talk about it," said Betsy, looking away.

"It was the same thing with what was left of the Woodward family, when I wrote *The Two Mrs. Grenvilles*. If I hadn't written it, someone else would have, and that someone else would have put in a lot of things that I chose to leave out. In both cases. Anyway, I think you're a terrific lady, Betsy, and I thank you for inviting me."

The next day, Gus said to Benny in the cafeteria of the courthouse, while they were waiting in line with their trays for the steam table, "There's something I think you ought to know, Benny. I had a call from one of those guys who was in court with Truman yesterday."

Benny, surprised, looked at Gus. "Yes?"

"He wanted to sell me some information about your brother-in-law," said Gus.

"What kind of information?" asked Benny, his voice tense.

"Of the druggy variety, I gathered."

"Jesus."

"He was looking for money. I said that we don't pay at my magazine. He seemed surprised at that. I thought you ought to know, because there're people covering this trial who do pay."

Later in the day, Shirley Baker said to Gus, "That was nice of you to tell us that, Gus."

"What he had to tell me, I didn't need to know. It had nothing to do with the case," replied Gus.

"My poor brain-dead brother," said Carmelita about Truman.

"What do you guys do nights?" asked Gus. "Do you sit home every night?"

"Sometimes we go to Denice Halicki's Bible class. Several nights a week, we go down to jail to visit O.J. He takes a big interest in family matters, like our brother Truman," said Carmelita.

"I mean, do you ever have any fun, or are you trapped in O.J.'s house all the time?"

"We go out to dinner at Jason's restaurant some nights. It's not actually Jason's restaurant, but it's where he cooks," said Carmelita.

"Jason's a chef?" asked Gus. Lefty Flynn, the man who killed Becky, had been a chef at Ma Maison on Melrose, a popular restaurant of the time with the film crowd, which went defunct in the wake of the murder and the trial. "I didn't know that."

"He's the sous-chef at a restaurant called Jackson's on Beverly Boulevard," said Carmelita.

"Is that the restaurant owned by Michael Jackson's son? I don't mean Elizabeth Taylor's friend Michael Jackson that Johnnie Cochran represented in the child molestation case," said Gus.

"We know. We know," said Carmelita. "The talk-show host Michael Jackson."

"Is that a known fact, that O. J. Simpson's son is the sous-chef at Jackson's?" asked Gus.

"Don't write about it, Gus. He doesn't want to be a tourist attraction," said Carmelita. "He'd lose the job if people started going there to look at him or ask him about his father."

"Okay."

During a break, Gus went up to Harvey Levin's cubicle in one of the media rooms on the eleventh floor of the courthouse.

"Harvey, how about having dinner at Jackson's on Beverly Boulevard tonight?" asked Gus.

"I thought we were going to Morton's," said Harvey.

"We were, but I just heard from Carmelita Durio that Jason Simpson is the sous-chef at Jackson's on Beverly Boulevard," said Gus. He leaned in and whispered as he spoke, so the television reporters in the cubicles around Harvey couldn't hear his news.

"No!"

"I promised Carmelita I wouldn't write about it, because it would become part of the O. J. Simpson tour of the city for all the O. J. junkies, but I didn't say I wouldn't go and have a look at him in his kitchen whites," said Gus. "He's never once spoken to me in the courtroom. Arnelle speaks. Jason doesn't."

"He probably won't come out of the kitchen if the waiters tell him we're there," said Harvey.

"We can yell, 'My compliments to the chef,' and clap and clap until he comes out," said Gus. "This is going to make a great scene for my novel, the overlapping of the worlds in Los Angeles. I go on Michael Jackson's radio show several times a week. He tapes me early in the morning at the Chateau before I leave for the trial, or sometimes he tapes me at night for the next day. I never hide the fact that I think Simpson is the killer, and I wonder if Jason listens to the show in the kitchen when he's preparing. In the novel, I'm going to have Jason in the kitchen at Jackson's listen to his boss's father's radio show and hear me tell the story about the time he tried to destroy the statue of his father with a baseball bat. And later in the story, carrying the bat forward in the plot, I'm going to have O.J. use that same bat when he smashes in the windshield of Nicole's convertible Mercedes-Benz. That scene, by the way, is going to be the introduction of Detective Mark Fuhrman into the story. How's that?"

"What time's the reservation?" asked Harvey.

10

In his "Letter from Los Angeles," Gus wrote:

O.J. Simpson has taken over my life. I start thinking about O.J. before six o'clock each morning, when the room-service waiter at the Chateau Marmont brings me my o.j. and coffee. By that time, I'm usually halfway through the New York Times, *where I read my friend David Margolick on the O.J. Simpson case before I read anything else; then I switch over to the* Los Angeles Times, *where I read Andrea Ford and Jim Newton on the O.J. Simpson case, even though I already know what they're writing about, because I was sitting in court the day before as it was happening, and then watched it all on television on the early and late news, as well as on* Larry King Live *or any other show that had special coverage. Once I have showered and shaved, it's seven o'clock, time to turn on the television set to see whom Katie Couric and Paula Zahn and Joan Lunden may be inter-*

viewing about the case. Then I hear the fax machine making sounds in the other room, and I know it's Craig Offman from Wayne Lawson's office at Vanity Fair *magazine sending me the pertinent pages of the* New York Post *and the* New York Daily News, *as well as Liz Smith, Cindy Adams, Richard Johnson and what* they *have to say about the case today. At 7:35, I'm in my rental convertible Mustang, barreling down Beverly Boulevard as I switch radio stations to hear the latest on the case, which I already know, until I arrive at the Criminal Courts Building on West Temple Street in downtown Los Angeles. Then we in the media line up to get our daily badges, which we pin to our jackets, all the time talking about the latest rumors in the O. J. case, or saying things to one another such as "You were great on Geraldo last night." At nine o'clock, we walk into the courtroom and take our places in our assigned seats, and then the door to the holding room opens and in comes O. J. Simpson himself, usually surrounded by Johnnie Cochran, Robert Shapiro, and Carl Douglas. We all stare at O. J. to see what kind of mood he's in or to which lawyer he's talking, and we watch him say good morning to members of his family. When Judge Lance Ito comes in, we do not rise, but we do rise on the bailiff's order to do so as the jury enters.*

*Then the trial begins again, and all day long
we watch it, except for our lunch break, when
we talk about it, saying such things as "Did
you notice the way O. J. looked up at the ceiling when they showed the picture of Nicole
lying in all the blood?"*

"Well, here comes O.J.," whispered Gus to Kim
Goldman, the dead young man's sister, as Simpson
made his afternoon entrance into the courtroom. As
always, it was impossible not to look at him. He
played out his scene with the lawyers and the camera. Carmelita and Shirley leaned forward in their
front-row seats and smiled at their brother, as they
did every time he entered the courtroom. The
Browns passively stared at him. The Goldmans, who
hated O.J., stared at him with hostility, always hoping he would look in their direction to see the extent
of their hatred. Although Simpson never looked in
their direction, his face assumed a haughty arro-
gance when he knew they were looking at him.

"I wish you'd stop calling him O.J., Gus," whispered Kim, cupping her mouth with her hand. "It
sounds too friendly. My father says it sounds like
you like him when you refer to him as O.J."

"Your father's absolutely right," said Gus, cupping his hand over his mouth. "You know, Kim, I've
been thinking the same thing myself. I hate calling
him O.J. What does your father call him?"

"The killer. The murderer. The monster," said
Kim.

"Let me start over again. 'Here comes the killer,'" said Gus. "How's that?"

"Now you're talking," said Kim, trying not to laugh.

"Don't you dare tell anyone I said that," said Gus.

"Except my father," said Kim.

"Gus, it's Charlie Wick."

"Hi, Charlie."

"I caught you with Dan Rather last night on the news," said Charlie. "Do you enjoy working with Dan?"

"I do. I like him very much."

"I notice every week he asks you the same thing —to predict the outcome."

"And every week I give the same answer: hung jury. There's no chance of a conviction."

"Say, Gus, speaking of the trial. As you probably know, the President's not well," said Charlie. "It's a terrible disease, Alzheimer's."

"Yes," replied Gus. He understood that the president Charlie was talking about was President Reagan, not President Clinton. During the Reagan presidency, Charlie Wick had been part of the administration in Washington, when he became head of the USIS. "I thought the letter the President wrote to the country to announce he had the disease was beautiful," said Gus. "I'm sure Nancy had a great deal to do with that. Please give her my best when you talk to her."

"It's Nancy I'm calling about, Gus," said Charlie. "Nancy is very homebound these days, taking care of Ronnie, and she spends a lot of time watching the O.J. trial on television. She's very much caught up in it, like a lot of people are."

"Amazing, isn't it, the enormous public interest in this trial?"

"Nancy would like to know if you'd have dinner one night to talk about it."

"Of course. I'd be very happy to do that, Charlie," said Gus.

"She knows every detail of the trial, and she's been reading you in the magazine and watching you on television, and she'd like to talk about it."

"Sounds good to me," said Gus.

"How about the Bel Air Hotel next Tuesday night?"

Somewhere along the line, Gus began to dislike F. Lee Bailey. After their early promise to remain open to each other, despite their different points of view as to the guilt of O.J. Simpson, when they had had dinner at "21" in New York many months earlier, before the start of the trial, they now no longer spoke when they passed in the corridors of the courthouse. Some of Gus's writings about the celebrated lawyer had displeased him. "He reintroduced the word *nigger* into our lives," Gus had written. The great friendship that Bailey had talked about at dinner between himself and Robert Shapiro, who had brought him on board as a member of the defense team, had disintegrated into hate. Each thought the other was leaking stories to the tabloid papers, minimizing the accomplishments of the other's career. He had been overshadowed in court by Marcia Clark, who caught him out in a lie, which caused a public temper tantrum. He claimed to have spoken personally to a black marine, Max Cordoba, who stated that Fuhrman had called him a nigger.

"Your Honor, I have spoken to him on the phone personally, marine to marine," Bailey said to the court, in order to validate his claim. In fact, Cordoba later declared on television that he had not had the conversaton that Bailey had claimed.

"Marine to marine" became a joke phrase in the media room on the eleventh floor of the courthouse whenever F. Lee Bailey's name was mentioned.

That night Gus sat in the dining room of the Bel Air Hotel with Charlie and Mary Jane Wick, waiting for the arrival of Nancy Reagan. He waved to the actress Candice Bergen and the film director Mike Nichols who were sitting a few tables away with John Calley, who had recently become the head of United Artists.

"The best movie Candy ever made was directed by Mike," said Gus.

"Do you miss the movies?" asked Mary Jane.

"Hell no," replied Gus. "Covering the O.J. trial's more exciting than any movie could ever be. I love being right there at the center of what everybody in the country's talking about and being able to comment about it. I feel lucky."

"I promised Nancy we wouldn't say a *word* about the trial until she gets here," said Mary Jane. "She couldn't *stand* F. Lee Bailey in court today."

They talked about their sons, who had known each other as children and were both in the film business. They talked about a long-ago weekend party they had all attended at Malcolm Forbes's château in Normandy. "Did I ever tell you that Jay Leno and I went up in one of Malcolm's hot-air balloons that weekend with this dowdy little lady who turned out to be the Queen of Romania?" asked Gus. They talked about the New York society figure Jerome Zipkin, whom Gus had portrayed as Ezzie Fenwick in his society novel *People Like Us*.

"Zipkin really hated me after that book," said Gus. "He tried to get Malcolm Forbes to disinvite me to his seventieth-birthday party in Tangier," said Gus. "Malcolm told me that."

"Nancy adored Zipkin," said Mary Jane.

"Oh, don't worry. I won't say anything about him when Nancy comes," said Gus.

"Here comes Nancy now," said Charlie, looking toward the entrance.

"Do I ask about the President's health, or is that not to be discussed?" asked Gus.

"Let her bring it up first," said Mary Jane.

Gus turned to watch as the former First Lady walked into the dining room with two Secret Service agents. People who noticed her whispered to their companions that she was entering the room, and many looked around and smiled greetings at her. She smiled back as she walked across the room. She stopped briefly to say hello to Mike Nichols and Candice Bergen.

"Give my love to your mother, Candy," she said, moving on.

Charlie and Gus jumped to their feet as she arrived at their table. She put out her hand to Gus in a forceful gesture and said, in an uncanny imitation of F. Lee Bailey, "Marine to marine."

Gus laughed. "This is called instant bonding," he said.

"Does he drive you as crazy as he drives me?" asked Nancy.

"Let me count the ways," said Gus, as they all sat down.

Gus had known Nancy and Ronald Reagan back in the days when they were still actors, long before he became the governor of California. The late film star Dick Powell, when he was the president of Four Star Television, a highly successful production company where Gus had been a vice president, once said to Gus, "See if you can get Nancy Reagan a part on *Burke's Law* next week, Gus. She called June last night and said she wanted a job, and I said I'd look into it." *Burke's Law* was a popular television series starring Gene Barry, with multiple cameo roles for name actors, that was then shooting on the Republic lot. June was the film star June Allyson, who was married to Dick Powell. She and Nancy had been under contract to MGM at the same time.

There were pictures of the Reagans in Gus's scrapbooks back in Prud'homme, Connecticut: "Ronnie and Nancy Reagan dancing under a marquee at Sid and Francie Brody's Fourth of July lunch party for Rudolf Nureyev, 1964," one caption read; "Nancy Reagan and Peach at General Frank McCarthy's and Rupert Allen's party for Italian film star Gina Lollobrigida, 1965," another caption read; "Nancy and Ronnie Reagan, Janet and Freddy DeCordova, Doris and Jules Stein, New Year's Eve at Alfred and Betsy Bloomingdale's, 1965," still another caption read.

In the years between then and the present, there had been almost no contact between them. As the Reagans moved up from their house in Pacific Palisades to the governor's mansion in Sacramento to the White House in Washington, Gus's fortunes were in reverse. He moved from the house in Beverly Hills to an apartment on Spalding Drive south of Wilshire Boulevard to a cabin in Oregon to a room in Greenwich Village. When Nancy Reagan, whom he once got a job for on *Burke's Law,* was the First Lady of the United States of America, Gus was living in a room without daylight, writing *The Two Mrs. Grenvilles* and hoping to make a comeback.

After he established himself in his second career as a writer, he had taken an occasional potshot at the First Lady during the White House years in articles he had written in *Vanity Fair,* particularly in reference to Jerome Zipkin's presence at so many White

House social events. He had used the word *un-seemly*. Further, Gus was a Democrat who had never voted for President Reagan. So he had been unsure how Mrs. Reagan would greet him when they met again until she said, "Marine to marine," and all anxieties vanished. Throughout the evening, Gus never stopped talking.

"The night before the jury went through Simpson's house on Rockingham, the defense, particularly certain lawyers from Johnnie Cochran's office, redressed the house," said Gus. "These are the same guys who keep saying in court each day, 'Your Honor, this trial is a search for truth.' Let me tell you about their idea of truth. They took down all the photographs of white people and replaced them with photographs of black people. On Simpson's orders, fires were lit in the fireplaces and vases were filled with flowers. They were going for the cozy, homey look. Meanwhile, Nicole's condo, where the murders took place, has been stripped bare, so the jury could get no sense of her life. Over at Rockingham, they put out a Bible that hadn't been there before, and at the top of the stairs they hung a copy of the Norman Rockwell painting of white federal marshals holding the hands of a little black girl as they lead her into a public school, which they had brought over from Johnnie Cochran's office. They wanted to show the jury that O.J. was proud to be a black man."

There was silence at the table as the four looked at each other.

"Want more?" asked Gus.

"Oh, yes."

"They removed a nude picture of Paula Barbieri from his bedside table, and they replaced it with a picture of his mother, Eunice, in her wheelchair."

"How do you know all this, Gus? I haven't heard this before," said Charlie.

"I have a mole on the defense team who keeps me up to date on what's going on," replied Gus.

"You're going to use this, aren't you?" asked Nancy.

"It'll be a great scene in my book, showing all the busy little bee lawyers taking down the white-people photographs and putting up the black-people photographs and the Norman Rockwell picture. I'm going to have them roaring with laughter as they make the changes, especially when they hang the Norman Rockwell. I'm going to call the chapter 'The Truth Seekers.'"

"It makes me sick to hear these things," said Charlie.

"It makes me sick, too," said Gus. "What they say is, they're just doing their job. From their point of view, lying is just part of their job. Jimmy Breslin said to me once, 'A courtroom is a place where people lie,' which I have come to learn is very true."

"I don't think that's the way it's supposed to be," said Nancy.

"The lawyers who are always proclaiming, 'Your Honor, this trial is a search for truth,' are the same ones who say O. J. was chipping golf balls at the time of the murders," said Gus. "Truth has become a joke word."

After dinner, Gus walked Nancy out of the dining room to her car. The Secret Service agents appeared behind them. Ahead, the parking boys directed her driver to bring her car forward. As they walked over the little bridge, Nancy looked down at the swans below and the lawn beyond.

"That's where Patti's wedding was," she said. "It was such a pretty wedding. Didn't last."

"Grafton's been divorced, too," said Gus. "I think it's great you've reconciled with Patti."

"I needed her," said Nancy.

"It's been wonderful seeing you again, Nancy," said Gus, as he kissed her good night on the cheek. "It's been such a long time."

"This has been great for me, talking about the trial," said Nancy. "Sometimes I get so frustrated by what's happening, so it's good to talk about it with someone who's actually there. Would you like to do this again?"

"Of course. It's my favorite subject. I never run out of stories."

11

In his "Letter from Los Angeles," Gus wrote:

It was from Robert Kardashian's house in the San Fernando Valley that O.J. Simpson, with a gun, a reported eight thousand dollars in cash, a passport, a fake beard, and Al Cowlings at the wheel, departed on his famous bolt for Mexico, or his bolt for Nicole Simpson's freshly dug grave to commit suicide, depending on which version of the story you believe. Shapiro and Kardashian claimed they had been upstairs in a conference room and didn't know Simpson and Cowlings were leaving. Also in the house at the time were Dr. Henry Lee, America's foremost forensic scientist, Dr. Michael Baden, a former New York City medical examiner, Dr. Saul Faerstein, a psychiatrist, Dr. Robert Huizenga, an orthopedic surgeon brought aboard by Shapiro, several nurses, et cetera. All claimed to have been unaware that Simpson and Cowlings had left the house. Kardashian, with Shapiro by his side, read Simpson's cover-every-base "suicide"

134

note at a hastily convened press conference. "He only had sixty dollars on him," Shapiro said on camera to offset the belief that his client was trying to escape. As for the fake beard, Shapiro's spin on that was that Simpson had been planning on taking his children to Disneyland, an interpretation that might work for Michael Jackson but which seems improbable for Simpson, who had not been having problems being mobbed by fans for a long time, particularly kids, prior to the grisly slayings in June. But, as they say out here, Shapiro was just doing his job.

Although Gus had once lived in Los Angeles for many years, he had never been so aware of what a small town the Hollywood community really was until his return for the trial. Everyone knew everything about everyone else. Like Robert Shapiro, whom everyone seemed to know in the houses where Gus went to dinner, Robert Kardashian, the great friend of O. J. Simpson, also began to come up more and more as a figure in the story who, outside of the courtroom, interacted in the social world in which Gus moved. Gus had written that Kardashian would always be remembered as the man caught on videotape walking off Simpson's estate on Rockingham the day after the murders, carrying a Louis Vuitton bag, which many people believed contained Simpson's bloody clothes. Gus knew before he met Kardashian that his former wife, the mother of his four children, was now married to the

Olympic Gold Medal winner Bruce Jenner. He knew that Kardashian was engaged to a rich and beautiful widow named Denice Halicki, who was in litigation with her late husband's brothers over his $14 million estate. He knew that Kardashian had sold his Beverly Hills house to Don Ohlmeyer, the president of NBC West Coast, three weeks before the murders of Nicole and Ron. Ohlmeyer, a close friend and outspoken advocate for Simpson, was a frequent visitor at the county jail where Simpson was incarcerated.

One Friday, Gus ran into Kardashian at the Grill in Beverly Hills. In court, they had never spoken. As Gus passed his table, Kardashian said, out of the side of his mouth gangster-style, "Why aren't you home writing?" Gus laughed. He stopped and introduced himself.

"I know who you are," replied Kardashian. "O.J. knows who you are, too. He turned around and said, 'Who's that guy?' I told him, and he said, 'He's the guy who wrote about the Menendez brothers.' O.J. had the cell next to Erik Menendez when he was first in jail."

"I know. After they moved O.J. to another cell, I heard Erik the parent killer told everybody he thought O.J. was guilty of murdering Nicole and Ron," said Gus. "If that's not the pot calling the kettle beige, I don't know what is."

They both laughed.

"Just to tie things up in a ribbon, did you know

that Jose Menendez was one of the top executives at Hertz Rent-a-Car when O.J. was doing all those commercials?"

Kardashian nodded as if he knew.

"But I bet you didn't know this: Jose's kids, Lyle and Erik, who were then young teenagers, worshiped O.J., and one time Jose and Kitty had O.J. to dinner as a treat for the kids. They never saw one another again until they met up in the county jail, where all three are charged with double murder."

"The minute I heard that Nicole was murdered, I knew that O.J. had killed her," said Cici Shahian. Cici had been one of Nicole Brown Simpson's best friends. She had stopped Gus in the hallway as he was leaving the office of Michael Viner, the president of Dove Books, where she worked.

"I used to see her almost every day. We jogged on San Vicente the day before she was murdered. We saw Kato. She wouldn't speak to him. She thought he was spying on her for O.J. She said, 'Nothing's free in life.' That's how Kato pays for his room at O.J.'s. She used to say, 'He's going to kill me and get away with it, and charm the world, because he's O.J. Simpson.' She knew. She foresaw what was going to happen. She just didn't know what day it was going to happen."

"We should get together and have dinner, Cici," said Gus. "I'd like to talk about Nicole. I can only think of her lying in a couple of gallons of blood in a short black dress with her throat slit. I can't get a feeling about her."

"I'll tell you what, Gus. I know you like to go to all the fancy restaurants, but I'm not in the mood for that. Why don't you come over to my apartment on Spalding Drive in Beverly Hills Tuesday night? I'll cook some lasagna, and I'll tell you about her, and I think I'll ask Faye Resnick and Robin Greer. The three of us, we were her best friends."

"Spalding Drive? What number Spalding Drive?" asked Gus.

Gus walked through the entrance of Cici Shahian's apartment building on Spalding Drive. He stopped in the middle of the redbrick courtyard and stood there, looking about, remembering. The scent of jasmine was in the air. Built in the Georgian style in the forties, the building retained a sense of elegance, although skyscraper apartment buildings on Wilshire Boulevard now dwarfed it.

He climbed the outdoor staircase to Cici's apartment. She answered the door.

"Michael Viner was supposed to come, but at the last minute he went to a screening of a picture at Bob Evans's house with Jack Nicholson," said Cici. "So it's just you and us girls."

"I think we can make do without Michael," said Gus. "What's Evans running?"

"Muriel's Wedding."

"I haven't seen a movie since the trial started," said Gus.

"You know Faye, Gus," said Cici.

"Hi, Faye."

"And this is Robin Greer."

"Hi, Robin."

"My aunt said to say hello to you," said Robin.

"Who's your aunt?"

"Jane Greer."

"God, I haven't seen Jane Greer in years. She was a beautiful woman," said Gus.

"Still is."

"Used to be married to Eddie Lasker when I knew her."

"Over and out long ago."

"Your aunt was great in *Out of the Past* with Robert Mitchum when she was at RKO," said Gus. "Give her my love."

Inside Cici's apartment, Gus kept walking over to the window and looking out on the courtyard of the building. Cici was in the kitchen, fixing the dinner. Faye Resnick and Robin Greer sat on the sofa, talking about Nicole.

"There was a viewing of Nicole's body in an open casket on the day before the funeral," said Robin. "Nicole didn't look anything like herself. She looked old and unhappy. It wasn't like looking at Nicole."

"We walked in to pay our respects to the family," said Cici, coming in from the kitchen. "O.J. was right there. We all knew in our hearts that he had done it, but we all hugged him. He gave each of us a different message. He said to Faye, 'You know, I loved her too much.' He said to me, 'Please help Arnelle to take care of the children.' At the funeral, I sat down, and Cora Fishman sat next to me, then Faye and Kris Jenner, who used to be married to Robert Kardashian. Who sits next to me on the other side but Kato Kaelin. He never looked at me. I said, 'Kato, what happened?' He never looked me in the eye. I turned and said to Cora, 'This guy knows something. He won't look at me.'"

"Robert Shapiro showed up at the wake with O.J.," said Faye. "Right there, with Nicole's dead body on view, he said to her mother, Juditha Brown, 'Are you sure your phone call to Nicole was at a quarter to eleven?' Juditha had initially made a mistake remembering the time of her call to Nicole to tell her she had left her glasses at Mezzaluna restaurant, where the family had had dinner after Sydney's dance recital. If it had been at ten-forty-five, that would mean that O.J. wouldn't have had time to commit the murders and still make his plane. Juditha wanted to believe that O.J. didn't do it."

"Nicole was secretive," said Robin. "I had begged her not to return to O.J. She told me about his abuse, but she didn't tell me she was seeing O.J. again."

"What I can't understand is why she didn't leave him earlier," said Gus.

"Her family," said Faye. "They wanted her to stay in the marriage."

"Why?"

"The money. Her father stopped speaking to her when she said she was going to leave him," said Faye.

"Dear God."

"Nicole felt that O.J.'s abusiveness to women had something to do with his father being gay," said Robin. "You did know the old man was gay, didn't you? Left the family, became a drag queen. Most people don't know that. You never hear about it. Nicole called O.J.'s mother, Eunice, after one of the beatings to ask her if she'd been beaten by her husband. She wanted to know if it ran in the family."

"Nicole never wanted the kids to know she was fighting with O.J. on the phone. She would say to them, 'It's my friend,' so they wouldn't know it was him. Nicole used to say, 'You don't get it. He doesn't love me. He's obsessed with me,'" said Cici.

A feeling of sadness went through Gus. Once Becky had said to Peach about Lefty Flynn, "He doesn't love me. He's obsessed with me."

"Why did Nicole go back to him, then?" asked Gus.

"I'll give you a straight answer, Gus. Nicole could not be happy being alone," said Cici. "She had to have a man. She had to have someone else with her. Every guy she went out with let her down, so she always went back to O.J."

"Do you think O.J. knew about Ron Goldman?" asked Gus.

"I know he did," said Faye. "I heard him mention Ron. He'd seen him in Brentwood, driving Nicole's Ferrari. It made him crazy."

141

"But they were divorced. She could see anyone she wanted," said Gus.

"She liked young guys, late twenties, early thirties, and that made O.J. crazy, too, because he was beginning to get on in years. All her boyfriends after O.J. were in that age group. Keith Zlomsowitch, Grant Cramer."

"Were Nicole and Ron having an affair?" asked Gus.

"Not yet," said Faye. "She liked him. It was going to happen, but it hadn't happened yet. I know that. That's the kind of thing she and I talked about."

"Maybe it was going to happen that night," said Gus. "I never could understand why Nicole lit the candles around the bathtub, unless she was expecting a night visitor and was setting the scene. Candlelight, soft music on the stereo, the scent of Rigaud in the air, and the handsome young waiter with the good pecs she'd already let drive her Ferrari. Come to think of it, Ron went back to his apartment and took a shower first and changed his clothes. If he was just going to Nicole's condo to return her mother's glasses, which she'd left behind at the restaurant, he wouldn't have needed to take a shower first, nor would he have had any way of knowing that Nicole had drawn a tub for him and lit the candles to get things started."

"What are you talking about, Gus?" asked Faye.

"That's the way I'm going to describe it in my novel," replied Gus.

They sat by the fireplace and continued to talk.

142

"How does O.J. react when they flash those pictures of Nicole's dead body on the screen?" asked Robin.

"He doesn't look," replied Gus. "He keeps his eyes averted from the screen. Either Carl Douglas or Robert Kardashian moves in and sits next to him and keeps him involved in conversation while the pictures are on the screen. Kardashian's gotten pretty expert in positioning himself so as to block O.J.'s face from the camera when the bloody pictures of Ron and Nicole are on the screen."

"Perfect," said Faye.

"How'd you like to do that for a living?" asked Gus. "Offer comfort and distraction to the killer when they show pictures to the jury of the people he killed?"

"I'll tell you something I bet you didn't know, Gus," said Cici, coming into the room, carrying her lasagna. "Everybody sit."

"What's that?" asked Gus, who was seated at the head of the table.

"Robert Kardashian's my cousin."

"He's your cousin? Good God. I didn't know that," said Gus.

"Yes. We're both Armenians. The Kardashians are a prominent Armenian family out here," said Cici.

"I didn't know that, either."

"Of course, Robert and I don't speak now, ever since the murder. We're on different sides. He went with O.J., and Nicole was my best friend. I *know*

143

O.J. is guilty. At Nicole's funeral, he couldn't look me in the eye. He knows that I know."

"There sure is a lot of overlapping among the players in this case," said Gus.

"Do you know, Gus, the strangest thing happened to me the Tuesday after the murders," said Cici. "The murders were on Sunday. O.J. came back on Monday from the golf tournament he went to in Chicago, and this—what I'm about to tell you— happened on Tuesday. I was driving my car, and I came to a stoplight. I was thinking, thinking, thinking the whole time about the murders, and all the signs that I hadn't picked up on, and I happened to turn and look out the window at the car in the next lane to me, and I swear to God, Gus, there were O.J. and my cousin Robert waiting for the light to turn green. I couldn't believe it. O.J. was on the passenger side. They were in Robert's car. They were talking so intensely to each other, they didn't notice me. All that I could think of was, Where have they been? What are they talking about? I felt like I was watching a strategy of lies being planned. When this thing is all over, I'll never speak to Kardashian again. Never!"

Gus got up and walked to the window and looked out over the courtyard.

"That must have been after O.J. and Kardashian went to LAX to pick up his golf bag, which he'd left in Chicago. That's when you saw them. I'll bet you money the bloody knife was in that golf bag. It could go right through the security in the golf bag, without

144

being noticed. He could have sent Kato, or Ron Shipp, or Al Cowlings out to the airport, but, no, he went himself, in the midst of his so-called grief and mourning for his slain wife. Something fishy there. I always wonder if all the pieces of this story are ever going to come together."

"What's keeping you so fascinated at that window, Gus?" asked Cici. "You've gone over there to look out about four times."

"My previous life," said Gus.

"What does that mean?" asked Cici.

"I used to live in this building," said Gus.

"You're kidding!"

"No, I'm not. Do you know who lived in this apartment that you have? Sydney Guilaroff. You probably don't even know who he is, or was. He was at MGM for years, the greatest of all the hair-dressers. The big ladies of the screen wouldn't do a picture without him. He did Joan Crawford, Norma Shearer, Garbo, Ava Gardner, Lana Turner, Cyd Charisse, all of them. They all loved Sydney. He did Marilyn Monroe's hair in the casket before they buried her. He did Natalie Wood's after she drowned, before they buried her. I remember Ava Gardner used to come here to the building to visit Sydney."

"I love hearing stories about Hollywood history, Gus," said Robin.

"Which apartment was yours, Gus?" asked Cici.

"Across the courtyard, with the two terraces, and the wrought-iron banister going up the stairs. That was mine. I lived there for quite a few years."

145

"That's the best apartment in the building," said Cici. "One of the big record-company executives lives there now."

"I moved here after my marriage broke up. Peach and the kids stayed in the house on Walden Drive. It wasn't a good time in my life when I was here. I was out of work, broke, too ashamed to see anyone. I began to go downhill, slowly at first, but it escalated. I used to sit over there nights and drink and smoke dope and snort cocaine to blot out what was happening in my life."

The three young women stared at him.

Gus turned back and sat down. "I led a very dangerous existence when I was drinking and using. Sometimes I'm surprised I'm still here," said Gus. "I almost got murdered in that apartment, but I only tell that story when I qualify at an A.A. meeting."

"I heard some of that from my aunt," said Robin.

"My drinking became public," said Gus. "George Christy alluded to it in his column in *The Hollywood Reporter.* So did Marvene Jones in her column. So did Bob Colacello in *Interview.* He wrote that I was all washed-up. Which I was, but I hated reading it. Finally, I had to give up the apartment. I couldn't pay the rent. I couldn't afford to put my things into storage, so I sold every piece of furniture in that apartment, every book, every plate, every piece of silver, even my Turnbull and Asser shirts with the monograms on them, and the Porthault towels. What I got from that sale was what I lived on until I got back on my feet again some years later."

"Is it a bummer for you being here?" asked Cici.

"No. I got through it finally," replied Gus. "It just brings back a lot of memories I'd managed to suppress."

"Where did you go when you left here?" asked Cici.

"Oregon. I lived for six months in a one-room cabin in the Cascade Mountains, in a place called Camp Sherman."

"What did you do there?"

"Licked my wounds. Started to write."

When Gus and Kardashian met again in court the following week, Gus wrote in his notebook, "Will you give me your telephone number?" and handed the notebook to Kardashian.

As Kardashian was writing down the number, Deputy Browning, who was known to the reporters as "Big Girl," pounced on Gus, enraged. Like her counterpart, Deputy Jex, she was filled with contempt for the media, mean as a hornet, and carried away by the importance bestowed on her by Judge Ito.

"I'll have you removed from this court," she screamed at him. Her face turned bright red and was twisted with anger.

Gus was startled, embarrassed, and bewildered.

Later, in the cafeteria, he told the writer Joe Bosco, "She was terrifying, but she was also ridiculous. Her reaction would have been appropriate if she had discovered me molesting a couple of children, not handing my pad to Kardashian for his phone number."

Gus was an expert mimic. By late afternoon, he had Shoreen Maghame of *City News* and Michelle Caruso of the *New York Daily News* roaring with laughter at his imitation of Deputy Browning.

That night, as he was dressing to go to his friend Tita Cahn's house for dinner, the telephone rang in his room at the Chateau Marmont. It was Jerrianne Hayslett, the director of media relations for Judge Ito.

"What happened today, Gus?" she asked.

"What do you mean?" asked Gus.

"With you and Deputy Browning."

"Oh, her. She got quite annoyed with me when I handed Kardashian my notebook to write down his telephone number."

"That's against the rules. Members of the media can't speak to lawyers in the courtroom," said Jerrianne, who was a stickler for rules.

"Oh, okay, I didn't know that. Rules like that should be posted. She was ridiculous, she was so mad, but I think everything's all solved," said Gus.

"No, it's not. She went to see Judge Ito and wants you to be permanently barred from the courtroom," said Jerrianne.

"You must be kidding," said Gus.

"I'm not. She was very serious."

"This is absurd, Jerrianne. She pounced on me, with her face contorted with anger that looked almost out of control. She was over the top. It didn't make any sense to be that angry about asking for a phone number. She could have had a heart attack, she was so mad."

"I can only tell you, Gus, that your seat in the courtroom is in jeopardy. I've just left Judge Ito."

"Something stinks here, Jerrianne. I don't want to sound paranoid or anything, but something's going on. I wonder if somebody put her up to that to keep me out of the courtroom."

"Save that for your novel, Gus," said Jerrianne, who was in a no-nonsense mood. "How are you going to handle this?"

"I'm going to fax a letter to Judge Ito. I'm going to tell him I am so law-abiding in a courtroom that the deputies at the Menendez trial gave me a gift of a lucite clock with the emblem of the sheriff's department on it at the end of the trial. I can't believe that Judge Ito would throw me out of the courtroom permanently without hearing my side of the story."

Tita Cahn's dinner that night was for Sean Connery and his wife, Micheline, who had just arrived in town from Spain to begin shooting Connery's new film. Tita was the widow of Sammy Cahn, the famed lyricist for whom Gus had been the stage manager years earlier on the television musical version of *Our Town*, which had starred Frank Sinatra.

Arriving late as usual, Gus cased the room from the marble hallway three steps up. There were orchid plants on every flat surface, in full lavender bloom, and sixteen or so famous faces were chatting on sofas, or leaning on the bar, or standing in small groups. As always at her parties, the guests were the high-powered of the film world. In a glance, he saw Sherry Lansing, the head of Paramount Pictures, and her film director husband, Billy Friedkin, who had directed the film *The Boys in the Band,* which Gus had produced when he was still in the movie business. Sidney and Joanna Poitier. Warren Beatty and Annette Bening. Angie Dickinson.

Tita, his hostess, came to the steps to greet him. They were old friends.

"Have I got a surprise for you," she said.

"You're lookin' gorgeous," said Gus, kissing Tita on each cheek. "Not a bad group for a Tuesday night in Beverly Hills. Sorry to be late."

"I never care if you're late, Gus, as long as you've got all the latest O.J. news," said Tita. "Did you see Faye Resnick on *Larry King* tonight? She's very gutsy, that one, the things she has to say about O.J. and Johnnie Cochran. Of course, I agree with every word. You know me and Johnnie Cochran. Just starting with the spelling of his name, for God sake."

"Johnnie has a very nice wife named Dale," said Gus. "I have to say that for him. A classy lady. I think he must wear those lavender suits and terrible ties for the benefit of the jury. Dale wouldn't ever buy clothes like that for him. I saw her shopping at Sulka in Beverly Hills last Saturday, buying him undershorts."

"Now, listen, Gus, you can't leave right after dinner tonight, like you always do, even if you have to be on *Good Morning America* tomorrow," said Tita. "I've got Michael Feinstein coming in to play after dinner, and Tony Danza's going to sing."

Tita's surprise for Gus was his seat at the table, next to Margaret Weitzman, the outspoken wife of the defense attorney Howard Weitzman, neither of whom he had met before. Howard Weitzman, who achieved a national reputation when he won an acquittal for John DeLorean in a drug case, had been O.J. Simpson's first lawyer after the murders. Three days later, he left the case and turned the reins over to Robert Shapiro. There had been much speculation in legal circles and a great deal of gossip in social circles that Simpson had confessed to Weitzman. Gus was thrilled with his seat at the table.

"I used to go out with Robert Kardashian before I met Howard," said Margaret.

"Everywhere I turn, I run into people who are connected to Robert Kardashian," said Gus.

"I'm not connected to him anymore, believe thou me," said Margaret.

"I hadn't realized Kardashian moved in such exalted circles as this," said Gus, perusing the table.

"No, not quite like this, but this is the kind of group he'd like to be in," said Margaret with a laugh. "We're both from Armenian families out here, and his family knows my family, and that whole number, and we went out for a while, but it was nothing serious. He was a nice-enough guy then, but I'd never

151

speak to him again now. I mean, this man *knows* the truth about what happened, and he's sticking with O.J."

"Oh, good, I like vehemence," said Gus, knowing they were about to become friends.

"And I'm vehement all right, at least on this subject," said Margaret. "How Robert Kardashian could line himself up with O.J. Simpson is something I will never understand. He called me once after it happened, and I said to him, 'Don't you *ever* call this number again,' and I hung up on him. None of his old friends will see him now, did you know that?"

"No."

"I'm so glad Howard got out of that case. You know, Gus, I don't know you very well, but I'm going to tell you something, even though Howard hates it when I say it. If my husband hadn't quit that case, I would have divorced him, I kid you not."

She paused for a moment, as if thinking how much to say. Gus knew never to interrupt when a storyteller was on a roll.

"You see, Howard and I knew O.J. and Nicole. I mean, we'd have dinner together, the four of us. Howard represented O.J. before, from back when he was arrested after Nicole's 911 call in '89. I always knew he beat her, so I hated him even before he killed her. Howard and I were home that Monday morning, and the telephone rang. It was O.J. calling from Chicago, where he'd gone to play at a golf tournament, and he said to Howard, 'Nicole's been murdered in L.A.' The news wasn't out yet. No one knew.

It was the first time we'd heard it. Howard said all the appropriate things. I mean, the news was shocking. Then O.J. asked Howard to be at his house when he got back from Chicago. He said, 'There's going to be a lot of media. I'm going to need some help dealing with the media. I'm flying home on the first plane.' Since he was calling from Chicago, it didn't occur to us then that he had anything to do with it. This was before we knew that he'd just left for Chicago the night before. I went with Howard over to O.J.'s house. I didn't like him, and he knew I didn't like him, but I wanted to tell him how sorry I was, because Nicole was my friend. We drove over to the house on Rockingham—it's not far from our house—and he was right, the media was already lined up outside the gates, CNN, NBC, CBS, ABC, the whole nine yards. By that time, of course, the news was out, everybody knew, and we drove in through the gates. When I opened the door of the car, I looked down at the driveway before getting out and, I swear to God, Gus, I saw blood on the driveway. I knew right then, before I walked into that house, what had happened. I knew he did it. I went in, spoke to O.J., told him I was sorry, and then I left before Howard and he went off into another room to talk."

"You have me transfixed," said Gus. "What happened with Howard and O.J. behind closed doors? Did he confess to Howard?"

"I can't discuss my husband's business—you know that, Gus," said Margaret.

"It was worth a try. You'd be surprised at how

153

often that trick works," replied Gus, and they both laughed. "Everyone I know thinks that Howard knows he did it and that's why he quit the case."

"My lips are sealed," said Margaret.

"I have a theory on why Howard allowed O.J. to be interviewed by Lange and Vannatter without being present himself," said Gus.

"Howard took a lot of flak for that from every quack lawyer pundit on television," said Margaret.

"I know. My theory is that O.J. didn't want him to be there. My feeling is that the decision was O.J.'s and not Howard's. O.J. was used to bullshitting cops. He'd been bullshitting cops all his life and getting away with it. Witness all Nicole's 911 calls that he bulled his way out of. But it's hard to bullshit two seasoned detectives who know their job if your lawyer's sitting there listening to your bullshit," said Gus. "Bullshitting's a private kind of thing."

"O.J.'s one of the great con men of all time," said Margaret.

"And his con job worked on Lange and Vannatter," Gus continued. "They only interviewed him for thirty-two minutes, and they kept their kid gloves on. Nobody got rough. Any other suspect in a double murder, they'd keep grilling for hours, until the killer got confused with his lies. But not O.J. They never even gave him a urine test, which would have determined what drugs were in his system, because no one had the nerve to ask the great football star to piss in a bottle, as if it was beneath his dignity."

154

"I think we're going to be good friends, Gus," said Margaret.

"I get that feeling, too," replied Gus.

"Don't tie up Gus for the whole evening, Margaret," called Tita, playing hostess from her end of the table. "We all want to hear what happened in court today. Come on, Gus. Only Gus could tell you that Johnnie Cochran's wife, Gail—"

"Dale," called out Gus, correcting her.

"Yes, Dale—she gets Johnnie's undershorts at Sulka in Beverly Hills," said Tita. "Stand up. Say a few words."

"What did you say to Judge Ito?" asked Jerrianne.

"I sent him a fax last night," replied Gus.

"I know. What did you say?"

"I told him I was law-abiding. I told him I respected the court system. I said I would never violate the rules of the court. I said I had never been reprimanded in any courtroom before. I told him the deputies at the Menendez trial gave me a gift at the end of the trial, I'd been so good, a lucite clock with the insignia of the Los Angeles Sheriff's Department on it that I keep on an antique table in the media room of my house in Prud'homme, Connecticut, next to the Bronze Star I won for saving a man's life in the Battle of the Bulge. I rather laid it on a bit, Jerrianne, as you can probably tell."

"He loved it. Everything's okay. Your seat is safe."

12

In his "Letter from Los Angeles," Gus wrote:

Ron Shipp provided one of the defining moments of the trial. He made all of us in the media realize that we could look at and listen to the same witness on the stand and interpret him differently; black journalists saw Shipp one way and white journalists another, and all felt confident of their take on him. Shipp, an African-American former L.A.P.D. officer, had been one of Simpson's best friends, as well as a friend of Nicole. I was so impressed by Shipp's testimony and sense of honor that he became for me a figure of nearly heroic proportions, a deeply conflicted man caught between duty and friendship, racked by guilt for not doing anything to halt the domestic violence he knew was going on in the lives of his friends Nicole and O.J., a violence that he came to believe resulted in murder. On the stand, he was treated with sneering contempt by defense attorney Carl Douglas, who managed to intro-

156

duce a drinking problem and suggested an adul-
terous Jacuzzi dip at Simpson's house on Rock-
ingham with a blonde not his wife. The word
blonde, *which he used several times for maxi-*
mum effect, was spewed out of his mouth like a
dirty thing. Shipp, maintaining calm, twice spoke
directly to Simpson from the witness stand. The
first time he said, "This is sad, O.J." The second
time he said, "Tell the truth, O.J." When I told
an African-American reporter my impressions of
Shipp, she looked at me as if I were mad. The
person she had seen on the stand was "a sneak, a
snake, a most disloyal figure."

"Sorry to be late, Katie. There was another bomb
scare at the courthouse, and I couldn't get to my car
because the police had the parking lot behind the
courthouse sealed off," said Gus, out of breath, rushing into the CNN studios on Sunset Boulevard.

"Go right into makeup, Gus," said Katie Spikes,
the producer of *Larry King Live.* "Sophie's waiting
for you. We're on the air in about eight or nine
minutes."

"Is Larry hosting the show from Washington?"

"No, Larry's here. He got in last night. We're
doing the show from Los Angeles all this week."

As Gus walked into the greenroom after makeup,
he looked in and saw Faye Resnick, who was already
in makeup.

"Hi, Faye," said Gus, who was delighted to see

her. "I didn't know you were on the show, too. God, we've got a lot to talk about tonight. Did you watch the trial today?"

"Watching the trial has become my lifework," said Faye. "Chris Darden was great today. I was cheering for him."

Gus turned and saw Judge Burton Katz, who was also seated in the greenroom and was also in makeup for the show. The two men stared at each other for an instant. Gus turned away from Faye and walked out into the hall again. Looking down the hall, he saw Katie about to go into the control room. He called after her.

"Katie, I'm not going to go on tonight," he said when he got to where she was.

"What do you mean, Gus? We're on the air in four minutes. I was on my way to get Larry," said Katie.

"I'm not going on the air with that guy in there," said Gus, pointing with his thumb to the greenroom.

"That's Judge Burton Katz. He's a retired judge who's covering the trial for the *Malibu Times*," said Katie.

"You don't have to tell me who he is, Katie," said Gus. "He was the judge in the trial of the man who killed my daughter, where the killer served only two and a half years in prison. We are not fond of him in my family."

"We didn't know that when we booked him, Gus," said Katie.

"I know that, Katie. I'm not blaming anyone. I'm

158

just saying that I will not go on the air with him. Tell Larry hello, and I'm sorry. I'll come back any other night he wants me."

"Sit in here, Gus, in this dressing room, just for a minute. Please don't leave. Let me tell Larry," said Katie.

In a minute or so, the door to the dressing room opened and Larry King came in. "I guess you've just lost me a friend, Gus," said Larry.

"What do you mean?" asked Gus.

"I sent Katz home."

"You didn't have to do that, Larry," said Gus. "I told Katie I'd come back any other night."

"You're a better guest," said Larry. "You have a seat in the courtroom. We better get into the studio. We're on in about a minute."

"Hi, Gus, it's Gillian Washburn. Listen, I read in the papers and heard on TV about Marcia Clark's child-custody problems. I can't believe that husband of hers is doing this to her during the most important case of her life. What a shit he must be. If you ask me, I bet the defense put him up to this. You ought to check that one out, Gus. George agrees with me on that. But this is what I was calling about: My kids are about the same age as Marcia Clark's two boys. I could have our nanny pick up Marcia's kids after school and bring them here to play. We have a pool and a court—they're probably too young for that— and a jungle gym, so Marcia wouldn't have to worry about them, and they'd be in good hands. We'd feed them and then have our nanny take them back to Marcia's home. Would you ask her?"

"Gus, would you like me to arrange for you to meet with Wolfgang and Marta Salinger?" asked Ernest Lehman, the Academy Award–winning screenwriter, whom Gus had known years before, when they were under contract to Fox. They were at an Academy screening at the Samuel Goldwyn Theater on Wilshire Boulevard.

"I'm pulling a blank, Ernie," said Gus. "Who are the Salingers?"

"They're old friends of mine, lovely people, very quiet, very distinguished," said Lehman, "but they've been in the news recently as the employers of Rosa Lopez."

"Oh, of course, the Salingers," said Gus.

"They've been next-door neighbors to O.J. for seventeen years. They've got some great Rosa stories to tell you. Rosa was a friend of O.J.'s maid, the one Nicole supposedly slapped. Wolfgang says Rosa *never* took the dog out for a walk that night, when she claims she saw the white Bronco on the street. No way. Wolfgang says the dog is old and blind, and he doesn't ever let it go off the grounds."

"Oh, yes, Ernie, I'd really like to meet the Salingers," said Gus. "Rosa's one of my favorite characters in this saga. She's going to play a big part in my novel."

"They liked it when you wrote in *Vanity Fair,* 'If Rosa Lopez is as lousy a housekeeper as she is a liar, I'd hate to see the inside of the Salingers' house.'"

For Gus, Rosa Lopez, the former maid for the Wolfgang Salingers, provided an epic memory of the trial. She was O.J. Simpson's alibi, promised to the jury by Johnnie Cochran in his opening statement. She said that she saw Simpson's white Bronco parked outside the mansion on Rockingham when she took the Salingers' dog for a walk at the same time the murders were taking place at Nicole's condo on Bundy. Therefore, Simpson could not have committed the murders. But it hadn't worked out. She had blundered badly on the stand.

That Friday, Gus said on the *CBS Evening News* with Dan Rather:

"The extraordinary good luck of the defense team continues. Lucky for them but sad for the prosecution, the jury did not hear Rosa Lopez get caught out in her lies during the expert cross-examination of Christopher Darden, and the defense will never bring her back. The publicity seeker has been caught out. She has left for San Salvador. She is history in this trial."

That Sunday, Gus continued about Rosa on his segment with Harvey Levin on KCBS:

"Although Rosa left the courtroom in shame, it was a different story entirely outside the steps of the Criminal Courts Building, where she was worshiped by the masses. The crowds cheered for her. She was wearing one of the four new dresses bought for her by Mr. Johnnie, as she called Johnnie Cochran on the stand. An African-American male of slender build and great height appeared on the top of a stone wall adjacent to the courthouse. All eyes, including Rosa's, shifted to him. He spread his arms wide in a crucifixion pose and unfurled an eighteen-foot-long pink banner, on which had been stitched in large yellow letters the words 'Dear Rosa, We love you. We believe you.' The cheers of the crowds became deafening. Rosa received her accolades, as if she were Evita being cheered by her people. Led by lawyers, she made her way through the dense throngs, past the dozens of video cameramen who walked backward to record the greatest moment of her life. When she arrived at her waiting car, where her driver held the door open for her, she turned to look back for an instant, as if to record it in her own mind, and stepped inside. The door closed behind her."

"I'm sorry I missed that," said Harvey.

"I felt like an extra in *Day of the Locust*," replied Gus.

"Do you think the defense paid her?" asked Harvey.

"She must have gotten something more than four dresses, a room at the Bellage Hotel for a couple of nights, and a town car with a chauffeur not in uniform," replied Gus.

Later, driving back to the Chateau Marmont, Gus said to Harvey, "What bothers me about that pink banner the guy dropped were the words 'We believe you.' They don't care that she lied. She's a heroine to those people because she tried to help O.J. They don't care if O.J. killed Nicole and Ron. They just want him to get off."

Message left on Connie Chung's answering machine in New York:

Connie, it's Gus Bailey. Sorry I didn't see you when you were in L.A. Jennifer Siebens told me if Dan Rather goes to Bosnia next week, I'm going to do the Friday segment of the *CBS Evening News* with you. Anyway, I've just heard this amazing story concerning you, and I want to verify it, as I'd like to use it for my "Letter from Los Angeles" in the next issue, due tomorrow morning, so I'm on deadline. I heard that you were doing a secret on-camera interview with O.J.'s mother, Eunice Simpson, at her condo in San Francisco last week. And that there were all sorts of ground rules agreed upon in advance between the network and Shawn Chapman, a lawyer in Johnnie Cochran's office, of what you could and couldn't ask the old lady. What I heard is that you made some sort of statement to the effect that women were very fond of her son O.J. And Eunice said, "Oh, yes, O. J.'s a regular Jack the Ripper." And then Shawn Chapman stopped the interview cold and wouldn't let you go on. I couldn't stop laughing when I heard the Jack the Ripper line. Is this true? If so, can I use it? It's a great story. Right up my alley. I'm at the Chateau

Marmont in Hollywood. Two-one-three six-five-six-one-oh-one-oh. Best to Maury. And love. Gus.

"Hi, Gus. My name is Moya Rimp. I met you yesterday in the corridor outside the courtroom. I told you I loved your monthly 'Letter from Los Angeles.' Do you remember? Red hair? Anyway, I know you're busy so I'll only be a minute. What I wanted to tell you in court yesterday is that my mother is the top real-estate woman in Brentwood. Pauline Rimp. Everybody knows my mother in Brentwood. Lou and Juditha Brown have given my mother the exclusive on Nicole's condo in Brentwood. They're dying to unload it. They want seven hundred thousand for it. At first they wanted a million. But not many people want to live in a house where a double murder took place. And it's been stripped to the bone. There's nothing in it, and it has kind of an eerie feeling about it. So, my mother and I are moving into the condo and bringing our own furniture and the dog to show how livable it is for a prospective buyer. My mother's a big fan of yours, too, and we all know O.J.'s guilty as sin, and we were wondering if you'd like to come to dinner so that you could see the condo where the murders actually happened. It's so much different when you're *in* it than it is when you see the photographs of it at the trial. For instance, the area where O.J. slit the two throats is tiny, really tiny. You ought to see it, Gus. Nobody in the media's been here yet."

"I'd love to come," said Gus.

"I don't want you to think I'm a nutcase or any-

164

thing. My mother's first cousin is Robert Altman, the film director, and Bob and Kathy both said they knew you, and they'll come, too," said Moya.

"I said I'd come even before I heard that extra added attraction," said Gus.

"You and Bob could stage the whole murder."

"Hi, Gus, it's Harry Benson" was the message on Gus's answering machine at his apartment in New York, where he had not been for months. Harry Benson was one of the great photographers, much in demand at all the top magazines. Gus had once gone on a shoot with Harry when he was photographing Leona Helmsley of the real-estate empire, at the height of her meanness, to see if he wanted to write her story for the magazine. He had declined the magazine story, but he enjoyed listening to Harry's stories about his adventures photographing Jimmy Goldsmith, Muhammad Ali, and Gloria Vanderbilt, and they always enjoyed seeing each other when they met.

"I'm not sure where you're staying out there in L.A., but I figured you'd keep checking your New York machine. I was going through some old proof sheets in the files at my office the other day, and I came upon this picture of O.J. I didn't remember I'd ever taken. It's from when he was playing with the Buffalo Bills. He's in the shower. He's laughing. You can see his dick. It's got soap on it, but you can see it. You're welcome to it if you want to use it in your book."

"I hear your dance card is always filled, Gus," said Mrs. Billy Wilder when she ran into Gus one Sunday night at Chasen's. "All anybody in this whole damn town wants to talk about is O.J. Simpson, O.J., O.J., wherever I go, and I for one am so damn *sick* of Mister O.J. Simpson, I wouldn't care if I never heard his name again."

Gus always thought that Audrey Wilder was one of the most stylish women in the world. Once she'd been a band singer with Tommy Dorsey. Then she went under contract to Paramount. Then she married the great film director Billy Wilder and kept him fascinated by her for forty years. *Glamorous* was the best word to describe her. She liked sequined dresses and diamond bracelets, and she had a lot of each. One of the chapters in Truman Capote's unfinished novel, *Answered Prayers,* was titled "And Audrey Wilder Sang," which she often did at the A-list parties in the upstairs room at the Bistro when Gus and Peach were married.

"My dance card is not always full," replied Gus.

"That's what everyone says," said Audrey.

"Highly exaggerated."

"I wanted you for dinner next Thursday, the twenty-first. Zubin and Nancy Mehta are in town and we're having a few people for dinner at Mr. Chow's. Do you think you can come?"

"I'm sure I can, but I'm always late," said Gus.

"I promise you, on my word of honor, we will

not talk about O.J. Simpson," said Audrey. "I'm not going to allow a word to be said about him for the whole dinner. There *are* other things happening in the world, and in Hollywood, than O.J. Afterward, you and Billy can go in a corner and talk about it to your heart's content, but not in front of me."

"Tell me about Marlene Dietrich," said Gus, steering clear of the banned subject of O.J. Simpson when he settled in at Audrey's left at Mr. Chow's in Beverly Hills. "I saw an amazing documentary on her the other night on the Arts and Entertainment channel, and Billy was quoted quite a lot." Dietrich was often described in biographies and gossip columns as the "great friend" of Billy Wilder. Gus knew perfectly well when he started the conversation that Audrey had always loathed Marlene.

She inhaled on her cigarette, looked at one of her rings, and then leaned in quite close so that the conversation belonged to them, not the table.

"Let me tell you about Marlene, Gus," she said, as she signaled to the waiter and pointed to her glass for a refill. "I'm not one of those Hollywood dames who uses the *C* word at the drop of a hat, but if I ever *did* use the *C* word, it's how I would describe Marlene, because that's what she was. Contrary to popular opinion, she did *not* have an affair with my husband, although she liked people to *think* she had. Did you ever read that piece of trash biography her daughter wrote? Maria whatever-her-name-is? Did you read what she wrote her mother said about *me* in that lousy book?"

"No, I didn't, but I'd certainly like to hear," said Gus. "This is the first time in months that I haven't had to talk about O.J. at dinner."

"Billy and Zubin are going to bend your ear on that subject before the night's over," said Audrey.

"Gus, can I talk to you in private for a minute?" asked Jerrianne Hayslett.

"Oh, God, what have I done now?" asked Gus. They walked down the corridor away from the other reporters. "I have been a model of proper decorum for Deputy Browning."

Jerrianne laughed. "It's not Deputy Browning," she said.

"My fax to Judge Ito must have been effective," said Gus. "Now Browning totally ignores me, as if I don't exist, and I hope it stays exactly that way. What's up?"

"Gus, you know all these famous people, so I thought you'd probably know this," said Jerrianne, looking around to be sure they weren't being heard. "What do you say to somebody who just got a nomination for an Academy Award?"

He repeated her question: "What do you say to somebody who just got a nomination for an Academy Award?"

"Yes," said Jerrianne.

"You'd say 'Congratulations,'" said Gus.

"Oh, no, Gus. In show business, it's bad luck to say congratulations. Or so we've been told," said Jerrianne.

"No, that's not right," said Gus. "It's bad luck to say 'Congratulations' to an actor on opening night. That's why people say 'Break a leg' instead. But if someone has just gotten a nomination for an Academy Award, it's absolutely appropriate to say 'Congratulations.'"

"No, I heard you *never* say 'Congratulations' to an actor," replied Jerrianne, rejecting his solution out of hand.

"Jerrianne, *who* are we talking about? If I knew that, I could tell you what to say," said Gus.

Jerrianne looked around them again. Then she said in a whisper, "Helen Mirren."

"Helen Mirren? You know Helen Mirren, Jerrianne?" asked Gus. "I'm very impressed."

"*Shhh.* No, I don't know Helen Mirren," said Jerrianne, smiling.

"I'm missing a beat in this story," said Gus.

"Well, this is just between us, Gus," said Jerrianne.

"Of course."

"Well, Sam Goldwyn—you know, the producer —sent the video of *The Madness of King George* to Judge Ito for the jury to see. They can't watch much television, in case there's something on about O. J. or the trial, and so the studios are sending over videos of all the movies that are up for awards. Judge Ito was so impressed with Helen Mirren's performance in that movie that he wanted to send her a note about her nomination," said Jerrianne.

"I see," said Gus, finding it strange that Judge Ito would have time to send a congratulatory note to an actress nominated for an Academy Award in the midst of the madness that the trial had become. "The judge could tell Miss Mirren that her nomination was richly deserved."

"I knew you'd know, Gus," said Jerrianne.

"Chateau Marmont."

"Mario? This is Gus Bailey. I'm still at the courthouse. Can you read me my messages, please."

"You've got a bunch here, Gus. Someone named Mary, no last name. Message says, 'John Gotti at the Marion Prison in Illinois has put a contract out on O.J.'"

"Oh, my," said Gus. "Go on."

"Sherry Lansing wants to know if you would speak about the O.J. trial for Stop Cancer at the Beverly Wilshire on the twenty-ninth. It's her charity. Martin, the concierge from Claridges in London, has an amazing story for you that ties into the Simpson trial. Howard Weitzman wants to know if you'd speak about the trial at his wife's surprise fortieth-birthday lunch party at the Bel Air on Saturday the nineteenth. Forty women. You're his birthday present to Margaret, he said. Harvey Levin says they're going to shoot your TV segment here in the lobby of the Chateau this Sunday rather than at the studio. More atmosphere, he said. Mrs. Norman Lear wants you for a dinner dance/book party on Tuesday for Ben Bradlee and Sally Quinn. Not black tie. Jennifer Siebens of CBS says Dan Rather's coming out here next week and wants to have coffee with you before you shoot the segment. Mrs. Ann Gartland, the wife of police captain Frank Gartland, would like you to attend a dinner at the Police Academy in Elysian Park on the tenth in honor of her husband's fortieth anniversary with the department. Chief Willie Williams will be there, as well as Gil Garcetti and Marcia Clark and Chris Darden. Mrs. Gartland would like you to sit at her table. Mrs. Connie Wald wants you for dinner on Saturday for Prince Rupert Loewenstein, who is arriving for a month. Your son Zander said that he was going to be at his mother's house in Nogales for the next week. Mrs. Randolph Hearst called from New York. She saw you on television, thinks you look tired, and need a weekend off from the trial. She'd like you to spend the weekend of the nineteenth at the Hearst Ranch in northern California. Wintoon, it's called, something like that. She said they'd send the plane for you."

"That's pretty swell," said Gus.

"You could do a book of your phone messages, Gus," said Mario.

"Stick them all in my box. I'll pick them up when I get back."

"One more. Call Graydon Carter. Important." Graydon Carter was the editor of *Vanity Fair* magazine.

"Gus, there's somebody you really ought to meet," said Faye Resnick. They were sitting in the makeup room at CNBC in Burbank, California, waiting to go on live with Geraldo Rivera in Fort Lee, New Jersey.

"Who?" asked Gus.

"I keep talking and talking about this guy to Chris Darden and Marcia, but nobody seems to do anything. Have you heard anything about this television pilot O.J. made just before the murders?"

"The *Frogman* pilot. I've heard about it, but I don't know anybody who's seen it. Isn't that where they taught O.J. how to use a knife?"

"It's called the silent kill," said Faye. "This guy I know trained O.J. to do the silent kill."

"I saw Arnie Kopelson last Sunday night at a screening at Len and Wendy Goldberg's house. We were talking about the *Frogman* pilot at dinner. Arnie helped finance that pilot, which I never knew before. He told me that he'd get a print of it over to me at the Chateau, but a couple of days later he said that there were no prints available," said Gus.

"I think they've been destroyed myself," said Faye. "This friend of mine can tell you everything. Mark Lonsdale. The pilot was his idea. It was really a stuntman's show. NBC said, we'll take the project, but you have to use O.J. in the lead."

"That would have been the request of Don Ohlmeyer, the president of NBC West Coast, for O.J. to get the lead. They're bosom friends. He visits O.J. in jail several nights a week. He's a total advo-

172

cate, very outspoken that O.J. didn't do it. Seems strange for the president of a network."

"Mark didn't mind having to use O.J. in the part," said Faye. "He said he had name recognition, and if the murders hadn't come along it would probably be on the air now."

"What did Mark think of O.J.?" asked Gus.

"He said he was a real prick with a sense of public image. He'd be difficult on the set and then, if he spotted a fan, he'd be charm itself."

"It's a deadly combination, massive ego and a failing career," said Gus. "I used to be in show business."

"You told me that at Cici's."

"Does it really show him slitting a woman's throat in the pilot? That's what I heard the other night."

"He grabs a girl by the throat and puts a knife up to her throat," said Faye. "Mark said that there were a lot of spooky similarities in the pilot to what later happened in real life, that didn't seem spooky when the pilot was being made."

"Like what?" asked Gus.

"There's a scene where he goes to his ex-wife's grave," said Faye. "And listen to this, Gus. There's a character in the pilot that O.J.'s character threatens to kill. The character's name is Goldman. O. J. says the line 'I'm going to kill you, Goldman.'"

"I'd better call this guy," said Gus.

13

In his "Letter from Los Angeles," Gus wrote:

Many people feel Johnnie Cochran won the case the day the jury was seated. The story made the rounds that Simpson said to Cochran after the jury was seated, "If this jury convicts me, maybe I did kill Nicole in a blackout." Cochran's mistress, Patricia Cochran, the Caucasian mother of his only son, revealed in an interview that Cochran had told her before jury selection, "Give me one black juror, and I'll give you a hung jury." And they say this case isn't about race.

The prosecution made a serious miscalculation during jury selection in thinking that black women would be sympathetic to the prosecution because of the issue of domestic violence. Nicole Simpson's cries on the 911 tapes were not as shocking to black people as they were to whites. Jury consultant Donald Vinson had warned that this would be so and was dismissed. An African-American woman married to a Caucasian wrote me: "I believe O. J. Simpson is not guilty; my

174

*husband believes he is. In our eight years of mar-
riage, this is the only disagreement we've had on
the issue of race. I feel that you, like my husband,
are unable to understand a black man's rage the
way that blacks understand it. In us, a black
man's shouts do not produce the same shock that
they do in the white community. Sometimes those
shouts accompany physical abuse, but very often
they do not. Rarely do they accompany murder.
So to black people, evidence of O. J.'s rage does-
n't translate to a belief in his guilt."*

Gus and the great film star Elizabeth Taylor were not
new in each other's lives when they began meeting
on Sunday afternoons at Elizabeth's house in Bel Air
to discuss the Simpson trial, with which she was consumed, in minute detail. Twenty years before, he had
produced one of her films, and they had remained
friends, although the film, which was ill-fated from
the first day of shooting in Cortina d'Ampezzo, Italy,
brought about the end of Gus's career in films. In his
journal, Gus had written extensively on the making
of that film, when nearly everyone of consequence
concerned with the project was drunk, drugged, or
disorderly, except for Henry Fonda, who was the single model of good behavior. It was there in Cortina
that Elizabeth told Gus one night, when they were
driving in the Dolomites during a blizzard, that she
couldn't remember when she wasn't famous. It was
there that her celebrated marriage to the great Welsh
star Richard Burton began to unravel and came to an

175

end in a very public manner. It was there that Elizabeth said to Gus, in the bar of the Hotel Miramonti at two o'clock in the morning, when they were both drunk, "You know, Gus, this is going to be the last picture you're ever going to produce." Gus knew when she said it that she was being prescient, not mean. He understood that she could see that his life was unraveling, as well as her marriage. He knew that what she said was going to come true.

"Come at three," her secretary, Randy, would say when he called to confirm the date with Gus. She was never ready when he got there, but he was not put out by that. Invariably, Jose Eber was still upstairs with her doing her hair. "Elizabeth is chronically late," Richard Burton had once said to Gus about her, when they were making the film in Cortina d'Ampezzo. Gus enjoyed looking at her superb picture collection and her exotic fish. He had portrayed her with great affection as the film star Faye Converse in two of his novels and had written a profile of her for his magazine when she came out of the Betty Ford Center, having dealt with the same problem that Gus had dealt with.

Elizabeth had an instinct for entrances, even when she was on a walker, which she now was. He jumped to his feet each time, complimented her on her beauty, and kissed her on each cheek. She made her way slowly to the center of a large white sofa and sat beneath the van Gogh painting that her art-dealer father, who had had a gallery in the Beverly Hills Hotel when she was a child star, had left her in his will years before. Behind a needlepoint pillow, there were always a lipstick and a mirror, which she occasionally put to use during conversation. Her health at the time of the trial was precarious, her most recent marriage had ended badly in an ugly blaze of tabloid publicity, and she rarely ventured forth beyond the gates of her estate. The trial occupied her days. She could remember every legal detail.

"Barry Scheck is brilliant," she said, "but I felt so sorry for poor Dennis Fung, the way Scheck went after him day after day. I mean, Dennis Fung didn't kill anybody."

"I couldn't understand how Judge Ito could have allowed Scheck's cross-examination to go on that long," replied Gus. "It was cruel. It wasn't necessary to humiliate Fung like that. It's one thing to knock a witness down, but it's another thing entirely to kick him when he is down, especially when every lawyer on the defense team knows O.J. did it."

"I almost couldn't look at him," said Elizabeth.

"This part you didn't see on TV: During the break, Johnnie Cochran was jubilant over what Scheck had done to Fung, and he went skipping down the hall to the men's room, singing, 'We're having Fung, we're having Fung.' It was disgusting, but then, even worse, back in the courtroom, Robert Shapiro handed out fortune cookies to some of the reporters, myself included, saying, in a Charlie Chan accent, 'These from Hang Fung Restaurant.' These are the same two guys who are screaming racist every five minutes."

"I'll tell you who I can't *staaaand* is Mr. F. Lee Bailey. Do you like him?"

Gus smiled. "I had lunch with Nancy Reagan yesterday at Marje Everett's house, and she can't stand him, either."

"Nancy and I were at MGM together in the old days," said Elizabeth. "She came to my wedding when I married Larry Fortensky at Michael Jackson's ranch. I never see her now that the President's so sick."

"She stays pretty much at home," said Gus.

"Tell me more about F. Lee," said Elizabeth.

"He has lifts in his cowboy boots to make him appear taller, and when he sips from a little silver flask he always keeps in front of him, his pinky finger sticks out."

"What's in that flask?" asked Elizabeth.

"It's not coffee, because he has a container of coffee in front of him. It's not water, because he has an Evian bottle in front of him. I don't know what it is."

"And this whole police conspiracy thing is ridiculous," said Elizabeth. "One minute they're accusing the L.A.P.D. of being inept, incompetent, and careless, and the next they're saying that they're all part of a brilliant conspiracy to frame O.J."

"Thank you, Johnnie Cochran, for that," said Gus. "Cochran's the one who said the police lab is a cesspool of contamination, during his opening statement. When you have a client you know committed the murders, what you do is blame the police for everything. It's surefire. I'm sure that every one of the black jurors has had his or her beefs with the L.A.P.D., and they want to get even, and Johnnie knows that. He's gotten rich over the years suing the L.A.P.D. for infractions against black people, so he knows how to play this game better than any lawyer in L.A."

"Listen, Gus, I *know* Johnnie Cochran, for God sakes. He's been here to this house, sitting right in that chair you're sitting in. He was charming, funny. I adored him. I'm the one who put him together with Michael Jackson, when Michael was having his, uh, his problems, and he did a brilliant job for Michael. Oh, have I shown you my latest acquisition?" She shook back the sleeve of her caftan and held a bracelet up to Gus's face. "Michael sent me this sapphire bracelet. Isn't it divine?"

"It's beautiful, Elizabeth, but you deserve a sapphire bracelet, at least, after what you did for him when he was in trouble with that kid who was suing him," said Gus. "Didn't you fly all the way out to Bangkok, or someplace, to be with him?"

"Twenty-two hours on the plane, thank you very much. My back—I couldn't move," said Elizabeth. "Don't tell anybody I'm on a walker, for God sake. I had a hip replacement, and one leg came out shorter than the other. That's all the tabloids need to hear."

"Speaking of Johnnie, or Mr. Johnnie, as Rosa Lopez calls him, I received an invitation in the mail to a testimonial dinner at the Beverly Hilton that is being co-hosted by Johnnie Cochran *and* Miss Elizabeth Taylor. Can you explain that one to me?"

"It's a dinner honoring my lawyer, Neil Papiano."

179

"I don't think you should go, Elizabeth," said Gus.

"I have to go. Johnnie and I are the hosts. Neil Papiano introduced me to Johnnie, and this whole thing was set up long before the O.J. Simpson trial."

"Johnnie will use it for a photo op—you can count on that. You of all people know when you're being used. He'll have pictures of the two of you on television and in every newspaper in the country, and it's going to look like you think O.J. didn't do it, if you're seen laughing it up with O.J.'s lawyer at the Beverly Hilton during the middle of his murder trial. First a child molester and then a killer."

"Michael is *not* a child molester," said Elizabeth, as if she had said the same sentence over and over again in previous conversations.

"Well, O.J. *is* a killer," replied Gus.

"I know you're right, Gus, but I don't know how I can get out of it. Neil's my friend, he's handling my divorce from Larry, and Johnnie Cochran's one of his best friends. I don't know what to do."

"You could check into St. John's—you know. That back of yours has been giving you trouble since the flight to Bangkok—and nobody could ever say you finked out. Make a videotape from your hospital bed that they can play at the dinner, wishing Neil well and saying what a great guy he is. They'll drink toasts to your good health at the dinner, and your picture won't be in the papers with Mr. Johnnie."

180

"Who's that guy with the ponytail who's always around?" asked Gus. It was the following Sunday afternoon, during his visit with Elizabeth Taylor.

"That's Jose Eber, my hairdresser," replied Elizabeth.

"No, not Jose. I know Jose. The fattish guy with the gray ponytail," said Gus.

"Oh, you mean Bernard."

"Yes. Who's Bernard?"

"Bernard Lafferty."

"Bernard Lafferty? You mean Doris Duke's butler Bernard Lafferty?"

"Yes."

"Isn't he supposed to have killed her?" asked Gus. "I mean, like helping the final exit along a bit, à la Dr. Kevorkian."

"No, absolutely not, Gus," said Elizabeth, bristling a bit. "That's a terrible story and completely untrue. Bernard adored Doris. She couldn't have done without him. You'll like him when you get to know him."

"I read in Bob Colacello's piece in *Vanity Fair* that he's a drunk," said Gus. "That's why the judge removed him as executor of her will."

"He's stopped the drinking. He's in the program, and he takes it very seriously," said Elizabeth.

"How did you get to know Bernard?"

"Doris Duke left me a million dollars for AIDS, and Bernard was the executor of the will. That's how I got to know him. And he's charming," said Elizabeth, in such a way as to let Gus know she didn't want to hear anything unpleasant about him.

Gus was aware of her enormous loyalties to her friends, especially those who were in trouble. "I didn't know you knew Doris Duke," he said, instead of what he had been going to say.

"Actually, I didn't know her very well," said Elizabeth. "I'd met her a couple of times, but she always did wonderful things for charity."

"Good for Doris. That was very generous of her," said Gus.

Gus called the writer Bob Colacello in New York. He and Gus had been at *Vanity Fair* together for years. Colacello was the authority at the magazine on matters pertaining to Doris Duke, the eccentric billionairess, whose death was under investigation.

"You won't believe whom I met, Bob," said Gus. "Bernard Lafferty."

"You're kidding!"

"I'm not. He was at Elizabeth Taylor's yesterday when I was there. He always seems to be there, according to the secretary. Elizabeth said Doris Duke left her a million bucks for AIDS and Bernard was the executor."

"Actually, Bernard gave the million to her AMFAR charity during the time he was executor and had the authority to do such things," replied Colacello. "He was a huge fan of Elizabeth's."

"Oh, I see," said Gus. "Well, I suppose that's one

way for a fan to meet his idol. Lay a million dollars on her favorite charity. Far more effective than a fan letter, I'd say. She'd have to invite you to dinner in return for that. It's rather noble in a way."

"Noble? How?"

"He gives away a million dollars from a multibillion-dollar estate, a mere pittance for Miss Duke, as Bernard calls her, but a contribution of consequence for Elizabeth's charity. It's called 'perfect balance.' He gets to become friends with Elizabeth Taylor, and the money goes to a great cause."

"That's one way to put it," said Bob. "What's he like?"

"Strange guy. Wears a drop earring. Carries a gold clutch purse. Seriously fat. Probably very companionable for Elizabeth, who doesn't see many people these days. He hardly said a word. Speaks with a brogue and makes grammatical errors, but he's very gentle. I can see why these rich ladies have him around."

The following Sunday, Gus was waiting patiently in Elizabeth Taylor's living room while Jose Eber was putting the finishing touches on her hair and makeup upstairs. Gus was using the time to make notes in his green leather notebook with the gold-edged pages, which he always carried with him, on what he was going to talk about later that evening on his weekly wrap-up of the Simpson trial on KCBS.

"I discover we have a mutual friend," said

Bernard Lafferty, who had been sitting so quietly on another sofa at the far end of the room that Gus had not noticed him.

"Oh, Bernard, excuse me, I didn't notice you were there," replied Gus. "I was just making some notes for my broadcast later."

"With Harvey Levin, I know. We always watch," said Bernard. He spoke in a lilting voice and sat with his hands folded in front of him. Although he was now a rich man living at Falcon Lair, the Los Angeles residence of Doris Duke, which had been built by the silent-screen star Rudolph Valentino, he maintained the manners and attitude of a servant.

"We have a mutual friend? Let me guess," said Gus, putting his notebook in the pocket of his blazer. "Oatsie Charles? Isn't she an executor of Doris's will also? I know Oatsie."

"Yes, she is, but I don't mean Mrs. Charles," said Bernard.

"C. Z. Guest? I've heard her speak of you, very affectionately, as a matter of fact," said Gus.

"She was a great friend of Miss Duke's, but I don't mean Mrs. Guest," said Bernard.

"Who, then?" asked Gus.

"I meant Faye Resnick."

"Faye Resnick? How in the world do you know Faye Resnick, Bernard?" asked Gus. "I'm always interested in how the social circles overlap."

"In the program. At the Friday-night meeting on Rodeo Drive. Faye and I are both in the program," said Bernard. "Elizabeth said you were in the program, too. I hope you don't mind my knowing that. Anonymity and all that."

"Oh, I don't mind," said Gus. "Richard Johnson broke my anonymity on Page Six of the *New York Post* not long ago. There are no secrets these days, Bernard."

"I know Faye wouldn't mind that I told you," said Bernard. "One day I saw her at the coffee machine. I recognized her right away. Her picture's been in the papers so much since the murders. It was shortly after her book came out, and she was taking a lot of hits in the media from people who said she was capitalizing on her friend Nicole's murder."

"I was one of those who misjudged Faye at first, but I've become a great admirer of her," said Gus.

"That day, she looked so forlorn, so unhappy and friendless. I spoke to her. I told her I'd been maligned in the media, too. I said people were saying that I killed Miss Duke, when I adored Miss Duke. It's hard when you are being misjudged unfairly, as we both were. We had something in common."

"I didn't know Faye was in the program."

"She's going to take a cake on her first anniversary next week at the Rodeo meeting," said Bernard.

14

In his "Letter from Los Angeles," Gus wrote:

Despair *was the operative word for the prosecution team as they watched criminalist Dennis Fung squirm under the relentless cross-examination of Barry Scheck, whose courtroom expertise surpassed that of every member of the defense team thus far. During the days that the attack was on, the prospect of defeat was written in the slump of the shoulders of Marcia Clark, Christopher Darden, and Hank Goldberg. Fung, who wilted more each day, was unprepared for the superbly crafted onslaught aimed at destroying his credibility and competence. Scheck, who possesses the requisite mean streak and unpleasantly curled lip of the successful defense attorney, was not satisfied with mere victory in felling Fung for his failure to collect evidence properly at the crime scene. He wanted humiliation, and he got it. In a cross-examination sometimes painful to watch—especially with Johnnie Cochran, looking like the cock of the walk,*

beaming his approval from the defense table—
Scheck verbally kicked and shamed his victim
with the insistent implication that if Fung was so
inept in gathering evidence, O.J. Simpson was
therefore innocent. From his chair at the defense
table, Simpson watched, haughtily amused by
his lawyer's brilliance.

George Vernon was a mysterious character in the media group. He had press credentials, but no one had ever heard of the paper that he wrote for. During lunch in the cafeteria, he often sat at a table by the Simpson family's table, which gave the appearance that he was with them. As time went by, there were those in the press group who began to wonder if he had not been planted by the defense to get information on how the members of the press were talking about Simpson privately.

"I don't like the way he's always hanging around, listening to what the reporters are saying among themselves," said Robin Clark, who was covering the case for the *Philadelphia Inquirer.*

"I bet he has a pipeline right into Carl Douglas's office," said Gus.

"I was in Chicago over the weekend, Gus," said George one day in the corridor. He had a habit of coming up from behind, which unnerved Gus.

"Oh?" replied Gus. He had never had good feelings about George and tended to stay away from him.

"People in Chicago don't like the way you're writing about the case, Gus," said George.

"Is that so?"

"People think you're biased, Gus," said George.

"Not all people think that. I get an awful lot of fan mail, George," said Gus.

"Not good to be biased, Gus."

"You're not threatening me, are you, George? Only last week you asked me to autograph one of my books for your daughter, and now you're giving me ominous feelings. If I thought that, I'd have to go right to Judge Ito," said Gus, speaking in a teasing voice, as if he were not taking seriously what George was saying to him.

"I'm not threatening you. I'm just telling you what people in Chicago were saying about you over the weekend," said George.

Sometimes during breaks, Gus chatted with Denice Halicki, the rich and beautiful young widow who was the live-in fiancée of Robert Kardashian at the time of the murders. Her husband of three months had been killed in a stunt accident on an action film he was producing, and he left her an estate of $14 million, which siblings of her late husband were contesting. She was often in the courtroom. She discussed with Gus the Bible group that she had formed, which was attended by O.J.'s sisters, by Dale, Johnnie Cochran's wife, and by several of the female lawyers on the case. Sometimes Roosevelt Grier, who was Simpson's spiritual adviser, came to talk to the group. Then one day Halicki stopped

188

coming to court. Gus first became aware that the engagement between her and Kardashian was in trouble when a tabloid reporter named Craig Lewis, who was at the time with the *National Enquirer,* sidled up to him in the courtroom one day and asked him if he knew that Kardashian was "making out" with a beautiful young lawyer from Johnnie Cochran's office. Gus had not been aware of that information, but he knew the young lawyer in question and liked her. He became arch at the time and said to the reporter, "I don't know anything about it, and I wouldn't tell you if I did."

When Gus asked Larry Schiller if it was true about the broken engagement, he replied that Denice had moved out and taken all the furniture with her, including the television sets. The story became the hot courtroom gossip of the day. Even Simpson's sisters, Shirley and Carmelita, were whispering about it. Later, after Gus discovered that Dr. Henry Lee, the famous forensic scientist, who was an expert witness for the defense, had also been in Kardashian's house when Simpson and Cowlings had taken off on the freeway chase, he asked Schiller how many people in all had been there. Schiller reeled off the names, but he specifically said that Denice Halicki had been out shopping and was not present at the time.

"I'm not sure if you'll remember me or not, Gus," said the woman on the telephone. "I met you in London several years ago when you were writing the

189

story on the breakup of Prince Andrew and Fergie. I was a friend of Steve Wyatt—you know, from Houston, Lynn Wyatt's son—and everyone was saying at the time that Steve, who was living in London, was having an affair with the Duchess of York, which he wasn't."

"Yes, I remember, sort of," said Gus. "Tell me your name."

"Schaffner. Eloise Schaffner."

"Didn't we have a drink together at Claridges?"

"We did."

"And it was Steve's friend Johnny Bryan, who was later photographed sucking Fergie's toes in the south of France, who was actually having the affair, as I remember," said Gus.

"You remember very well. I have another story to tell you."

"I'm off the duke-and-duchess circuit these days," said Gus. "I'm all mixed up with race and murder now."

"Which is what my tale is about," said Eloise. "I happen to be a good friend of Mick Jagger and Jerry Hall and Keith Richards and Ron Wood, and the bunch of them."

"You've piqued my curiosity," said Gus.

"Do you remember when the Rolling Stones were on their tour and played at the Rose Bowl in Pasadena last year?" she asked.

"I do. Robert Shapiro got a standing ovation from the crowd when they flashed his picture on the screen," said Gus. "I almost puked at the time."

"Same concert. Different cast of characters. My story's about A. C. Cowlings, O.J.'s friend," said Eloise.

"You've piqued my curiosity further," said Gus.

"It turns out A. C. Cowlings is a great fan of the Stones, particularly Keith Richards. He called the public-relations people handling the concert, told them who he was, like he's a great celebrity, asked for complimentary tickets, which they sometimes give to famous people, and also a backstage pass that gave him access to the dressing rooms of the Stones themselves."

"Poor dead Nicole and Ron have foisted a whole new circle of celebrities on us," said Gus. "My friend Joe McGinniss, the writer, was on an American Airlines plane the other day, in first class, and Cowlings was on board. Joe said he had a man with him to keep people from going over to talk to him about the case, like a bodyguard. All of a sudden, he's become Denzel Washington. When the plane landed, a public-relations person came on board and escorted him off the plane before anyone else. All this attention for the man who was driving the getaway car for his killer friend during the freeway chase. Don't get me started on these people. I get too worked up at some of the things I hear. Go on."

"The PR people gave him the tickets and the pass. It was good publicity to have him there. After the concert, he was in Keith Richards's dressing room. He wanted to party with Keith. He wanted to go back to the Four Seasons, where they were all staying. The more Keith resisted him, the more he told him about the night of the murder."

"I can just see him, sucking up, dispensing tidbits of murder gossip, making himself irresistible to his idol."

"From what I gather, he told Keith everything," said Eloise.

"What do you mean, 'everything'?" asked Gus. "Did he say O.J. killed Nicole and Ron?"

"I don't know the specifics. I was only told that he told everything."

"Will Keith Richards talk?"

"No, of course not. But I thought maybe you could do something with the story."

"Good story. I don't know how I can use it in *Vanity Fair,* though. It's what they call hearsay. I have to get the story directly from Keith, which you say he won't do. Al Cowlings is an interesting character in this story. I believe he probably knows more than anyone else about these murders. I've never understood why the police and the lawyers keep treating him with kid gloves. I don't understand why they didn't arrest him for aiding and abetting. When this trial's over, I'm going to write a novel about it. What you just told me would be a great scene in the book. The Rolling Stones concert at the Rose Bowl. It's got everything. It'll be an even greater scene in the miniseries. It'll show Shapiro on the giant screen, waving to the crowd, experiencing the ecstasy of fame as if it were an orgasm. It'll show the fans cheering him because he's representing O.J.

Simpson, the football star. In the novel, I'll change everybody's name, so I can get away with a lot of stuff I couldn't get away with in nonfiction. I'll have the character based on Cowlings, the arriviste celebrity, made famous by his proximity to a murderous event, arriving backstage with a bag of the white stuff—which I'll have him call 'toot'—as a gift, to ingratiate himself. The more blow he takes, the more he'll talk. I remember reading in the *National Enquirer* at the time that a porn-star friend of Al's said she asked him where the murder weapon was, and she said he answered, 'With the fishies.' I'll use that line in the scene with the character based on Keith Richards, and I'll have the Keith character keep him going until he finds out the body of water the knife was dropped in. Are you still there, Eloise? I'm sorry. I get carried away when I start thinking of the novel. I hope you're not calling from London."

The trial was in its afternoon break. Reporters on deadline rushed to the telephones, while others waited for their turn. Larry Schiller, who wrote Simpson's best-seller jailhouse book, *I Want to Tell You,* had become an inner-sanctum member of the defense team, with a regular courtroom seat next to Shirley and Benny Baker and Carmelita Durio.

"Do you know how Schiller got his seat in the courtroom, sitting with O.J.'s family?" asked David Margolick, the *New York Times* reporter.

"No," said Gus. "I just know that Judge Ito was

really pissed that he was sitting there and had Jerri-anne Hayslett kick him out for a few days."

"Johnnie Cochran went to Judge Ito and begged him to rescind his ruling on Schiller's seat," said Margolick. "He told Ito that Schiller was paying the defense team their salaries, because the only money they were getting from O.J. was from the book Schiller wrote with O.J., declaring his innocence."

"That should be a clue to the outcome," said Gus.

Although Gus made no bones at all about how he felt concerning Simpson's guilt, he had developed a curious friendship with Larry Schiller during the trial. It was from Schiller that Gus got his information about the defense team that he published in his "Letter from Los Angeles" each month. They often had lunch together in the cafeteria and occasionally had dinner together, along with Schiller's fiancée, Kathy Amerman, a photographer. Gus believed early on that Schiller also thought Simpson was guilty, despite being his collaborator on *I Want to Tell You.*

"If I tell you this, Gus, you have to promise me you won't use it," said Larry Schiller. "It could get back to me."

"Okay."

"The lawyers hate having to go down to the jail at night to visit O.J. It's okay the first couple of times, but he drones on and on and on, telling the same stories night after night, how he didn't do it, how no one's looking for the real killer, how could they be doing this to him, keeping him in jail. I heard last night he talked for forty-five minutes without stopping. I heard all that stuff when I was doing the book with him. It gets real boring, let me tell you."

"The lawyers all know he did it, don't they?" asked Gus.

"That's the one thing that they never talk about," said Schiller.

"You play a dangerous game, if I read you right, Larry," said Gus one day. "They think you're one of them, and you get to hear all the backstage stuff. You get to talk to O.J. in jail. Believe me, I'm not being critical. I'm fascinated."

Schiller just smiled and said nothing.

"Why do I sense that there's a book churning inside you?" said Gus. "You're going to have stuff none of the book authors are going to have, like McGinniss and Bosco and me. You get to listen to Cochran and Shapiro and Scheck when they don't have to censor what they say."

Schiller smiled and said nothing.

"I just hope you don't get murdered when they find out what you're doing," said Gus.

In his novel, Gus decided to base a character on Schiller named Joel Zircon. At first, he thought of the character as a double agent, but later, as the trial went on, he changed it to a triple agent.

He and Gus were chatting in a corner.

"Don't blame Johnnie Cochran for playing the race card, Gus. They're all part of it, no one more than O.J., and O.J.'s giving the orders," said Larry.

195

"You have to admit, Larry, it is a little hypocritical that a black man who turned his back on blacks, who liked only white women, white country clubs, and white neighborhoods, should now use the race card to help him beat a murder rap."

"Don't carry it too far, Gus," said Larry.

"Does Cochran listen to him?"

"You'd be surprised at how much input O.J. has in the strategy of his defense. Just because he spelled his kid's name wrong in the suicide note, don't ever mistake this guy for a dummy. When there's a strategy session at night in Cochran's office, O.J. is on a speakerphone from jail."

They were interrupted by Barry Scheck, who walked up to them.

"Gus, I wonder if I could talk to you for a minute," said Scheck.

"Sure," replied Gus.

"Up at the end of the hall," said Scheck as he turned in that direction.

"He's going to let me have it for what I wrote about him in the magazine," said Gus to Schiller. "God, I hate these scenes. Chris Darden was pissed at me the other day for something I wrote about his brother."

Scheck was standing by the water fountain. His face bore a troubled expression, not the anger that Gus had expected. He seemed uncomfortable, as if he had something to say but didn't know how to say it.

"I, uh, I see you hanging around with the Goldman family," he said finally.

196

"Yes, I've grown very fond of the Goldman family," replied Gus. "Judge Ito assigned me the seat next to them."

"Yes, I know." He stood there awkwardly for several moments. "I am haunted by the Goldman family," he blurted out, in what was like a low wail of pain. "I can't look at them. That family could be my family."

Gus, astonished, stared.

"I know they must hate me," he said. "You know, in every job there are things to do that you don't want to do." He looked at Gus. "I'm working for this guy—" He stopped. The two men stood there, having shared a moment of such intimacy that they couldn't look at each other.

"Barry, would you like me to tell the Goldmans what you said?" asked Gus.

"Yes," said Barry quietly. Just then, Deputy Jex opened the doors of the courtroom to indicate that the break was over.

"I had an extraordinary conversation with Barry Scheck today," said Gus. He was sitting on a bench in the corridor outside the courtroom. Next to him were Kim Goldman and her stepmother, Patti.

"Lucky you," said Kim Goldman.

"It was about you, about your family, all of you, so let me tell you. Hold the comments until I finish," said Gus. "He told me he was haunted by your family. He said that he couldn't look at you. He seemed to be in deep psychic pain when he was talking. He said that your family could be his family. He said he knew that you must hate him. He said that there're things in every job you have to do that—"

Gus stopped. Patti had tears in her eyes. "I don't know what to say," she said.

"Bullshit," said Kim. "He wants you to write him up well, Gus."

"No, I didn't feel that, Kim. I can always tell when I'm being used or conned. I have to tell you, I believed him," said Gus. "I think he's deeply anguished."

"Then if he's so anguished, he should quit the case," said Kim. She stood up and walked away.

"You made a mistake about me in your 'Letter from Los Angeles,' Gus," said Denice Halicki, who called on the telephone as he was getting dressed to go to dinner at the house of Sue Mengers, the retired Hollywood agent, who was hooked completely on the Simpson trial. "Jack's coming," said Sue when she invited Gus. When people in Sue's sphere said Jack, they always meant Jack Nicholson.

"I did? I made a mistake about you? What?" asked Gus.

"You said I was shopping on the day of the freeway chase and wasn't in the house at the time," said Denice.

"I did, yes."

"Who told you that?"

"I can't tell you my source."

"It was Larry Schiller, wasn't it?"

"Can't say."

"Get real, Gus," said Denice. "Do I look like the kind of stupid bimbo who would be shopping at Neiman Marcus in Beverly Hills when the eyes of the whole country were focused on *my* house in the San Fernando Valley, where O.J. Simpson was living with Paula Barbieri from the night after the murders to the freeway chase? You can't think I'd miss that, Gus."

Gus laughed. He was fond of Denice and had missed seeing her in court. It had never seemed right to him that she was not present at the time of the freeway chase. He realized that she would not have missed a possible historic occasion in her own house. He wondered why Schiller had fed him incorrect information.

"Sometimes I call Schiller 'the Triple Agent,'" said Gus.

Denice laughed at the name and immediately began calling him that herself. "Let me ask you something: Did you also hear from the Triple Agent that I had taken all the furniture when I moved out on Robert?"

"And the TV sets, too," Gus replied.

"They spread these stories about me. The furniture and the TV sets were all mine, from my previous house. Triple Agent didn't tell you that, did he? Oh no. Don't you see what he and Robert are trying to do? They're passing around information like this

199

about me in order to discredit me, in case I ever decide to tell what *I* know about those four days between the murders and the freeway chase, when O.J. was living in *my* house. That house belonged to Robert *and* me, not just Robert."

"Hi, Gus, it's Judy Hilsinger."

"Hi, Judy," said Gus. Judy had publicized all of Gus's novels on the West Coast, and they had become friends.

"Whose party are you off to tonight?" asked Judy. "I like to live vicariously through your social life."

"I'm having dinner at Drai's with Michael Viner and three of the four hookers who wrote the book *You'll Never Make Love in This Town Again*. At a center table. For all to see. Top that, please," said Gus.

"What happened to the fourth hooker?" asked Judy.

"Gossip has it that the fourth hooker is suing Michael for sexual harassment, which never happened, so she's not coming," said Gus. "Michael thinks Bob Evans put her up to it as revenge because he's so pissed off at what the girls said about him in the book."

"Gus, what can I say? You lead a magic life," said Judy. "Now listen. I know you're busy, and I hate to bother you with this, only it could be important for you. In the first place, have you ever been to Marbella? Spain."

"Yes, why?"

"Do you remember having lunch at the Marbella Club?"

"Yes."

"There's a guy who came to see me in my office who lives part of the time in Marbella, has a house there, I think. He said he had lunch with you at the Marbella Club with Peter Viertel and Deborah Kerr."

"Good God, that was years ago. I was doing an article for the magazine on Adnan Khashoggi, who owns an enormous villa in Marbella, although he was in the slammer in Switzerland at the time for some sort of financial malfeasance."

"I remember that article," said Judy. "Didn't Khashoggi get furious with you and threaten to sue or something?"

"He did, yes, but we've made up. We had a rapprochement at the Bel Air Hotel, quite recently, as a matter of fact, when he came up to me at a party of Paige Rense's and shook hands and engaged in pleasant chatter. Now he's my new best friend."

They both laughed.

"This guy who was in my office this afternoon is named Charlie McCracken. Does that name mean anything to you?" asked Judy.

"No, but my curiosity is building," said Gus.

"Do you remember having lunch at the Marbella Club with Peter Viertel and Deborah Kerr and another man?"

"I distinctly remember having lunch that day with Peter Viertel at the Marbella Club, and I remember for a fact that Deborah was *not* with us. Peter and Deborah were at that time very much in marital turmoil. It was the hot gossip of the Marbella smart set. He was involved with a married woman, and Deborah was at the house in Klosters at the time," said Gus.

"Maybe this guy's full of shit," said Judy.

"It's possible that Peter may have introduced me to somebody at the club, who turns out to be this guy in your office, but he didn't have lunch with us. I was talking to Peter about Khashoggi, and I was taking notes. Who is this guy? What about him?"

"He wants to see you. He asked me to set it up. I can't tell if the guy's for real or what. He said he's a friend of O.J.'s and Nicole's. Apparently, he knows something no one knows, but—"

"But he doesn't want to get involved," said Gus, finishing her sentence.

"How did you know I was going to say that?" asked Judy.

"Because I hear it all too often. People have things to tell, sometimes important pieces of information, but they don't want to get involved themselves. It makes me crazy, although I also kind of understand why they don't want to get involved. The publicity is terrible. If you have anything untoward in your own background, as most of us have, it's going to come out if you have to take the stand, even though it has nothing to do with the murders. I wouldn't particularly relish having to be cross-examined by Johnnie Cochran or Carl Douglas, or have Barry Scheck sneering at me, minimizing my life on national television."

"Would you want to see him?"

"Of course. What's his name again?"

"Charlie McCracken. He's only in town for tonight and tomorrow. He wanted to have dinner with you tonight."

"I told you I have Michael Viner and three of the four hookers, and no guy-from-Marbella-with-whom-I-did-not-have-lunch is going to change that plan for this evening," said Gus.

"How about breakfast before you go to court in the morning?"

"Can't. I'm on *Good Morning America* at four-ten A.M., meaning I have to get up at three-fifteen, to discuss what happened in court today. I always come back to the hotel after the program and try to get in an hour's sleep before I go down to court. So I don't think it's going to work out with your friend."

"He's not my friend. I never met him before," said Judy. "Apparently he had a phone call, or so he says, on the night of the murders that he wanted to tell you about."

"All of a sudden, I'm deeply interested," said Gus. "Tell him to meet me in the lobby of the Chateau Marmont at ten-thirty tonight. Tell him I have to be up at three o'clock and only have half an hour to talk. Tell him to be succinct."

———

"Do you remember that day when we had lunch at the Marbella Club?" asked Charles McCracken. Gus and McCracken had settled on a sofa at the far end of the Chateau Marmont lobby, drinking Pellegrino water. He had found when meeting with strangers who wanted to tell him things that it was easier to terminate a conversation in the lobby than it was when they went up to Gus's suite, where people tended to linger. McCracken was casually but expensively dressed in beige linen trousers, cream-colored silk shirt, loafers, and no socks. Later, Gus wrote about him in his journal, "McCracken looked like he belonged to all the best clubs in the world."

Gus, whose stock-in-trade was that he remembered everyone, didn't remember him at all but pretended he did by nodding affirmatively. They talked about Peter Viertel. They talked about Deborah Kerr. They talked about Adnan Khashoggi. Then Gus looked at his watch, shuddered at the lateness of the hour, and called a halt to the chitchat.

"Now, let me get this straight," Gus said. "You had a call at your house in Marbella, Spain, on June 12, 1994, the night of the murders, from someone who was at Nicole's condo on Bundy *after* the murders but *before* the police arrived?"

"That's right," said McCracken.

"And the caller was *not* O.J.?"

"That's right. You see, Gus, I've known O.J. and Nicole for years, like twenty, or something like that. I played golf regularly with O.J. And I know the Browns very well, Juditha and Lou and the sisters.

204

That's why I never thought O.J. was guilty, for the longest time. I always thought it was somebody else who had done it, but I've changed my mind since I've been here and talked to a few people, the Browns included."

"Was the somebody else you thought had done it the one who called you that night?" asked Gus.

"This is what I can't talk about at the present time," said McCracken.

"You knew about the murders in Marbella before the police knew in West Los Angeles?" Gus asked again. "Is that what you're saying?"

"That's right," McCracken replied.

"If you're not going to tell me, why did you want to see me?" asked Gus. "I fail to see the point of this nocturnal visit, as I have really learned nothing that is of any value to me."

"When the trial's over, I'll tell you then," he said. "You're the one I'd like to tell this story to."

"Big fucking deal," said Gus. "If some of you people who know stuff that is pertinent to this case don't speak up, this man who killed two people is going to walk. Listen, I have to go to bed. I have to be up at three to be on *Good Morning America*." He started to get up. "Was it Jason Simpson who called you that night?"

"No."

"Was it Al Cowlings?"

"No. I can't talk about it."

"Was it Marcus Allen?"

"No."

"I know for a fact that Nicole was seeing Marcus Allen again. Faye Resnick told me, and I find her very reliable," said Gus. "There are even some people who say that he may have been at the condo on Bundy at some point on the last day."

"I don't know," McCracken said.

"It's a funny thing about guys like O.J. They don't blame their friend for fucking their ex-wife. They blame their ex-wife for fucking their friend. It's a growing-up-in-the-projects sort of mentality, I guess," said Gus.

"Marcus got married at O.J.'s house after O.J. knew about the affair," said McCracken.

"That will be a good scene for my novel. O.J.'s reception for his ex-wife's lover's marriage to a beautiful blonde. It will be a terrific way to establish the house on Rockingham for what's to follow," said Gus. He got up to end the evening. "One of the three hookers I had dinner with tonight at Drai's said Marcus Allen had the biggest dick she ever saw. It must be true. Faye Resnick said the same thing in her book. Nicole called it Driftwood, apparently. We had a very enlightening conversation, as you can see. My new best friend said Marcus tried to piss on her once, after he'd spent the night with her girlfriend in the next bed, but she said, 'No way, Charlie.' It's a whole chapter in her new book, apparently. I had no idea that water sports, as pissing is known in the trade, were such a big deal with the movie stars. Good night, Mr. McCracken," said Gus.

"I'll be in touch when the trial's over," said McCracken.

Gus was standing at one of the three urinals in the men's room on the ninth floor of the Criminal Courts Building. As he was finishing, Barry Scheck came in and stood at another. They nodded to each other. Then Gus walked over to the sink to rinse his hands.

"Say, Gus," said Barry. He looked straight ahead toward the wall in front of him. "Do you remember that conversation you and I had the other day?"

"Of course, Barry," said Gus, who had been astonished by the intimacy of the conversation that had occurred. He noticed that Barry's voice was brisk, businesslike. The torment of Wednesday had vanished by Friday. Before he spoke, Gus knew what he was going to say. He had told someone on the Dream Team what he had said to Gus, and the someone had said, "Are you crazy?"

"I just want to make it absolutely clear to you that I believe O. J. Simpson is totally innocent," said Barry as he finished at the urinal and began to adjust himself.

"Oh, Barry," said Gus, mock disappointment in his voice, as he turned and left the men's room.

"You know, I wasn't going to write that up, Joe, but I think I will now, after what he just said to me at the urinal," said Gus to Joe McGinniss when he came out of the men's room. "I'm no longer touched by him, like I was the other day. I've been thinking, Joe: In the novel, I'm going to have Scheck tell his partner Peter Neufeld—who doesn't seem to like me much—that he told Gus Bailey how guilty he felt about the Goldmans, how he couldn't look at them, and how he knew they hated him. I'm going to have Barry be as moved by the conversation as I was, when he's telling the conversation to Neufeld. And then I'm going to have Peter Neufeld go fucking ballistic, up in their suite in the Bellage Hotel off Sunset. 'What do you mean you told that fucking Gus Bailey you couldn't look at the Goldmans? Can you imagine what he'll do with that in *Vanity Fair*? That's just the sort of bullshit they print! You tell him—' That fight will lead directly into the urinal scene I just told you about. Got it?"

"Gus, do you remember Bill Bixby?" asked Joe Torrenueva, as he was cutting Gus's hair in his salon on Wilshire Boulevard in Beverly Hills. Gus and Joe were old friends, from the days when Joe had worked as a trainee barber under Jay Sebring, the celebrated hairstylist who changed the way men's hair was cut in the early sixties in Hollywood. Paul Newman, Steve McQueen, Robert Wagner, and Warren Beatty were some of his clients, with whom he also partied. Jay was murdered with Sharon Tate, Abigail Folger, and a few of their friends, in the Charles Manson massacre at Sharon Tate and

Roman Polanski's house on Cielo Drive in Beverly Hills in 1969.

"Bill Bixby? The TV star? Of course," said Gus. "I never knew him very well when I lived out here, but he was a very nice guy, as I remember."

"He left me money in his will when he died," said Joe. "He was that kind of guy. Do you remember his wife?"

"I think I do," said Gus. "Wasn't she French? She was very beautiful, wasn't she?"

"Yes. French and beautiful. Her name was Brenda Benet. She and Bill had a little boy, whom they both worshiped. A beautiful kid, but he was sickly. He had a respiratory problem. He'd been in the hospital a lot. Then out of the blue, Brenda left Bill."

"Why?"

"She fell madly, crazily in love with someone else. In a million years you'll never guess who broke up their marriage."

"Who?"

"Al Cowlings."

"What? Al Cowlings! All these guys keep showing up, don't they? Just like O.J., Al had his beautiful blond wife," said Gus.

"They never married. I'm not completely sure she was divorced from Bill," said Joe. "One time Brenda and Cowlings were going skiing in Aspen together, and Brenda wanted to take the little boy with them to teach him to ski, but Bill said no, absolutely not. He said the air was too thin in Colorado, and the boy shouldn't go. Brenda said the child hadn't had an attack in over a year, and she took him with Al to Aspen. A couple of days later, the little boy had a respiratory attack, and he subsequently died."

"Oh, what a terrible story," said Gus.

"Are you going to have a manicure, Gus? Kathleen's free now."

"Okay, but go on, don't stop. What happened?"

"Brenda went into this tailspin of despair and guilt."

"Of course. That poor woman. Think of the guilt she must have felt. What happened to her?"

"She killed herself."

"How?"

"Shot herself in the face."

"This is a horrible story, Joe," said Gus.

"Bixby always said he could have imagined Brenda taking an overdose, but he couldn't imagine that she would ever shoot herself in the face."

15

In his "Letter from Los Angeles," Gus wrote:

A. C. Cowlings, who is called Al by his friends, remains one of the great mystery characters in this story. A former University of Southern California Trojan and National Football League player, Cowlings has been O. J. Simpson's closest friend from their childhood days in the projects in San Francisco. Simpson's first wife, Marguerite, the mother of Arnelle and Jason, had first been Cowlings's girlfriend. Some people will tell you that Al's a swell guy; others will tell you just the opposite. Cowlings was driving his old pal in the white Ford Bronco on the famous June seventeenth freeway chase, five days after the murders and one day after Nicole's funeral. While crowds on the sidelines cheered for their hero's safe getaway, Cowlings was calling all the shots, with one hand on the wheel and the other on a cellular phone. His best friend, who was holding a gun to his head at the time, was being transformed during that ride from a mere sports

211

star into a criminal legend, part of the folklore of America, and Al Cowlings, always there for O.J., was helping to make it happen.

Cowlings has mostly been out of the news since a grand jury elected not to indict him for aiding and abetting a fugitive from justice. Recently, he surfaced again at the Los Angeles Airport, with a garment bag in one hand and an airline ticket in the other. A Chicago-based CBS television reporter named Bryon Harlan, who happened to be in Los Angeles to cover the Unabomber's threat to blow up an airplane at LAX, spotted Cowlings and, good reporter that he is, attempted to interview him. The incident that followed was recorded on video by Harlan's cameraman.

"We're from CBS News," said Harlan, holding out a microphone.

"I don't give a fuck where you're from, CBS News," replied Cowlings.

Harlan politely persisted.

"Hey, I'm traveling, man! Get the fuck out of my face," said Cowlings. He lunged forward, swung the garment bag at Harlan, and struck him.

"You shouldn't have hit me, man," said Harlan.

"No, I should have knocked your fucking head off. That's what I should have done," said Cowlings, walking away.

For my money, Al Cowlings knows a lot more about these killings than he's telling.

"I went to the Palm for dinner last night," said Gus during lunch in the cafeteria of the courthouse with his friend Cynthia McFadden of ABC News, with whom he'd covered three trials. "The place was packed. Who do you think was the biggest star in the room, sitting at the number-one table, with people streaming by from other tables to stare at him? Guess."

"Sinatra," said Cynthia McFadden.

"No, not Sinatra. Sinatra I could understand."

"Who?" asked Cynthia.

"Al fucking Cowlings," said Gus.

"Didn't you write something nasty about him?" asked Cynthia.

"Of course. Several times. I said on television his best friend's murders have made him *somebody,*" said Gus. "He was being *somebody* last night and eating it up."

"Did he recognize you?"

"Yes."

"Did he speak?"

"No. When he left, he had to pass right by my table, but he elaborately turned his head the other way, talking to some middle-level show-business executive he was with, with terrible cuff links, who was joyous to be seen with such an important person as A. C. Cowlings at the Palm. When he got to the

213

front door to leave, he turned around and stared at me. He really gave me a dirty look, and then he went out the door."

"You should be careful, Gus. You're too free and easy with your opinions about this case," said Cynthia. "Some people are getting pissed off at you."

"So George Vernon tells me," said Gus. "He said people in Chicago didn't like the way I was covering the case."

"Who's George Vernon?" asked Cynthia.

"George-from-the-newspaper-nobody-ever-heard-of George," said Gus. "People think he's a defense plant in the media. I wish Cowlings had stayed a little longer. Tina Sinatra, Frank's daughter, was there at another table. They still keep a caricature of O.J. Simpson up on the wall. When Tina became aware that she was sitting right beneath it, she stood up on her seat in the booth and draped her napkin over O.J.'s picture. There were cheers in the restaurant."

"I hope you're going to use that in your 'Letter from Los Angeles,'" said Cynthia.

"Tina said I could. I asked her permission last night," replied Gus. "I don't want to get on the wrong side of the Sinatras. I've always had this problem with her father. Did I ever tell you about that?"

The only person to whom Gus told the story about Judge Ito writing a fan letter to Helen Mirren was Harvey Levin, the investigative reporter for KCBS in Los Angeles who was covering the Simpson trial. Every Sunday evening, as a Los Angeles lead-in to *60 Minutes,* Gus and Harvey did a wrap-up of what had gone on during the week at the trial of the century. Harvey handled primarily the legal aspects of the case, while Gus told the stories of what was happening to the personalities of the trial. Harvey had wanted Gus to tell the Helen Mirren fan letter story on the air, but Gus had declined.

"Are you crazy, Harvey? I don't want to lose my seat in the courtroom," said Gus. "Ito already had Jerrianne Hayslett express his displeasure to me that I wrote in the current issue that the courtroom looked like a gangster's wake because of all the floral tributes. Between Ito and Jerrianne, they'd have me back in Prud'homme, Connecticut, if I told about his fan letter to Helen Mirren. Jerrianne told me Ito watches us."

Gus had first met Harvey fifteen years before, when Harvey covered the trial of Lefty Flynn in the Santa Monica courtroom. Back then, before Gus understood about reporters and journalists, he thought Harvey was too aggressive in his questioning during the family's period of grief, but he came to admire him for the outrage he felt over the outcome of the trial. Each placed the blame squarely at the foot of the judge. By the time they met again years later at the Simpson trial, Gus had become a seasoned courtroom observer, and Harvey had become a star investigative reporter for KCBS. They greeted each other like old friends. They saw things the same way. They hated to see killers walk free or receive only a tap on the wrist.

Harvey usually picked up Gus late Sunday after-noon at the Chateau Marmont in his convertible BMW, and they planned what they were going to say on the air on the drive to the KCBS studio on Sunset. They moved in different circles, and each liked to hear the O.J. gossip the other had picked up. Harvey liked to hear Gus's stories of the parties he had been to and the people he had met that week.

"The other night at Sue Mengers's house, her gay black butler was passing the peas, and he told me that he was very disappointed in O.J.'s body when he saw those pictures of him stripped down to his Jockey shorts," said Gus.

"Stop it!" said Harvey.

"I couldn't stop laughing when he told me," said Gus.

"Was Nicholson there?"

"I sat with him in a corner for about forty min-utes talking about the case," replied Gus. "He knows every detail. I have another tidbit for you you're going to like, but we can't use it on the air."

"Tell me."

"Ito's written another fan letter," said Gus.

"No!"

"The other night I went to dinner at Marje Everett's house. Do you know Marje? She used to be the head of Hollywood Park. She lives across the street from Ray Stark. She's a great friend of Nancy Reagan, Merv Griffin, Elizabeth Taylor. She loves music, and she likes people to stand around the piano after dinner and sing. Sometimes Van Cliburn's there, and he plays. Or Johnny Mathis. Sometimes Jo Stafford sings. Candy Spelling knows the lyrics to practically every song ever written. The other night David Foster was playing the piano. You know David, don't you? The composer? Nice guy. I just met him recently. Beautiful wife, Linda Thompson, who used to be Elvis Presley's girlfriend. I was sitting on the piano bench next to him. Johnny Mathis was singing "Always," standing by the piano. When he finished and everyone was clapping, David said to me, 'Gus, I had the nicest letter from Judge Ito the other day.'"

"No!" said Harvey.

"Yes. Naturally, my ears perked right up. 'Oh?' I said, casually, like I wasn't riveted, which I was. David more or less had the letter memorized. He's going to fax me a copy. It went something like this— I had him tell it to me twice: 'Dear Mr. Foster, Over last weekend, when Mrs. Ito and I were driving in Arizona, we decided to play some of the new CD's that our friend Arsenio Hall sent us, and one of them was yours.'"

"Unbelievable," said Harvey. "You wouldn't tell this on the air tonight, would you?"

"I told you I wouldn't. Ethics, you know. There's more to the letter that I can't remember, about how pretty the music was, that kind of thing."

"I like the Arsenio Hall name-drop," said Harvey. "I hope you're going to use it in your book."

"Of course. And I know a thing or two about name-dropping," said Gus. "Doesn't it seem odd to you, Harvey, that between Laura Hart McKinny and her tapes, Detective Mark Fuhrman and Captain Peggy York, a courtroom full of lawyers who don't like him, and a jury that's started to, that Ito should still find the time to write a fan letter to David Foster about his new album, which he and his cop wife played last weekend while driving in Arizona?"

"Unbelievable. Now, what are we going to talk about tonight?"

"I want to talk about the hostility that's building each day between Johnnie Cochran and Chris Darden," said Gus. "Cochran knows how to push Darden's buttons, and Darden falls for it every time. Cochran treats him like an Uncle Tom in front of the jury. Chris is really in a terrible position in this trial, being a black prosecutor trying to put a black sports hero into prison for life without parole. I heard that he got booed in his church last Sunday because he's part of the prosecution team, and he's a very sensitive guy. That's got to be hard to live with while this trial is going on. And on top of all that, his brother's dying of AIDS. Did you know that? That's what I thought I'd talk about, not the AIDS part, but the rest, about getting booed in church. Shapiro got hissed at the temple. Did you hear that?"

16

In his "Letter from Los Angeles," Gus wrote:

The opening night of the opera is a great social event in any city, and Los Angeles on May sixth was no exception. All the swells and all the music buffs turned out. Black-tie. Big dresses. Big jewels. Big stars. That kind of night. Baroness Di Portanova of Houston, the Countess of Dudley of London, and Nan Kempner of New York added a touch of out-of-town glamour to the already-glamorous occasion. The Founders Room was packed to the rafters during intermission. Champagne flowed. The candlelit Grand Promenade was the scene of the party afterward.

The opera was Verdi's Otello. *Plácido Domingo sang the part of Otello, the dark-skinned hero, and June Anderson was Desdemona, his fair, blond wife. Sometime during the second act, husbands began to turn to wives, and wives to husbands, and whisper, "It's like O. J. and Nicole." The scene onstage and the tragic denouement seemed eerily reminiscent of the ter-*

rible events that had occurred in Brentwood a year before. Obsession. Jealousy. Suspicion. Spousal abuse. Rage. Violence. Otello's hands. Desdemona's throat. Murder.

"The jury should see this," said Mrs. Marvin Davis, the wife of the billionaire oil-and-real-estate tycoon.

"June!" said Gus, rising, when June Anderson, dressed in silver, made her diva entrance into the Grand Promenade for the party that followed the opera. "You were great!"

"Gus!" replied June. "I was wondering if you'd be here."

They kissed on each cheek.

"I wouldn't have missed this," said Gus.

"I told you back then in Las Vegas when we got those gold plate awards that I'd be in Los Angeles to sing *Otello* with Plácido," said June.

"You did indeed," replied Gus. "I remember the conversation distinctly, and I remember that I said, oh, no, I wouldn't be in L.A. then. I said it wasn't a place I liked to be. But here I am, and here I've been for months."

"Apart from the trial, how has it been for you, being here?"

"I keep running into people who used to be in my life, before the deluge," said Gus. "People who stopped speaking to me when I was down and out now say things to me like, 'You know, Gus, I always knew this was going to happen to you.'"

"Do you call them on it?"

"Of course not; it doesn't matter anymore. That's the way of the world. The person that I am now has very little to do with the person they used to know when I lived here."

A committee member approached, papers in her hand. "Miss Anderson, I've been asked to escort you to Mayor Riordan's table, and the Marvin Davises have asked that I bring you by their table on our way to the mayor's table."

"I'll be right there," replied June. She returned her eyes to Gus to finish their conversation, as she pulled the matching stole of her silver dress over her shoulders, indicating with a gesture that the air-conditioning was too cool. "Finish, Gus."

"So I'm glad I came, even though I told you that time in Vegas that I never wanted to come back here," said Gus. "I'm glad the trial's taking so long, even. Wherever I go out here, I keep bumping into my past. By the time I cool, I don't want to have any unfinished business in my life."

"I don't think you're about to cool, Gus," said June.

"And isn't this a much too serious conversation for an opening night, when I'm monopolizing the star while Mayor Riordan and the Marvin Davises are waiting for her?" said Gus.

"Do you remember us watching the freeway chase at the Mirage Hotel in Las Vegas?" asked June.

"Do I remember?" said Gus. "I'll never forget that night. I'm using that scene in my novel—the two of us in the suite watching the freeway chase while they're waiting for us downstairs to give us our awards. You don't mind being a character in my novel, do you?"

"Mind? I'm thrilled," said June.

"What a lot has happened since that night."

"I read your coverage of the trial every month, and I see you on television with Dan Rather on Friday nights," said June. "Hung jury, I hear you predict each week."

"Yes, hung jury, that's what I say every week, like a mantra. Tonight everyone in the audience was seeing the similarities between Othello and Desdemona and O.J. and Nicole. There was literally a buzz going through the Dorothy Chandler Pavilion. Could you feel the audience reaction on stage?"

"Oh, yes," said June.

"Only Othello had the class to commit suicide," said Gus.

June laughed.

"Othello didn't hire a bunch of expensive lawyers in Venice to help him lie his way out of it the way O.J. has," continued Gus. "Othello didn't put his family through what O.J. is putting his family through: Poor old mom in the wheelchair and his sisters uprooted from their lives in another city. Think of how much work it has to be for them to pretend they believe his lies. Othello wouldn't have done that."

"I see you haven't changed your mind on his guilt since Las Vegas," said June.

"Hell no, I haven't. I'm more convinced than ever," said Gus. "It's his blood at the scene of the crime that's going to put him away, if there's any justice in the world. But this case isn't about justice anymore. This case is about getting a guilty man acquitted, no matter what they have to do to achieve it."

"Miss Anderson," said the committee member who had been standing by waiting to escort her to the mayor's table.

"Listen, I'm tying you up here, and you're the star of the evening. Your fans are all waiting, glaring at me, in fact," said Gus.

"I want you to meet Plácido," said June.

"I talked trial with Plácido for half an hour one night at the Marvin Davises," said Gus.

The next day Gus had lunch in the cafeteria of the Criminal Courts Building with the television superstar Barbara Walters, who was out from New York to observe the trial for several days, and his great friend Cynthia McFadden, who was reporting on the trial for ABC. Walters was lining up post-trial interviews for *20/20*. McFadden and Gus had covered the William Kennedy Smith trial and the Menendez brothers trial together, and they both had houses in Prud'homme, Connecticut, which they had not been to for nearly a year.

"I think we can say we're sitting with the biggest star in the cafeteria today, Cynthia, and it's a pretty star-studded day, with Sydney Biddle Barrows and

Heidi Fleiss to our left, and the entire Dream Team except Bob Shapiro to our right," said Gus.

"Barbara practically caused a mini-riot just now coming down on the elevator," said Cynthia. "'May I have your autograph, Miss Walters?' 'May I have your autograph, Miss Walters?'"

"Oh, stop it, you two," said Barbara.

"I heard you had dinner with Kato Kaelin," said Gus.

"How did you hear that?" asked Barbara.

"Gus has unimpeachable success when it comes to who's where for dinner every night," said Cynthia.

"They weren't exactly hiding out," said Gus. "You can't go to Spago and think you're not going to be reported on when you're Barbara Walters and America's most famous houseguest, Kato Kaelin. Two people called me from the restaurant. What did you think of him?"

"He's cute," said Barbara. "You can't help liking him."

"I bet you'll get more out of Kato than Marcia did when he was on the stand," said Gus. "I think it was a mistake for her to get pissed off at him and declare him a hostile witness."

"He said she wasn't ever nice to him when they met before he took the stand," said Barbara.

"I never thought Kato was one of the bad guys," said Gus. "He's a Hollywood type we all know, a freeloader, but not a bad guy. My feeling about him has always been that someone scared the you-know-what out of him before he took the stand."

"Like who?" asked Barbara.

"I don't know who exactly, but I remember all the people connected with the defense who called Kato the day after the murders, when he was staying at Grant Cramer's apartment in West Hollywood," said Gus. "O.J. called Kato several times at Grant's. Shapiro called him there. Skip Taft, O.J.'s business manager, called him. Cathy Randa, O.J.'s assistant, called. All the team players. They were working out the story line of the murder night. I happen to know for an absolute fact that on the night after the murders, O.J. and Shapiro had Kato in a corner in the kitchen of the Rockingham house questioning him and questioning him, trying to get the alibi set. You ought to talk to Grant Cramer, Barbara. He was one of Nicole's boyfriends after she split with O.J., and he introduced Kato to Nicole."

"I thought I was the only one who knew about Grant Cramer," said Cynthia. "How do you know him, Gus?"

"He was in the miniseries of *An Inconvenient Woman*. Played the hustler. And I used to know his father and three of his mothers when I lived out here," said Gus.

"You've got Hollywood connections, Gus," said Cynthia.

"The point of all this is that the story Kato Kaelin told on the stand and the story that Kato Kaelin told

Grant Cramer when he moved into his place the day after the murders weren't quite the same," said Gus.

"You're going to use that in your novel, aren't you?" asked Cynthia.

"Hell yes. It's already written," said Gus. "I have the character based on Kato say to the character based on Shapiro, 'But that's not the way it happened, sir. O.J. and I *didn't* go to McDonald's. We went to Burger King, and we bought crystal meth from Ron X, and I paid with O.J.'s hundred-dollar bill.' And then I have O.J. say, 'No, no. *This* is the way it happened, Kato.'"

17

In his "Letter from Los Angeles," Gus wrote:

What's happened to the Brown family? They almost never come to court anymore. Occasionally Tanya, Nicole's youngest sister, and her fiancé, Rico, come by, but the family as a unit has not been seen for weeks in their section of reserved seats. To my way of thinking, it is a mistake for them not to come. The Goldman family, particularly Kim, Ron's sister, and Patti, his stepmother, almost never miss a day, and they pay strict attention, even during the boring parts. In many people's minds, Kim Goldman has become the conscience of the trial. On the other side of the aisle, the Simpson family are equally constant in their attendance. You have to say this for the Simpsons, no matter how you feel about the guilt or innocence of the defendant: They're a united family in their support of O.J., and they're respected by everyone. When Carmelita Durio, Simpson's sister, wheeled her mother, Eunice Simpson, who was dressed from head to

toe in purple, into the courtroom one day, every-
one stepped back to let them pass.

Gus attended a dinner at the Police Academy in Elysian Park in downtown Los Angeles, where several hundred police officers and their wives were honoring Capt. Frank Gartland, the second in command to police chief Willie Williams. Gartland was celebrating his fortieth year with the L.A.P.D. Scattered around the room among the police officers were all the members of the prosecution team— Marcia Clark, Chris Darden, Bill Hodgman, Hank Goldberg, Cheri Lewis—who were treated by all as the celebrities they had become, as well as Suzanne Childs from the district attorney's office. Gus was seated at the head table, as the guest of Captain and Mrs. Gartland. Just before the guests were asked to quiet down for the invocation by Monsignor Gerald O'Hagan, he ran into Pattijo Fairbanks of the D.A.'s office, with whom he had become friends during the Menendez trial.

"I had a bit of an ick with Juditha Brown the other day," said Gus.

"Tell me," replied Pattijo.

"I am bewildered, utterly bewildered, by the fact that they hardly ever show up at the trial," said Gus. "How could they not go to the trial anymore? It's the last business of their daughter's life."

"Two murders do not make a dysfunctional family functional," replied Pattijo, who had been in the department for years and had seen it all. Gus took out his green leather notebook to write down what she said. "Don't you dare quote me on that, Gus."

Gus put his notebook away. "I called Juditha and asked her why they'd stopped going."

"Oh? And what did Juditha answer?" asked Pattijo.

"She said, 'It's my least favorite place to be, Gus,' and I replied, 'Of course it's your least favorite place to be, but you should be there all the same, Juditha. The jury should see that Nicole had a family and that her family is devastated by her loss. The Goldmans are there every day. No matter how tough it is, they take it.'"

"What did she say?"

"She said, 'I have Nicole's children to take care of, Sydney and Justin. This is a terrible period for them.' And I answered, 'I know. I understand that, but you also have three daughters. Their presence in the courtroom would be of greater value to the outcome of the trial than touring the country to raise money for battered women.'"

"I bet she didn't like that," said Pattijo.

"She didn't. She said, 'I think you're being a little impertinent, Gus. I thought you were friendly to our side.' I said, 'Of course I'm friendly to your side, Juditha. You know that. I'm the only one who has the guts to tell you what I'm telling you, that you're not going over with the jury, and you're not going over with the media.'"

"You might have gone too far, Gus," said Pattijo.

"I know it," replied Gus. "I'm all for raising

money for battered women, but that's what Denise Brown should do *after* the trial, not during the trial. It makes it look like she's trying to get famous on Nicole's death."

"You didn't say that to her, did you?"

"No, but I did ask her about that picture of Denise in the *National Enquirer,* hugging some cheap gangster in Boston. Don't you think the defense must be eating that up?"

"And what did she say?"

"She said it didn't mean anything, that picture. She said, 'My daughter is a very hugging sort of girl. She hugs everyone.'"

"Oh God," said Pattijo.

"I've gone through what the Browns and Goldmans are going through, and I know what I'm talking about. The Goldmans are playing the scene correctly, but the Browns aren't. Someone from their family *must* be in the courtroom at all times."

"Your call must have had some effect," said Pattijo. "At least Tanya and Rico have started to come."

"True, they have. But I just wish Tanya and Rico would stop necking in the courtroom," said Gus. "It's not a good look in front of the jury. Chris Darden told them to cut it out. They're all nice people in that family, but they don't seem to have any judgment."

"My wife's a big fan of this writer here," said Captain Gartland during his remarks, pointing to Gus. "I don't usually read the kind of fancy magazine he writes for, but Ann got me to start reading his accounts of the Simpson trial, after she told me he always sticks up for the police. I don't have to tell anyone in this room that when the defense has no case, they turn things around and blame the police for arresting the wrong guy, as Mr. Johnnie Cochran and his team are doing to Detectives Phil Vannatter and Tom Lange, two of the finest detectives in this department."

The room broke into applause, and Gartland continued. "My new friend here wrote that, uh— wait a minute, I've got it here; I knew I wouldn't be able to remember it. Here it is: 'In court, Cochran acted as if it was an impertinence on the part of Detectives Vannatter and Lange to have had the temerity even to *suspect* that such an eminent person as Mr. O.J. Simpson might be the killer when they went to his house on Rockingham after the discovery of the mutilated bodies, even though Simpson had a record for beating up his wife in the past and smashing the windshield of her Mercedes-Benz with a baseball bat.'"

Before leaving New York for Los Angeles to cover the trial, Gus had had a drink with an English friend, Victoria Weymouth, in the bar of the Westbury Hotel on Madison Avenue and Sixty-ninth Street. As he was bringing her up to date on the latest news about the murders in Brentwood, a beautiful woman walked into the bar from the street entrance. Tall, dark-haired, purposeful in her stride, she walked past his table on her way to the lobby. Gus, astonished, recognized her. He turned and stared after her.

"I've lost you, Gus. Whom are you staring at, for God sake?" asked Victoria, an interior decorator of note, who was then doing up a Fifth Avenue apartment in the English style for an Australian billionaire. "What movie star is that?"

"That's the sister of Nicole Brown Simpson, whom we've just been talking about. Her name's Denise Brown. These things happen to me all the time. I'll be talking about somebody, and the person appears."

"Serendipity, they call it," said Victoria.

"When the police called to tell the family Nicole had been murdered, Denise said straight off on the telephone, 'O.J. did it.' She knew, and O.J. wasn't even a suspect at that time. Would you excuse me for a minute, Victoria. I can't let this opportunity pass by."

He followed Denise Brown into the lobby. She was standing at the desk, asking for her messages.

"Miss Brown, I'm Gus Bailey," he said when he caught up with her. He could tell that she had never heard of him, as there was no recognition at the sound of his name. "I'm a writer for *Vanity Fair* magazine. I've recently covered the Menendez trial in Los Angeles, and I'm going back shortly to cover the O.J. Simpson trial."

"I'm sorry, I'm not giving any interviews," replied Denise. He saw that she was wary of being approached in this manner.

"I don't want an interview," he replied. "I just wanted to introduce myself to you before the trial starts. May I give you a card? If you tell Gil Garcetti that we met, or Pattijo Fairbanks in the D.A.'s office out there, they'll give you a rundown on me. I'm prosecution-friendly."

"How did you find out that I'm staying here at the Westbury?" she asked.

"I didn't find out. I didn't follow you here. I just happened to be having a drink in the bar with an English friend, talking about your sister's murder, as a matter of fact, and you walked by my table. Of course, I recognized you right away. You look so much like Nicole. I look forward to seeing you in California."

With that, he turned and went back into the bar.

When he saw her again some weeks later, in the corridor of the courthouse, Denise Brown greeted him as if they were old friends. "Hi, Gus. I want you to meet my mother and father, Juditha and Lou Brown. This is Augustus Bailey, the writer. He's the one I told you about. We met in New York at the Westbury. He's covering the case for *Vanity Fair.*" She turned to Gus. "You see, I checked you out. I hope I wasn't rude that day."

"You weren't. Just wary," replied Gus. "Which is probably a good thing to be, with all the publicity this case is getting."

"Tell me. Privacy has gone right out the window in our lives," said Denise. "There are reporters outside our house. They follow me in my car. It's awful."

As the weeks went on, Gus and Denise often talked together and sometimes even laughed together. Gus liked her. One day in court, she cupped her hand over her mouth and said to Gus, "The trial of the century is turning into the joke of the century, and you can quote me on that." He said to his editor about her, trying to describe her, "Her emotions are right out there. She cries, she laughs, she snorts with derision, she smiles with approval. She likes or she doesn't like you. There're no blurs with her."

"I was haunted by what Officer Riske said on the stand about waking up Sydney and Justin in the middle of the night, when he went to the condo to investigate the murders," said Gus. "What terror those kids must have felt, being told to get dressed by a cop in uniform."

"Oh God," said Denise, shaking her head at the memory.

"How old are the kids?"

"Sydney's nine and Justin's seven."

"It must have been frightening for them, sitting in the back of a police car all that time, in the alley behind the condo, not knowing anything, not being told anything," said Gus.

"Sydney said she knew something had happened

to her mother. She said that to Justin in the police car on the way to the station," said Denise.

"The poor little things," said Gus.

"The other night, Sydney said, 'Mommy's here. I can smell her perfume.' It's so sad."

"I'm sure you've thought of this, or Marcia and Chris have, but if the kids' dog, the Akita, hadn't gone out and looked for someone to bring back to discover the bodies, the children might have discovered their mother when they woke up," said Gus.

Carl Douglas walked by. Gus and he looked at each other but didn't speak. Gus said to Denise, "There goes the seeker of truth." Gus had written in his "Letters" that hardly a day went by when either Douglas or Johnnie Cochran didn't make a pronouncement to the court in sanctimonious tones that the trial was a search for truth.

"I don't know how those guys can look at one another without laughing when they're talking about searching for truth one minute and the next they're selling the jury a bill of goods that O.J. was chipping golf balls at Rockingham at the time that a Colombian drug cartel was killing Nicole over on Bundy because they mistook her for Faye Resnick, when they all know perfectly well that O.J. did it," said Gus.

"Write about it," said Denise.

"In my novel, I've already planned this scene where the Dream Team sits around a conference table in Johnnie's office and makes up this stuff. In the scene, I have them screaming with laughter, wiping the tears off their cheeks, as they come up with the idea of having O. J. chipping golf balls."

Denise nodded her head in Douglas's direction and said, with derision in her voice, "They want to put her on the stand."

"Who?"

"Sydney."

"Why? She's only a kid, and her mother's dead."

"She told them at the police station that her mother was crying on the telephone with a friend that night," said Denise.

"Surely O. J. wouldn't allow his team to put his daughter on the stand, as if she hadn't been through enough already," said Gus.

"Get real, Gus," said Denise.

Gus could visualize the courtroom appearance of the beautiful nine-year-old Sydney Simpson. "My God, it would be like a scene from my novel," he said. "Sydney would be seeing her father for the first time since he held her hand at her mother's funeral. Can you imagine how that would play in front of this jury? Ito may as well hand him his acquittal right now if he allows that to happen."

Denise put a stop to that line of thought. "Over my dead body is that child going to appear in this courtroom," she said, rising from the bench and walking away.

"I went to the reopening of the Beverly Hills Hotel the other night," said Gus, when he was visiting

Elizabeth Taylor on Sunday afternoon. The famous hotel had been closed for renovations and redecoration for several years, after it had been purchased by the Sultan of Brunei.

"How *was* that?" asked Elizabeth. Although she rarely went out to parties, she liked to hear what was going on.

"A rat fuck," said Gus. "Too many people. Too many photographers. You would have hated it. Anyone you would have known came early and left quickly."

"Richard and I once lived in a bungalow at the hotel," said Elizabeth.

"Peach and I used to use the hotel like it was a Beverly Hills country club," said Gus.

"How does it look? I hear it's all done over."

"They didn't ruin the Polo Lounge, and they didn't ruin the coffee shop. They kept the Don Loper banana-leaf wallpaper, but the chandeliers and the gilded chairs in the lobby look like imports from the Sultan of Brunei's palace, which is not high on my list of good looks in interior decorating."

"I figured."

"There was a woman there I used to know when I was in the picture business whose daughter is getting married in a big fancy wedding next Saturday. The matron of honor is supposed to be Marcus Allen's wife, Kathryn, who's her daughter's best friend. Are you up on Marcus Allen?"

"The football star," said Elizabeth.

"Marcus was a protégé of O.J.'s. He was a

younger version of O.J., a great player, and they became great friends. The fans loved him. Handsome. Rich. Moved in Hollywood circles. Loved the ladies. The ladies loved him. The story goes that after O.J. and Nicole split, Marcus started having an affair with Nicole, which freaked O.J. out. Faye Resnick told me this. In typical macho style, O.J. took out his fury on Nicole, not Marcus. When Marcus married Kathryn—young, beautiful, blond—O.J. gave them their wedding reception at his house on Rockingham."

"I think I saw the video of the wedding on *Hard Copy,* or one of those shows," said Elizabeth.

"I saw it, too," said Gus. "They even look alike, kind of. Now, this part of the story I can't verify, but several people have told me that the affair with Nicole started up again. They believe he may even have been in Nicole's condo on Bundy on the day of the night of the murders. He flew to the Cayman Islands later that day. There's a record of that. Both the prosecution and the defense want to talk to him. Your friend Johnnie Cochran thinks it will show that O.J. was not the insanely jealous man the prosecution says he was, because he gave Marcus his wedding reception. This lady I used to know in the picture business, the mother of the bride, told me that she had just talked to Marcus before she came to the party, and he said that neither he nor Kathryn was going to come to L.A. for the wedding. If he came to L.A., they could subpoena him, so they're not going to leave Kansas City. He doesn't want to get involved in this trial. If he stands up for O.J., he'll lose all his endorsements, and it could rock the marriage. Besides, he probably knows O.J. did it, and he doesn't want to lie."

"It's like O.J.'s everywhere," said Elizabeth.

"I saw Bernard Lafferty there," said Gus. "He came over and spoke to me. Is he still in A.A.?"

"Last I heard. Why?"

"I just wondered. He was in black tie, looking very smart," said Gus. "And he had on the biggest diamond studs I ever saw on a man in my life."

"I told him not to wear those," said Elizabeth, shaking her head. "It doesn't look right when he's having all this bad publicity."

"They looked like they could have been Doris Duke's earrings," said Gus.

"They probably were," said Elizabeth.

"Bernard introduced me to this young guy he was with, Andy Cunanan, a Latino type, who was all done up in a Gianni Versace dinner jacket. Very eager to please, instant first names, like we were old friends, that sort of thing. 'Hi, Gus, I met you at Ray Stark's one night. At the dinner for Marcia Clark.'"

"Is that true?" asked Elizabeth.

"He was there. Skip Hartley brought him that night. I remember him because he was so interested in the paintings, which everyone else just took for granted. He said, 'I watch you on TV with Dan Rather, and I read you in the magazine.' He was full of compliments, said all the right things, but he kind of gave me the creeps."

"Just what poor Bernard doesn't need in his life right now," said Elizabeth.

"Then the kid got really pushy, and he said something like, 'You ought to put me in one of your books, Gus. I'd be a great character, and Keanu Reeves could play me in the miniseries.' So I said, 'Well, you've got to *do* something in life before someone's going to write a book about you.'"

When Gus got back to the Chateau Marmont after court, he called Frank Bowling, the manager of the Bel Air Hotel. Gus had known Bowling when he was the manager at the Connaught in London and at the Carlyle in New York. Their paths often crossed at parties in both New York and Los Angeles.

"Frank, this is a rather odd request, which is why I'm not calling the maître d'," said Gus. "There's no court on Monday, and I want to come to the hotel for lunch in the garden, but I'm bringing Heidi Fleiss, the Hollywood madam. She's about to be sentenced to three years in the slammer, and I happen to have great sympathy for her. There won't be any problem, will there? Ex-clients in the lunch crowd, or wives of ex-clients, that sort of thing, who might make a fuss? Her black book's like a name-drop of Hollywood, you know."

"Of course not, Gus," said Bowling.

"I was thinking of the booth at the far end, the one Anthony Hopkins was sitting at when I saw him there last Saturday," said Gus.

"No problem."

"One other thing while I have you on the phone," said Gus. "Wendy Stark tells me that there's a guy who lives on Bristol Circle, a block away from O.J.'s house on Rockingham, who goes to the bar of the Bel Air every afternoon and tells anyone who will listen that he found bloody sheets and towels in his trash barrels that had been put out for pickup the next morning. Do you know anything about this guy?"

"I'll introduce you to him, if you'd like," said Frank.

"You're a prince, as always, Frank," said Gus. "Do you think he'd talk to me?"

"He talks to everybody else," said Frank.

"That's the trouble with these guys with information," said Gus. "I see it happen over and over again. They're big shots talking about what they know, but they won't go to the police because they don't want to get involved. Meanwhile, the Dream Team is running circles around the prosecution in the trial."

"Oh, speaking of the trial, Gus, I had the nicest letter from Judge Ito yesterday," said Frank.

"You did? What about?" asked Gus. "Not a fan letter, is it?"

"Sort of, I suppose," replied Frank. "He said that he and Mrs. Ito had had dinner here in the dining room at the Bel Air the night before, and he complimented me on the food and the service, and the courtesy of the staff."

"Perfect," said Gus.

"He said he had especially enjoyed the dessert tray," said Frank. "And he ended the sentence with an exclamation point."

Later, Gus called his editor Wayne Lawson in New York.

"Don't you think it would be interesting if I could locate the law clerk who takes Ito's dictation when he writes these fan letters? Don't you think it would be interesting to know what's going through the guy's mind while he's typing how good the raspberry tart was at the Bel Air Hotel when Ron Shipp's on the stand saying, 'Tell the truth, O.J.'? If you don't think it's right for the magazine, I'll save it for the novel."

Early on, when the trial of Heidi Fleiss, the Hollywood madam, was the talk of the town, Gus had written in one of his "Letters" that Heidi Fleiss would probably do more jail time for her victimless crime than O.J. Simpson or the Menendez brothers for their double murders. He meant it cynically, but he meant it. Heidi had been touched by what Gus wrote, and a meeting between them had been arranged.

When she arrived a few minutes late at his table in the garden of the Bel Air Hotel, he wanted to say to her, but he didn't have the nerve, that he never would have taken her for a madam. Her predecessor in the role, Madam Alex, whom Gus had met through Wendy Stark—who knew everyone—had the madam look, both in dress and manner. Heidi was wearing an oversize T-shirt, dark glasses, and a baseball hat on backward, which she took off when she sat down, letting her hair fall to her shoulders. She looked like a California girl on her way to the beach for the afternoon.

"I'm a wreck, Gus, a wreck. The idea of jail absolutely terrifies me," said Heidi. She ordered iced tea. "I honest-to-God don't know if I can handle it."

"I hear you're writing a book," said Gus.

"I need money. I have to pay my lawyer who lost the case for me," she said.

"Are you going to name names in your book?" asked Gus.

"No," she replied.

"Why not?" asked Gus. "That's the only way you're going to make any money on your book. From the names I've heard on your client list, people would be running to the bookstores to get copies."

"I don't know. That's what everyone tells me," said Heidi.

"Was O.J. ever one of your customers?" asked Gus.

"I don't talk about my customers, but no, he wasn't," said Heidi. "I could tell you a couple of stories, though, of things I heard about him."

"Let me ask you something. Are any of these rich and famous guys who utilized your services helping you out on your legal fees?" asked Gus.

"Get real, Gus," said Heidi, shaking her head. "I haven't heard from one of them since I got in all this trouble, not a single one."

"You know, it would be so easy for a couple of those guys who make ten or twelve or fifteen million dollars a picture to stuff a bag full of cash that couldn't get traced to them and have their business manager deliver it to you."

"Don't I wish it," said Heidi.

"If I'd been one of your clients, I'd have sent you over a bag of cash, pronto," said Gus, and they laughed.

"Oh, there's Gus Bailey. Hello, Gus." The woman's voice was one that Gus recognized, although he was still immersed in the injustice of Heidi's story. He jumped to his feet to greet Nancy Reagan and Betsy Bloomingdale, who were joining friends in the next booth. "Hi, Betsy," he said. "Hello, Nancy." They exchanged the requisite society kisses. Then Gus ventured, "May I present, uh—"

The three ladies stared at each other, fascinated, although no one spoke. In the several seconds that the encounter lasted, Heidi Fleiss met eye-to-eye the former First Lady of the United States Nancy Reagan and the celebrated international socialite Betsy Bloomingdale, just as Betsy Bloomingdale and Nancy Reagan met eye-to-eye the celebrated Hollywood madam, Heidi Fleiss.

It's perfect, thought Gus, watching the moment. As always, he could imagine it as a scene in his novel, the constant overlapping of the different elements of Los Angeles. He longed to reach in his pocket and extract his notebook and pen and start making notes, but he restrained himself for propriety's sake.

"Big hug," said Betsy, and the ladies scrambled to their table. Gus sat down again with Heidi.

"I can't fucking believe what just happened," said Heidi.

That night, Gus called Peach's house in Nogales, Arizona. He had received a message that Zander was going to be there visiting his mother. The trial had so monopolized Gus's thinking that he had not returned the call.

"Hi, Marisella, it's Gus."

"Hi, Mr. Bailey," said Marisella.

"Is Zander there?"

"He's here, but he's out."

"Will you ask him to call me at the Chateau Marmont this evening at six-forty-five? Or tomorrow morning at six-forty-five. Either one. He knows the number. We keep missing each other, and I'm impossible to get hold of most of the time because I'm at the courthouse. How's Peach?"

"She's pretty good. She's doing just fine, and she's always happy when Zander's here," said Marisella. "She likes watching you on the TV shows. We all do. Alicia, Gloria, all the nurses, they run into

Mrs. Bailey's room and say, 'Mr. B.'s on *Oprah*,' or whoever's show it is. We love it when you're on *Oprah*. Is she nice?"

"Oh, yeah, she's great, but she's in Chicago and I'm in L.A. when I'm on, so we're not face to face. Tell Peach I'm on *Good Morning America* at seven-twelve tomorrow morning," said Gus.

"I'll tell Gloria, too. She'll be on duty then. Mrs. B. sometimes forgets."

"Give her my love."

Gus had two sons, Grafton and Zander. Grafton, divorced, lived in New York and was a director in the film business. Zander, unmarried, lived in San Francisco, worked with troubled children, taught school, and was writing his first novel. Their mother, Peach, had multiple sclerosis and lived in a large house she had built outside of Nogales on land that had once been part of her father's cattle ranch. Gus and Peach had long been divorced, but they had never become unmarried. The death of Becky fifteen years earlier had bound them together in a closer way than when they had been married to each other. Gus was fond of saying, when he gave a Thanksgiving or Christmas toast at Peach's house in Arizona, "We may be a fucked-up family, but we're a family."

"Sorry I'm so hard to reach, Zander," said Gus, when they finally connected. "You have to get me between six and seven-fifteen in the morning, or six and seven-fifteen in the evening. Otherwise I'm never here."

"That's okay. I know how busy you are at the trial. I really liked the last 'Letter,'" said Zander. "Were you in the courtroom for the glove debacle?"

"I certainly was. It was high drama all the way," replied Gus. "It made me realize why O. J. was such a great athlete in his time, the way he tried on that glove and played the scene to the jury. Everyone in the courtroom knew the glove fit, but he seized the moment and made the touchdown. The guy has an instinct for survival."

"What's it like for you being in L.A. for such a long time?" asked Zander. "After Becky, I can remember hearing you say you never wanted to go back there."

"Strange, Zander. I keep running into people from my past," said Gus. "I'd forgotten how hard I'd slammed the door shut when I moved away from here."

"What's it like running into Judge Katz at the trial?" asked Zander.

"I avoid him. I never speak. I told you what happened on *Larry King*, didn't I? He's like a bad memory to me," said Gus. "Listen, how's Mom?"

"She hardly talks anymore," said Zander.

"I know, but I think she still listens. I think she likes to hear what's going on. When I call over there, Marisella, or whatever nurse is on duty, holds the phone up to her ear. I never ask how she's feeling anymore. I just start telling her about the trial, or who was at dinner at Connie Wald's the night before and who I sat next to."

"I don't think she remembers," said Zander.

"It doesn't matter. If it entertains her at the moment, that's enough," said Gus.

"Dad, the reason I called, the group that Mom started, Justice for Homicide Victims, wants to know if you'd speak at a victims' rights fund-raiser they're having in Los Angeles. They're trying to get Gil Garcetti, too," said Zander.

"Of course."

"They were afraid to call you at the Chateau because you're so busy, so they asked me to do it," said Zander.

"Tell them to fax me where and when, and I'll be there," said Gus. "Have you talked to Grafton lately?"

"He's as busy as you are. He cast Kate Capshaw, Uma Thurman, and Kiefer Sutherland for his movie," said Zander.

"Not bad for a first outing as director," said Gus. "I haven't read the screenplay, have you?"

"Yes."

"And?"

"He wrote it, too, you know, he and Adam Brooks."

"Is it about me?"

"Not really. More about Mom."

"How's your book coming?"

"Okay."

"I understand that answer. Okay. It ain't moving, it means."

"You got it."

"They're shooting the miniseries of *A Season in Purgatory* over on the old MGM lot in Culver City, and I haven't had time to go to the set once," said Gus.

"Who's in it?"

"I can't remember."

"That's not like you, Dad."

"I know. I'm usually a pain in the ass when they're shooting one of my books, but O.J.'s taken over my life," said Gus. "I don't even read about Bosnia. If it's not about O.J., I'm not interested. Listen, I have to go. I'm glad you're in Arizona with Mom."

18

In his "Letter from Los Angeles," Gus wrote:

Detective Mark Fuhrman's entrance into the courtroom was electric. For eight months, he has been portrayed by the defense as the archvillain of the Simpson case. Stories of his alleged racism have been brilliantly fed to the media by Simpson's lawyers, and they had first appeared in an article by Jeffrey Toobin in the July 18, 1994, issue of The New Yorker, *thereby gaining such notoriety and credibility that there was probably not a juror in the box who had not heard them. A similar defense tactic had been used in the William Kennedy Smith case in Palm Beach in 1991, when a vilifying article attacking Patricia Bowman, who had brought rape charges against Smith, appeared in the* New York Times *shortly before the trial began. The William Kennedy Smith and O. J. Simpson defense teams even employed one of the same private investigators, Pat McKenna, and the same forensic scientist, Dr. Henry Lee. The racist* profile and the framing of O. J. Simpson have become part and parcel of the persona of Detective Mark Fuhrman.

Anticipating the appearance of Mark Fuhrman on the stand was like waiting for the late arrival of a television star at a party. People kept looking toward the door of the courtroom. The lawyers kept walking back and forth. Outside the courtroom, the bailiffs barked orders for people to step back behind taped lines on the floor, just as they do when the sequestered jury arrives and leaves. When Fuhrman finally appeared, surrounded by four Los Angeles police officers serving in the role of bodyguards, he looked like nothing so much as the handsome lead in a cop series.

Fuhrman is to the Simpson case what Dr. L. Jerome Oziel was to the Menendez case: a major participant with a flawed record of his own, a person on whom hate can be heaped in tones of righteous indignation. As Dr. Oziel's deplorable ethics distracted jurors from the brutality of the murders of the Menendez brothers, so the alleged racism of Detective Fuhrman was meant to distract jurors from the crimes of O. J. Simpson. Even though the accusations of his having framed Simpson are fanciful, without proof of any sort, the allegations from Fuhrman's life made him fair game to be portrayed by the defense as a man whose deeds are as hateful as the murders Simpson is accused of committing.

251

Gus, remembering back to their initial meeting at dinner at "21" in New York, watched carefully as F. Lee Bailey cross-examined Detective Mark Fuhrman. He remembered Bailey saying that night, "Any lawyer in his right mind who would not be looking forward to cross-examining Mark Fuhrman is an idiot." His moment had come in the trial, and the courtroom sat in stunned silence.

"Do you use the word *nigger* in describing people?" he asked.

"No, sir," replied Fuhrman.

"Have you used the word *nigger* in the last ten years?"

"Not that I recall, no," replied Fuhrman.

"You mean if you called someone a nigger you have forgotten it?"

"Look at the look on juror number five's face," whispered Gus to Kim Goldman, who was sitting beside him.

"And number six," she whispered back.

"I'm not sure I can answer the question the way you phrased it, sir," said Fuhrman.

"Are you therefore saying that you have not used that word in the past ten years, Detective Fuhrman?" Lee Bailey was enjoying himself enormously.

"Yes, that is what I'm saying," replied Fuhrman.

That night Gus went to a small dinner given by the film star Kirk Douglas and his wife, Anne, at L'Orangerie on La Cienega Boulevard, the most elegant restaurant in town. Gus had known the Douglases from the period of his life when he and Peach were still married and lived nearby in Beverly Hills. There were photographs in Gus's scrapbooks at his house in Prud'homme, Connecticut, of the Douglases' youngest son, Eric, at the third- and fourth-birthday parties of Gus's daughter, Becky.

Among the other guests that evening were Frank Sinatra, his wife, Barbara, and Dani Janssen, the widow of the actor David Janssen, who had become a famous hostess in the movie colony. Although in failing health and inclined to be cranky, Sinatra retained his legend status. People turned to stare as he entered the restaurant under the watchful eye of his wife, and he acknowledged the looks he received from the patrons at every table, having long ago accepted his position on the top rung of the ladder of the Hollywood firmament. Kirk Douglas greeted him on his arrival at the table with the appropriate deference of a grand duke greeting an absolute monarch.

Barbara Sinatra was a stunning, witty blonde whom Gus had met years before on a yacht in Acapulco when she was married to Zeppo Marx, one of the Marx Brothers. Throughout the evening, she fussed over Frank, making sure he was comfortable, checking on his drink, repeating bits of conversation he had not heard, and ordering his dinner for him from the maître d'. "Mr. Sinatra will start with the boiled egg and caviar," she said.

Gus had known all four of Sinatra's wives:

Nancy, who was called Big Nancy, Ava Gardner, Mia Farrow, and Barbara, as well as his two daughters, Nancy, who was called Little Nancy, and Tina. But Sinatra had never liked Gus, and, consequently, Gus had never liked Sinatra. The genesis of Sinatra's dislike had never been clarified. People said, "Oh, that's Frank. That's the way he is." They had once worked together on the television musical of *Our Town,* but Sinatra had barely noticed Gus at the time in his lowly stage-manager position on the production.

In the past, long ago, when Frank was married to Mia Farrow, who was a friend of both Gus and Peach, there had been a few unpleasant incidents. People still said from time to time when they were talking about Sinatra, "Do you remember that time at Swifty Lazar's party in the upstairs room at the Bistro when he was so terrible to Peach?"

Later, when Gus changed careers and became a writer, he repaid Sinatra for his rudeness to Peach by basing a running character on him named Dom Belcanto, a legendary singer with Mafia connections, in several of his novels. Gus believed in getting even with certain people; he used to say, "It's the mick in me." In his Hollywood novel, *The Winners,* which had been a flop, he used the embarrassing incident at the Daisy nightclub in Beverly Hills, when Sinatra paid the captain, George Winona, fifty dollars to hit Gus, who was sitting at another table with Peach. George carried out his assignment because he was afraid not to. "I'm sorry, Gus, he made me do it,"

George had said with tears in his eyes as he struck Gus. Even then, years before he was a writer, Gus said to himself, "This would be a terrific scene in a novel."

After Gus's return to Los Angeles for the Simpson trial, he and Sinatra met for the first time in years at a dinner at the Gregory Pecks', where Sinatra was seated to the right of Veronique Peck and Gus to her left. The trial was the topic of conversation, as it always was, and Gus became the center of attention rather than Sinatra, who was used to being the center of attention wherever he went. The dynamic between them had changed, at least for the period of the O. J. Simpson trial. Gus was no longer afraid of him. If Sinatra had verbally attacked him the way he had once attacked Peach, Gus would have countered in kind. In the one moment their eyes connected, Gus felt that Sinatra understood that. They did not speak to each other that night, or any of the nights that followed, when they met at the Marvin Davises', or the George Schlatters', or the Kirk Douglases'.

No sooner were they seated at the table for eight than Kirk began to talk about the trial, which he watched every day on television. He was in distress over F. Lee Bailey's cross-examination of Detective Fuhrman that day in court.

"Gus, why, why, *why* did Detective Fuhrman say he hadn't said the *N* word in ten years? Why did Marcia Clark let him say that? It's going to come back to haunt him, believe me," said Kirk, in a wailing tone of voice.

"My source in the D.A.'s office tells me Chris Darden and Marcia hardly speak to Fuhrman, they're so pissed about the racist stuff," said Gus.

"That's stupid," fumed Kirk.

"Of course it is."

"I met Marcia one night at Ray Stark's."

"I know. I was there," replied Gus.

"Of course you were. I sat next to her at dinner. She seemed like a smart woman. She should have anticipated the question. F. Lee Bailey's a helluva smart lawyer. He's not going to let a chance like that go by. She should have prepped Fuhrman. She should have asked him the question, Have you ever said the word *nigger,* and worked out the answer with him. There's all kinds of answers like, 'Yes, I may have said it years ago, when I was a cop on the beat in South Central Los Angeles, dealing with the gangs, and I wish I hadn't said it.' But no. He said, 'I *never* said the word *nigger!*'"

"I know it's not very nice to say, and I probably shouldn't even say it, but I suppose *everyone* has said the *N* word at some time or other," said Anne Douglas.

"Frank said it this morning," said Barbara Sinatra.

"You're coming to our dinner tomorrow night at Chasen's for Margaret Thatcher, aren't you?" asked Charlie Wick.

"Of course, Charlie. I'm looking forward to it," replied Gus.

"And Sir Dennis, as he's now called," said Charlie. "And she's *Lady* Thatcher now. We knew her in the Washington years."

"Yes, I know. I told Mary Jane I might be a little late if I go on Larry King's or Geraldo's show first," replied Gus. "I never know for sure until the last minute."

"Lady Thatcher said all anybody talks about in the United States is the O. J. Simpson trial, and she's not really up on it. I wonder if I could pull you aside to fill her in on the broad strokes of the case."

"Sure, I'd be happy to, Charlie. I mean, how often in life do you get to chat up a former prime minister? You have no idea how many entrées O. J. Simpson is providing me with."

"Apparently you know Queen Noor, Gus," said Veronique Peck, when she called him at the Chateau Marmont. "Didn't you write about her in *Vanity Fair?*"

"Yes, I interviewed her in Amman just before the beginning of the Gulf War," replied Gus. "She drove me around in her Jeep. She had her chauffeur drive me to Petra, and I had dinner at the palace with her and the king. Why?"

"She and King Hussein are coming to town for an event at the Reagan Library," said Veronique.

"As friendly as I got with her, I always had to call her Your Majesty," said Gus.

"The Stanley Sheinbaums are giving a party for

them on Sunday and want you to come. You met the Sheinbaums at our house one night, when the Sinatras were there and Barbra Streisand. Do you remember?"

"I remember very well," said Gus. "A star-studded evening, as they say on *Entertainment Tonight.*"

"Stanley thought you might fill the king and queen in on the trial," said Veronique.

"Fine, I'd like to," said Gus, jotting down in his green leather notebook another social entrée courtesy of O.J. Simpson. "Use this in novel," he wrote.

"The Sheinbaums live on Rockingham, directly across the street from O.J.'s house, so there should be a terrible traffic problem that night, between the tourists gawking at O.J.'s house, the police guarding O.J.'s house, and the Secret Service and the motorcycle cops guarding the king and queen. It's going to be a nightmare, Gus. Why don't you drive over with us? They always recognize Greg and wave us right through, so we don't have to wait."

"I do a Sunday-night wrap-up of the trial with Harvey Levin on KCBS from six-thirty to seven, so I couldn't come to your house until after that," said Gus.

Gus counted sixty-eight L.A.P.D. motorcycles lining the driveway of the Stanley Sheinbaums' house on Rockingham as Gregory Peck's car, with Greg driving, inched its way forward. Police officers carrying walkie-talkies and clipboards with guest lists, checked the occupants of each car.

"Oh, yes, Mr. Peck, if you pull out of line here, you can go ahead of these cars. Chuck Pick is at the front door with the parking boys. I'll tell him on the walkie-talkie you're coming," said the officer.

"That's awfully nice of you, Officer," said Greg. "It's quite a mob scene."

"What's tying up the traffic is all those tourists trying to get a look at O.J.'s house across the street," said the officer.

"That's really quite a nice house of O.J.'s, isn't it?" said Veronique Peck, looking out the window as they moved forward.

"I just interviewed the next-door neighbors, the Salingers, who've lived next door to O.J. for seventeen years," said Gus. "They liked him as a neighbor, before the murders, I mean. They said he really loved that house, that it meant everything to him, like it was the fulfillment of his dreams. He kept the house through two divorces, and the wives and kids moved to condos with no backyards. He's that kind of guy."

"Is anyone living there now?" asked Veronique.

"Oh, yes. His sisters, Carmelita and Shirley, and Shirley's husband, Benny, and his mother, Eunice, when she's in town, and Jason, the son by the first marriage."

"What's he like?" asked Veronique.

"He never speaks in court. He's the sous-chef at Jackson's on Beverly Boulevard," said Gus.

"O.J.'s ruined this neighborhood, ruined it," said Veronique. "Everyone's up in arms over it. Mike Ovitz wants to turn it into a gated community, so *no one* can drive through."

"The value of everyone's property has dropped,"

said Greg. "Thousands of cars go through here a week now."

"The poor Sheinbaums. It's a nightmare for the people living here," said Veronique.

"Dina Merrill's buying a house a block or so down on Rockingham," said Gus.

"She'll be sorry," said Veronique.

Inside the house, Gus thanked the Sheinbaums for inviting him. Betty Sheinbaum was a daughter of Harry Warner of the Warner Brothers Studio Warners. In his film-producing days, Gus had known her daughter, Sarah, when they both had films showing at the Cannes Film Festival. He said hello to Warren Beatty and Stefanie Powers. David Margolick introduced him to Jesse Jackson.

"Are you going to be visiting O.J. in jail while you're in town, Reverend Jackson?" asked David.

Jackson gave Margolick a cold look and a noncommittal answer.

"Reverend Jackson didn't seem to like your question," said Gus.

"He looked pissed off that I'd asked it," said David.

"I noticed," replied Gus. "Do you remember the way the Kennedys always had a Catholic priest in the Palm Beach courtroom during the William Kennedy Smith rape trial? 'Father Murphy wouldn't be here if Willie did it' was the subliminal message to the jury. The Menendez brothers had a priest who sat with the family, too—I suppose to show what nice Catholic boys they were. I'm surprised the

260

Dream Team doesn't have any of the black leaders, like Jesse or Al Sharpton, in the courtroom."

"This trial is right up your alley, Gus," said Queen Noor. They were in a corner of the Sheinbaums' living room, talking about the case. "This has all the things you write about and get indignant about. The rich and the powerful in a criminal situation. You said trials are different if the defendant can afford million-dollar lawyers. You told me that was what interested you."

"What a good memory, Your Majesty. I remember the conversation, and I later wrote it in my journal, in case there's ever a memoir in my future. We were in your Jeep, going out to the refugee camps. That was an amazing experience for me."

"I don't always see *Vanity Fair,* but I have read a few of your pieces about the trial," said the queen.

"There are more complicated issues this time than in the kind of trials I usually cover. This time, there's race and fame thrown into the mix, along with the power and the money. What I'm beginning to realize is that the people who believe in him don't care if he did it or not. They want him to be acquitted. As a story, it's irresistible, but as an experience to be involved in, it has become like an obsession with me. Nothing else interests me."

"We watch the trial on CNN at the palace, but we're not caught up in it the way everyone is here. I've never seen anything like it. All anyone talks about is O.J. Simpson," said the queen.

"It's become something bigger than a murder

trial," said Gus. "I think people are beginning to feel that. It's telling us a great deal about ourselves as a country. There has never been a murder trial in this country that has so involved the nation for such a long time."

"Darling, you remember Gus Bailey, don't you?" said the queen as her husband came up to join her.

King Hussein smiled and greeted Gus with a handshake.

"Your Majesty," said Gus, giving the little bob of the head that is a requirement when meeting royalty. "Whenever I see you on television or read about you in the papers, I always remember that wonderful night at the palace when you had several of the journalists who were waiting to get into Baghdad for an off-the-record dinner. Judy Miller of the *New York Times,* Chris Dickey of *Newsweek,* and the other ten or so. That was a great night."

"I remember," said the king, nodding his head.

"I remember the queen chiding Chris Dickey for chain-smoking all through dinner," said Gus.

"Gus and I were just talking about—" began the queen.

"Yes, yes, I know, the O.J. Simpson trial," said the king.

"Go on, Gus."

"The trial seems to be exacerbating the racial tensions of the country. There's an ugly feeling with the crowds outside the courthouse carrying placards —blacks and whites screaming insults at one another. We are looking at each other suspiciously."

Graydon Carter, the editor of *Vanity Fair* magazine, sent a fax to Gus at the Chateau Marmont to call him at his apartment in the Dakota that evening.

"I just read your 'Letter' for the next issue," said Graydon. "I love the part where the real-estate agent's daughter arranged for you to go to Nicole's condo on Bundy, and you and she and some guy acted out the murders."

"No matter how many pictures you've seen of that patio, it's still a shock when you see how little it is," said Gus. "So much violence took place in such a tiny space. It was creepy being there. I almost felt I could hear the sound of the scuffling of Ron's sneakers and O.J.'s Bruno Magli shoes on the walkway."

"Who was the other guy?"

"Robert Altman, the film director. He's a cousin of the real-estate woman selling the house for the Browns. He was O.J. I was Ron. Moya was Nicole."

"Why didn't you use Altman's name in the article?" asked Graydon.

"I didn't want him to think I was using him," said Gus.

"It makes it a better story if it's Robert Altman, the great film director, participating in a reenactment of the murders on the actual site where they happened than just some anonymous guy," said Graydon.

"Is there still time to make some changes?" asked Gus.

"Write it tonight and fax it to Wayne in the morning," said Graydon. "Now, listen, Gus, do you think there's any chance you can take a few days off from the trial and fly over to London?"

"Oh God, I don't think so," said Gus.

"The magazine's having a fund-raising dinner at the Serpentine Gallery. Princess Diana's going to attend. It would be good if you could be there."

"I really don't know how I could take the time off," said Gus.

"The princess told me she liked the articles you wrote on Jackie Onassis and Queen Noor," said Graydon.

"Oh, great," said Gus. "I'd rather interview Princess Diana than anyone in the world," he added.

"It's a long shot. I just thought it would be a good thing for you to meet her under these circumstances," said Graydon. I had Dana check with Garcetti's office, and it's going to be a three-day weekend at the trial. Ask the judge for a day on each side. You could take the Concorde both ways. We'll put you up at Claridges."

"Can I let you know?"

That night, Gus wrote in his journal, "Fifteen years ago, when I was still down-and-out, or maybe just beginning to get up, if anyone told me I was going to have choices like this to ponder over in my future—Princess Diana or O.J. Simpson—I'd have thought it was camp."

264

"If O.J. walks, what do you think his life's going to be like?" asked Larry Schiller. They were sitting in a restaurant in Venice Beach. Schiller's fiancée, Kathy Amerman, was with them.

"Different, very different from the kind of life he led before the murders," said Gus. "No endorsements —I think that's over for him, even if he walks. And no television series. I don't even think his friend Don Ohlmeyer has enough clout to put him on television. And this I know for a fact: His country-club days are over. I hear there's going to be a mass exodus of members from the Riviera Country Club if he should ever show up on the golf course there again. What do you think? You're my only link with O.J."

"I'll tell you what the plans are, but you can't use this, Gus, either on television or in *Vanity Fair.* They'll know it came from me," said Schiller. "Save it for your novel."

"Okay."

"First, after the acquittal, about ten days after, there's going to be a Pay-Per-View television appearance that could net him somewhere up to twenty million dollars. That would pay off all the lawyers and leave O.J. more than enough to resume his old life. The show's going to feature his children from both marriages, his family and friends, and his lawyers. The interviewer, who's not settled on as yet, is going to be Barbara Walters or someone of comparable stature."

"I feel like puking," said Gus. "Kill two people and get rich on it. Who's making all these arrangements? Skip Taft? Robert Kardashian? They ought to be ashamed of themselves."

"Calm down, Gus. Calm down," said Larry.

"Oh God, would I love to write about this. There would be a white riot in Los Angeles if people knew such plans were afoot while this trial is going on."

"You can't write about it," said Larry.

"I know. I know."

"Don't you guys ever get sick of talking about O.J. Simpson?" asked Kathy Amerman.

"Just let me finish this point," said Schiller. "After the Pay-Per-View, O.J.'s going to drop out of the spotlight for two years, raise his children on a ranch in Wyoming, or someplace like that, away from things, and then return slowly to Los Angeles to restart his life."

"He's got it all figured out, hasn't he?" said Gus. "I keep thinking about poor Nicole and Ron."

"Could we talk about something else, please, besides O.J.?" asked Kathy.

"How about Princess Diana? Do you want to talk about her?" asked Gus. "I happen to have a little news in that department."

"Yes, now you're talking," said Kathy. "Don't you think she got a raw deal when she married the Prince of Wales and nobody told her he was in love with that country lady, whatshername?"

"I agree," said Gus. "There's a chance, just a chance, I might get to interview her. Graydon Carter wants me to take a couple of days off from the trial and fly over there to meet her."

"You're going, aren't you?" said Schiller.

"I don't know," said Gus. "Do you think I should?"

"Of course. Are you crazy? That's major stuff."

"I'm afraid I'll miss something," said Gus. "Suppose O.J. stands up in court and says to the world what he said to the Reverend Rosey Grier in jail— 'All right, goddamit, I did it. I killed them both'— and I miss the moment because I'm chattin' up Princess Diana over in London. I'd be mortified."

"It ain't going to happen," said Schiller.

"Are you out of your mind, Gus? Of course you should go to London," said Harvey Levin. "It's a slow part of the trial. You're not going to miss anything."

"What'll I tell Ito? I don't want to lose my seat in the courtroom," said Gus.

"Tell him the truth. Tell him you might get to do an interview with Princess Diana. He's the biggest starfucker in the world. He'll keep your seat for you," said Harvey Levin. "You wait. He'll probably say, 'Please give my best to the princess.'"

"Please give my best to the princess," said Judge Ito when he told Gus that his seat in the courtroom would be safe.

"I will, Your Honor," replied Gus.

19

In his "Letter from Los Angeles," Gus wrote:

"I want all the citizens of Los Angeles to remain calm," said an enraged Johnnie Cochran, in a sentence that said one thing but that could be interpreted as meaning another, during a press conference in which he blasted Judge Ito for ruling that only two of the forty-two uses of the word nigger *on the Fuhrman tapes could be presented to the jury. "The cover-up continues," said Cochran, in a menacing manner, I felt, suggesting that Judge Ito himself could be part of a conspiracy against Simpson. Many people were shocked by Cochran's statement, myself included. It evoked, as it was intended to, memories of the riots and the burnings after the Rodney King verdict. Later, in a sidebar in the judge's chambers, Ito told Cochran that he was going to overlook his public outburst. Hello? He fines poor Marcia Clark at the drop of a hat for the slightest untoward thing, and he overlooks a public statement on television by the lead de-*

fense attorney that suggests he is a part of the conspiracy to frame O. J. Simpson. What is going on here? I have heard it suggested that the defense is holding it over Ito's head that they know his wife, Capt. Margaret York, the highest-ranking female in the L.A.P.D., lied under oath when she said she didn't know Detective Mark Fuhrman, so that her husband could keep the gig. I've heard that's what Fuhrman is saying behind closed doors. It has become increasingly clear to those of us who attend the trial every day that Mr. Cochran is running the courtroom, not Judge Ito.

The baggage handler at LAX recognized Gus as he got out of the limousine *Vanity Fair* had provided for him and handed him his bag.

"I have two carry-ons, and I'm checking this one," said Gus. "Be gentle with this. It has my computer."

"You're the O.J. guy, right?" asked the baggage handler.

"One of them," replied Gus.

"I see you on *Larry King*," he said. "I want to show you something, as long as you're here. See this trash dispenser? In the trial, this is the dispenser they said in court that O.J. put the bag in that night, with the murder weapon, or whatever, when he was flying to Chicago after the murders. Let me tell you something—they didn't even *have* this kind of trash bin until later. Here's the kind over here that he put the bag in. See? If the police had asked me at the time, I would have told them that, but, oh no, they didn't do a good search. Anyway, these trash bins get filled up real quick and the cleanup crew empties them every half hour or so."

"So bye-bye murder weapon within thirty minutes after he dropped it in there," said Gus. "Gone forever."

"You got it."

The night before Gus met Princess Diana, he went to a dance given by Evelyn Rothschild, of the banking family, honoring the twenty-first birthday of his daughter. Gus had first known Evelyn years before, when he was a frequent visitor at Gus and Peach's house in Beverly Hills before his marriage. The dance was held at the Royal College of Art, which had been transformed into a replica of El Morocco, the famous New York nightclub of the thirties and forties, by the popular social figure and decorator Nicky Haslam. Gus was well seated at a zebra-striped banquette between the Duchess of Marlborough and the widow of Henry Ford.

"Oh, my dear, the grandeur of it all," said Gus's friend Caroline Graham, commenting on the splendor of his *placement.*

"O.J. Simpson has improved my social position," replied Gus. It was a line that he often used these days. "People's interest in O.J. is insatiable, even over here in the duchess set. I never used to be as well seated as I am these days."

"I understand you're a writer," said the Duchess of Marlborough, as she picked up Gus's place card, squinted at it, replaced it, and finished her sentence, "Mr. Bailey."

"Yes."

"Evelyn said you're at that awful O.J. Simpson trial in California," said the duchess. "I don't follow it. It doesn't interest me in the slightest. They say he's so famous, but I never heard of O.J. Simpson before. I couldn't care less about football, and someone told me those movies he made were ghastly. I don't understand why it's getting all this attention. How long are you staying? Are you going to be in town next week? There's an opening of my dog paintings at the Hahn Gallery on Albemarle Street."

After dinner, there was an unpleasant situation between Gus and one of the guests, the genesis of which dated back to long before the Simpson trial. It had to do with a previous murder in high places which Gus had written about. John Aspinall, the gambling figure and zookeeper, took great offense at Gus's presence at the Rothschild dance when Mrs. Ford introduced the two men.

"You mean this is Gus Bailey?" Aspinall asked, his face reddening with rage and a look of fury appearing in his eye.

Aspinall had disliked an article Gus had written about Lord Lucan on the occasion of the twentieth anniversary of his disappearance from England, in which Gus had suggested that a select group of rich and powerful men were keeping the alleged murderer of his children's nanny in stylish exile, with a reconstructed face. Perhaps in Africa, where Aspinall had a house, Gus had suggested. Perhaps on the coast of Mexico, where Jimmy Goldsmith had an eighteen-thousand-acre fiefdom. Perhaps in Old Prud'homme, Connecticut, where Lord Lucan's sister had a New England saltbox.

"If Lucky Lucan is dead, these guys wouldn't get so excited and upset when I suggest he's still alive," said Gus, after Aspinall had gone off in search of the host.

"Does that sort of incident happen to you often?" asked Mrs. Ford, who witnessed the encounter.

It goes with my territory, I suppose," said Gus. "There're a lot of people I seem to piss off, like Aspinall with the red face who was just here. A lot of people at the O. J. trial aren't mad about me, either."

"Does that bother you?"

"No, not really," said Gus. "I always know the side I'm on. I don't want to go to Johnnie Cochran's house for dinner any more than I want to go to John Aspinall's house for dinner. There's a long list. The way I look at something like what just happened is, I can turn it into a really good scene in a novel."

"Hello, Gus," said Carolina Herrera, the New York dress designer and social figure, who had recently brought out a line of cosmetics. She and her husband, Reinaldo, who worked at *Vanity Fair,* were New York friends of Gus's and had come over for the weekend of parties.

"You're the new Estée Lauder, I hear," said Gus, greeting her. They hadn't seen each other since the trial started.

"Don't I wish," said Carolina. They kissed on each cheek. "How does it feel to be away from the trial for a couple of days?"

"I feel guilty," said Gus. "I'm so afraid I'm going to miss something. I called L.A. three times today just to check in, and I did two interviews on Sky Television, all about O.J."

"I read in one of your articles that you have become friendly with O.J.'s sisters," said Carolina.

"I have," replied Gus. "They're very nice people."

"Do they think he's guilty?"

"No, they firmly believe he's not guilty. We never actually talk about did he/didn't he do it when we're together, but they must know how I feel, and I have to respect how they feel. I know they read my 'Letters from Los Angeles' in the magazine. They go to church. They have jobs. They're good people. They didn't do anything wrong. For their lives, they're doing the right thing. He's their brother, and they're there to support him."

"That's a difficult position for them," said Carolina.

"Sometimes I wonder how much O.J. was there for them before all this happened, but they were called into service to play family. My feeling is, not much. People I know who were friends of O.J. and Nicole and used to go to the house on Rockingham when they had parties tell me he never had his family around, just Nicole's family."

"His daughter's beautiful, isn't she?" asked Carolina.

"Arnelle. Yes, she's beautiful. She's the only one in the whole family who has O.J.'s looks. Arnelle and the daughter of Shirley and Benny, Terri, are first cousins, more or less the same age, but they're not friendly. They don't pal around together at the trial. It's as if they're from different social positions," said Gus. "The poor-cousin syndrome."

"If I sent something to O.J.'s sisters, could you get it to them?" asked Carolina.

The British writer Brian Masters heard Gus discuss the O.J. Simpson trial on Melvyn Bragg's radio show the morning after the Rothschild dance and called him at Claridges. He said he was writing an article on Claus von Bülow, who had been living in London since his acquittal at his second trial of charges of attempted murder of his wife, Sunny, who remained in a coma at Columbia-Presbyterian Hospital in New York. Gus had covered the trial for *Vanity Fair* magazine.

Using a camp-funny voice to lighten up the seriousness of what he was asking, Masters said, "As you are the only one living who still thinks he was guilty, would you give me a quote, Gus?"

"Oh, no, Brian," replied Gus. "I don't think so."

"Why?"

"I wrote everything I have to say about him," said Gus. "It's been years."

"Ten."

"I wouldn't say anything against him," said Gus.

"How about something for him?"

"Oh, no. I wouldn't do that, either."

Over the years at *Vanity Fair,* Gus had interviewed or written about some of the most famous women in the world: Jacqueline Kennedy Onassis, Imelda Marcos, Queen Noor, Audrey Hepburn, and Elizabeth Taylor, among others. Whenever Graydon Carter asked him whom he would like to interview the most, he always answered, "Diana," meaning the Princess of Wales. "Fifty years from now, they're not going to be writing books and musicals about Princess Margaret and Princess Anne. They're going to be writing about Diana. She upstaged the British Royal family. The aristos hate her. The crowds love her. She's a great character," said Gus.

The beautiful young Princess Diana walked toward Gus, smiling, welcoming, holding out her hand in greeting. "Don't tell me they've let you out of the trial!" she exclaimed, acknowledging in that sentence who he was and what he did for a living.

He replied, "Briefly, Ma'am," taking her hand and bobbing his head in the appropriate manner.

"I hear the O.J. Simpson trial is all anyone talks about in America," she said. "They say people watch it on television all day long."

Although Gus was not unused to being in the presence of august beings, he suddenly found himself beset with shyness in front of the princess. He had not expected her to be so warm and friendly. He wanted to tell her how much he admired her, but he was momentarily speechless.

As if she understood his dilemma, she asked him more about the trial. "Does it get boring, sitting there in the courtroom day after day?"

He looked at her. He saw that she really wanted to know the answer. "Sometimes the legalities get boring, Ma'am. Sometimes Judge Ito lets the lawyers go on too long. But the event is never boring. For me, it's like watching a movie as all these extraordinary people interact with one another. By the way, Judge Ito asked me to give you his regards."

"He didn't!" said the princess, delighted.

"He did. I had to get his permission to come so that I could keep my seat," said Gus.

"Have you ever talked to O.J. Simpson, just you and he?" she asked.

"No, I haven't," said Gus. "No one can get near him. If I even tried to speak to him, I'd lose my seat, but his friend Robert Kardashian told me he reads what I write about him. We've looked at each other in the courtroom. One day our eyes actually locked for a long moment."

"And what happened?"

"His eyes were wary at first, and then they softened, and I could see he was playing with me, like a cat with a mouse. I thought I could see the very beginning of a smile, as if he thought he was winning me over. I could actually feel the charm that everyone who knows him talks about. I thought to myself, in other circumstances than these, he would have won me over."

"If you could ask him one question, what would it be?" asked the princess.

"I wouldn't ask him about his blood at the scene of the crime, or the murder weapon, or the bloody clothes, or the cuts on his finger," replied Gus. "He's got all those answers down so pat he could pass a lie-detector test now. I'd ask him something that would throw him, something that would get him angry."

"Like what?"

"I'd say, 'Did you say anything to Nicole or did Nicole say anything to you before you slit her throat, or did you just grab her from behind?'" said Gus.

"Would you like to hear what I think is going to happen?" she asked.

"Of course," replied Gus.

"I think O.J.'s going to be acquitted," said the princess.

"I was afraid you were going to say that, Ma'am."

"Well?" asked Graydon. "How was she?"

"She was so nice. She was so available in conversation," answered Gus. "I thought it would be uphill, but it wasn't for a minute."

"What were you and she talking about so earnestly?" asked Graydon.

"O.J. Simpson," said Gus, and they both laughed. "That's all we talked about the whole time."

"What did she say?" asked Graydon.

"She thinks he's going to be acquitted. I always get a jolt when I hear people say that. Deep down I have this terrible feeling that she might be right, but I'm not at a point where I can deal with even the possibility of that thought."

"You're not letting this trial get to you, are you, Gus?" asked Graydon.

"It's all I think of morning, noon, and night."

"Listen, you're in London. Have some fun. Think about something else. You have a prize seat for dinner," said Graydon. "Between Joan Collins and Princess Salima Aga Khan."

"I never used to get seats like that before O.J. came into my life," said Gus. "You know something, Graydon? No one talks to me about anything except O.J. anymore. It's like my career began with this trial. People just look at my face and start talking about O.J."

"It's all the television, I suppose," said Graydon.

"Last night I was leaving Evelyn Rothschild's dance at about one-thirty in the morning, and I couldn't get a taxi on Kensington Gore for the longest time. Finally an off-duty taxi passed me on his way home. He went about half a block beyond me and then did a U-turn and came back. He lowered his window and then asked in a Cockney voice, 'Where are you going?' I said, 'Claridges,' and he said, 'Hop in.' I did. I could see him looking at me in the rearview mirror. Our eyes met. He said, 'How's the trial?'"

"No!"

"Yes. He recognized me from sitting next to the Goldmans in the courtroom. He watches the trial on Sky Television here in London. I couldn't get over it. He wanted to hear everything, and I told him everything. By the time we got to Claridges, he was my new best friend."

20

In his "Letter from Los Angeles," Gus wrote:

The infinite charm of Dr. Henry Lee, who is invariably referred to in the press as America's foremost forensic scientist, is legendary, especially when he talks to juries—beguiling them, amusing them, instructing them, making them feel like mini-authorities on blood splatter and shoe prints. If he suggests to the jury that there might have been a second set of shoe prints at the crime scene on Bundy, which would imply an alternate killer to the defendant on trial, that's probably what they're going to believe, even though there wasn't a second set of shoe prints. But, as they keep saying out here, he's only doing his job. I have never been one to contribute to the hagiography of Dr. Lee, having seen him give a quite similar courtroom performance when he was an expert witness for the defense at the William Kennedy Smith rape trial in Palm Beach.

Gus was having dinner with Harvey Levin and the *Hard Copy* reporter Pat Lalama at Eclipse.

"You have to say this about Dr. Henry Lee, he had the jury in the palm of his hand," said Harvey.

"Dr. Henry Lee always has the jury in the palm of his hand," replied Gus. "Dr. Lee has taken charm to a new level."

"He bugs you, doesn't he?" asked Pat.

"In a word, yes," replied Gus. "When he was on the stand in Palm Beach during the William Kennedy Smith rape trial, where he'd been hired by the Kennedys, he told exactly the same joke he told today on the stand, and the jury ate it up in Palm Beach just the way the jury ate it up today. He said, in a Charlie Chan singsong voice, 'You people all look alike to me,' and all the ladies on the jury were captivated. It's shtick. It's showbiz. Get the dopes on the jury to love you, and you can feed them anything."

"Do your imitation of Dr. Lee for Pat, Gus," said Harvey.

"Gus, it's Danny Selznick, a voice from your past." Gus was in his room at the Chateau Marmont, writing his "Letter from Los Angeles" that he had promised Wayne Lawson he would fax the following morning.

"Hi, Danny," replied Gus. Danny Selznick was the son of the great film producer David Selznick and the great stage producer Irene Selznick, who was the daughter of Louis B. Mayer, the founder of Metro-Goldwyn-Mayer. When Gus and Peach were married, they often saw Danny when they went to dinner at David Selznick's house during his marriage to Jennifer Jones.

"I'm calling from a pay phone on the highway in Martha's Vineyard," said Danny. "You're going to think this is a very strange call after such a long time."

"I won't think it's strange," replied Gus. "You should hear some of the calls I get."

"There's a woman out there, who's a friend of mine, who wants to meet you," said Danny.

"To what end?"

"She reads you in *Vanity Fair.* She watches you on television. She agrees with you on everything. She has some information she wants to tell you about the case, something she knows," said Danny.

"And she called you in Martha's Vineyard to have you call me here in Los Angeles?" asked Gus.

"She knew I knew you," said Danny. "She was nervous about calling you at the hotel."

"Why?"

"You've gotten famous, Gus. It scares some people off."

"Tell her it's only O.J. fame. It's not real fame," said Gus.

"She's a photographer, and she supplements her income by working in a photo lab in Culver City. Remember Culver City?"

"Home of your grandfather's MGM," said Gus. "'More stars than there are in the heavens.' Isn't that what they used to say about MGM?"

"Now called Sony Studios," said Danny.

"Not by me," said Gus. "I still say MGM."

"One of the private investigators for the defense stopped in the photo lab where she works awhile back, probably thinking it was an out-of-the-way place, to have some crime-scene prints made. It was about a six-hundred-dollar job, and he paid in cash."

"Interesting," said Gus. "She wants to tell me about the pictures?"

"She wants to *show* you the pictures. When she realized what they were, she made an extra set for herself. For which she could get fired, as I'm sure you're aware."

"Not to mention sued," said Gus.

"Are you interested?"

"I'd say so, Danny."

"She doesn't want to come to your hotel, because someone might see her there with you."

"Okay."

"She wants to know if you could meet her in the lobby of the Century Plaza Hotel on Sunday afternoon at three o'clock."

"I'm going to see Elizabeth Taylor at three. Could she make it at two?" asked Gus.

"I'm sure she can."

"What does she look like?"

"She knows what you look like."

"Should I not know her name?" asked Gus.

283

"Julie Coolidge," replied Danny.

"That's a very Connecticut-sounding name," said Gus. "You don't hear names like that much anymore, especially in murder circumstances like these."

"Thanks, Gus."

"I find I rather enjoy all these clandestine meetings I go to, Danny," said Gus. "It gives me faith in mankind that so many people want to come forward with information that *might* be helpful in convicting a killer. In no other case I've ever covered have I seen such passion as I have seen in this case, on both sides."

"Having any fun out there?" asked Danny.

"Oh, sure. I go out every night. It's different from the old days out here. By the way, I've seen a bit of Jennifer."

"Jennifer?"

"Jones, your former stepmother. She looks great. I went to a dinner the Livingstones had for Andrew Lloyd Webber before *Sunset Boulevard* opened out here, and I sat next to Jennifer."

"We haven't been close since Dad died," said Danny.

"Oh, I didn't know that," said Gus. "Listen, thanks for the call, Danny."

After checking his car with the parking valet, Gus walked into the marble-floored lobby of the Century Plaza Hotel in Century City. The lobby was vast, a city block long. He looked around for a likely location where a secret rendezvous might occur between strangers and headed toward a sunken bar area, down several steps, where people were sitting on bar stools. He stood at the top of the steps next to a potted palm, on display, since he was the one to be found. As he usually did at a new location, he pulled out his green leather notebook and wrote a quick description of where he was. Good for detail in the book later, he wrote.

"Gus?"

He looked up. He thought she looked just the way someone with the name Julie Coolidge should look. "Julie," he replied, putting out his hand.

"I'm Danny's friend."

"I jumped to that conclusion," said Gus. "How do you know Danny?"

"I'm doing a coffee-table book on stills from *Gone With the Wind,* which his father produced, and he's been an enormous help."

"Did you by any chance go to Smith?" asked Gus.

"Yes. How in the world did you know that?" she asked.

"You have that look. Listen, it probably isn't the best idea to sit at a table in this bar. Too many people. Too much noise to talk over. Especially if we're going to look at crime-scene pictures."

He could see that Julie was nervous.

"I see a lonely patch of marble planters and two chairs over there by the elevator bank," said Gus.

They headed in that direction.

"I read you. I watch you on TV. I agree with you about this case," said Julie when they were in place.

"Danny told me," replied Gus.

"O.J.'s so guilty, and I have a feeling that he's going to get away with it," said Julie. "I'm a photographer by trade, but I have a job in this photo lab in Culver City for rent money."

"I know. Who came to see you?"

"Two men. I don't know their names. They weren't any of the people you see on television, like Carl Douglas or Kardashian. These were new faces to me. I felt they were probably private investigators. They needed prints made in a hurry. I couldn't do it while they waited the way they wanted me to. There were too many. I said that I would work late that night and they could come back in the morning. When I saw the pictures that night, I couldn't believe what I was looking at. I almost fainted at some of the pictures of Nicole and Ron. I had no idea it was quite as bloody as that. But there's this one particular picture I want to show you. It's of Ron Goldman's watch. Look at the time. It says ten o'clock."

As Gus leaned forward to take the batch of photographs that Julie removed from a manila folder in her tote bag, his attention was diverted by a woman with a Botticelli hairstyle who passed by his chair on her way to the elevator bank.

"My God," said Gus, looking at the woman. Following several feet behind her was a man with a beard.

"What?" asked Julie.

"Do you see that rather harried woman in the yellow formless dress?"

"Yes."

"Do you know who she is?"

"No."

"That's Laura Hart McKinny, followed by her unhappy-looking husband," said Gus. "She's the woman who has the tapes where Detective Mark Fuhrman says the *N* word forty-something times."

"The screenwriter. I've read about her," said Julie.

"A screenwriter who's never sold a screenplay, as Peter Bart just pointed out in *Daily Variety*. She's O.J. Simpson's savior. This woman's tapes are manna from heaven for the defense. They are the blockbuster Johnnie Cochran promised the court that they would be. She was on the stand Friday, and she's going to be back on the stand Monday. Want some good dish?"

"Sure."

"Laura Hart McKinny and Fuhrman were lovers. That's what hasn't come out. I have a source on the defense team who lets me listen to the tapes nights at his house in the San Fernando Valley. Not just the 'nigger-nigger-nigger' stuff, which Cochran rightly called a blockbuster. I listened to this one tape where Fuhrman's playing the guitar while he's talking to her, and at one point in the song he says, 'I have to take a leak.' Hello? I said to my source, 'That sounds like they know each other pretty well. Do you think they were having an affair?' He didn't know. So I called my friend Anthony Pellicano, the famous private investigator, who's a great friend of Mark Fuhrman's. I said, 'Anthony, tell me, were Fuhrman and Laura Hart McKinny lovers?' He replied, 'For six months. Mark broke off with her when he met Caroline, whom he's now married to.' In my frame of reference, that puts Laura Hart McKinny into the wronged-woman category, which would make me question her motives in this case. Apparently Chris Darden has love letters that she wrote to Fuhrman."

They watched as Laura Hart McKinny and her husband got on the elevator and then returned to the photographs.

"Do you ever talk about anything else?" asked Julie.

"Almost never," replied Gus. He returned to the pictures of the crime scene. "It makes me feel faint to look at these pictures of Nicole lying in all that blood. Don't let it slip your mind that his kids were upstairs while this slaughter was going on. I wonder why they haven't made more of the fact that Nicole was barefoot."

He shuffled through the stack of pictures. "Oh, my God, look at this one. There's O.J. stripped down to his Jockey shorts, and that's Dr. Henry Lee on his knees in front of him with a Rolleiflex camera. This has to be the inside of Kardashian's house in the valley. This must have been taken *before* the freeway chase. You've got to give Shapiro his due. He brought in the big guns like Dr. Lee and Dr. Michael Baden to be expert witnesses on O.J.'s team practically the day after the murders. He certainly recognized a guilty client when he saw one."

"What exactly is an expert witness, Gus?" asked Julie.

"Some people call expert witnesses whores of the court," replied Gus. "Let me explain it this way. Dr. Michael Baden was paid a hundred thousand dollars by O.J. to say that it took fifteen minutes to kill Nicole and Ron, so therefore O.J. couldn't possibly have done it and still make his plane to Chicago. Got it?"

"Got it," replied Julie.

"Could you get in any kind of trouble if I wanted to print this picture of O.J. in his Jockey shorts and Dr. Henry Lee on his knees in front of him in *Vanity Fair*?"

"Benny," called out Gus to Benny Baker when he saw him getting coffee in the cafeteria. "When court's over, could you bring your car around to where my car is parked in the lot? Don't ask me to explain it. You'll understand."

Carolina Herrera, true to her word, had sent a huge box of fragrances, powders, creams, and lotions representing all her products as gifts for the sisters of O.J. Simpson. Each was beautifully wrapped in silver paper.

"I couldn't very well take these up to the court-room to give to you without causing a bit of a media incident," said Gus as he began handing over the boxes out of the trunk of his car to Benny and Shirley Baker, who put the packages into the trunk of their car.

"Who is this lady who sent us these things, Gus?" asked Shirley as she smelled the scent of powder through the silver wrapping paper.

"Her name is Carolina Herrera. She's a famous dress designer in New York, and all these packages are from her line of cosmetics," said Gus.

"Why would she send them to us?" asked Shirley.

"I saw her when I was in England last week. Naturally, she asked me about the trial, as everyone does. I started telling her about you and Carmelita. I said I admired you, the way you're dealing with what you're going through. She was very interested in hearing about you."

"This is very nice of her," said Shirley.

"She even thought of you, Benny," said Gus. "Here's some Herrera shaving soap and aftershave."

"Gus, if you'd get me the address, I'd like to write Carolina Herrera a thank-you note," said Shirley.

Gus was sitting in the backseat of a limousine with the beautiful model Cheryl Tiegs, heading down Sunset Boulevard for the premiere of *Waterworld* and the party afterward. "Come on, Gus. It will do you good to get out of the courtroom. We'll be Kevin's guests. They're sending a car, tickets, the works. I'll pick you up at the Chateau. Oh, it's black-tie," Cheryl had said when she called to invite him. Kevin was Kevin Costner, the star of the controversial film that had cost so much to make. "You'll like Kevin."

"I met him the other night at Barbara and Marvin Davis's," said Gus.

"I've been wanting to tell you about this friend of mine who's a friend of O. J.'s. A really good friend for a long time. Golf buddies, like that. He also knew Nicole."

"This guy doesn't live in Marbella, does he?" asked Gus. "He didn't get a call on the night of the murders, did he?"

"No, different guy. He went to visit O.J. in jail the other day for the first time. He said he looked O.J. right in the eye and he asked him, 'Did you do it, O.J.?' And O.J. said, 'No, man. You know I never could have done that. I loved Nicole.'"

"My heart is breaking," said Gus.

"You know what, Gus? My friend didn't believe him. And O.J. knew he didn't believe him. He could see it when their eyes met. He's not going back to visit him again."

"His con-man performance doesn't seem to be working on some of his friends the way it did in the beginning," said Gus. "Right after his arrest, all of his buddies met in Shapiro's office, and O.J. spoke to them on a speakerphone from jail and swore to them one by one that he didn't kill Nicole, and they all believed him, and some of the guys even cried at the injustice of his being in jail. But loyalty goes only so far when murder is the issue. I heard Alan Austin also stopped going down to jail to visit him. Do you know Alan? He owns that building in Beverly Hills where the Giorgio Armani shop is. Years ago, when I was under contract to Twentieth Century-Fox as a television producer, Alan was under contract at the same time as an actor. Later he became a great friend of O.J.'s. Used to play golf with him all the time. As a matter of fact, he was playing golf with O.J. at Riviera on the morning of the murders. He's the one who told me how O.J. blew up at Craig Baumgarten on that morning during the game. He said O.J. got so angry at Craig, he kind of lost it. Alan absolutely refused to believe that his friend could ever have done such a thing. He was blindly loyal, but I hear that lately he's stopped going down to jail. He said every time he asked O.J. about the blood—how come his blood was at the scene of the crime—O.J. never could give him a straight answer....Hey, look up ahead, Cheryl. Klieg lights. Fans in the bleachers screaming for the stars. Army Archerd doing interviews. This is a real old-fashioned Hollywood premiere, like Peach and I used to go to when I was still in the business."

"Get ready, Gus. We're going to have to walk past all those cameramen and photographers when we get out of the limo. Look, there's Kevin in the car ahead of us."

Grafton, it's Dad. I'm mortified. I just heard on *Entertainment Tonight* that it's your birthday today. I never thought I'd get to the point where I'd hear about my son's birthday on television. Please forgive me. I am consumed with this trial. It has taken over my life. It is all I think about, or talk about, or even dream about. I have friends who have died while I've been here, and I haven't written condolence notes yet. I think it's great you got Kate Capshaw and Uma Thurman for the movie. Zander's in Nogales with Mom. Give him a call. Anyway, happy birthday. Are you going to be at Carrie Fisher's party Saturday night? I hear Chris Darden and Gil Garcetti are going. No word yet on Marcia Clark.

"Did I ever tell you this, Gus?" asked Harvey Levin, ready to launch into another story about the case. "It fit right in with what you were saying the other night. About two weeks before the trial started, I was in Shapiro's office in Century City. This was before Johnnie Cochran took over. Shapiro was still in charge. He did the same sort of thing with me that he did with Jeffrey Toobin, when he leaked to Jeffrey the stuff about Detective Mark Fuhrman's racism. He was playing cutesy. I was asking him questions about the defense strategy, and he said, 'I would never be a source, but if you should happen to *see* anything in my office.' He took a sign and turned it around. There, in a childlike spidery handwriting, were three possible defense strategies. Number One: O.J. didn't do it. Number Two: Contamination of the evidence. Number Three: Conspiracy to frame. That part was all fine, but I kept looking and saw that it was signed Henry Lee. I said something like, 'Is that Dr. Lee's handwriting?' and Shapiro said, because I apparently wasn't supposed to have seen the signature, 'That's not what I was showing you,' and then he kicked me out of his office."

Gus was having dinner in the garden of Roddy McDowall's house in North Hollywood. Elizabeth Taylor was to have been there, but she had backed out at the last minute. The others were Mart Crowley, the playwright, and Gavin Lambert, a writer who was working on a biography of Nazimova, the great stage actress who became a great film star. They talked about Natalie Wood, whom they had all loved. They talked about *Waterworld,* which they had all hated. They talked about Don Ohlmeyer, the president of NBC West Coast, who had just pulled the plug on *Gai-Jin,* a miniseries based on James Clavell's novel, which Roddy had flown to Japan to shoot.

"This guy Ohlmeyer goes to visit O.J. in jail several nights a week," said Gus.

"And he canceled my pilot," said Roddy.

"Do you know anything about the *Frogman* pilot at NBC?" asked Gus.

"Only that O. J. Simpson had the lead, right?"

"Exactly," said Gus. "One of Ohlmeyer's conditions for making the pilot was that O. J. have the lead. What I've heard is that they had a technical adviser who taught them how to use knives to kill."

"Am I right in remembering that the cops at O. J.'s house after the murders watched that tape of the pilot?" asked Roddy.

"I read that, too," said Gus. "The thing is, there're no copies of that pilot anywhere. They must have destroyed all the copies so the prosecution couldn't subpoena them."

"Who was at Sue Mengers's last night, Gus?" asked Mart.

"Gore Vidal. Jack Nicholson. Like that," said Gus.

"What did Gore have to say?"

"He said he thought Marcia Clark was getting very Roz Russell," said Gus.

Gus was sitting in a box at the outdoor Greek Theater watching Johnny Mathis's concert with Nancy Reagan, Marje Everett, and Merv Griffin. At the suggestion of the Secret Service, they remained in their box during the intermission.

Gus, leaning toward Nancy Reagan, picked right up on the conversation he had been having with her about the trial when the overture started an hour earlier.

"Johnnie Cochran acted as if it was an impertinence on the part of the detectives outside the gates of Rockingham to have even *suspected* that such an eminent person as O.J. Simpson might be the killer," said Gus. "What kind of damn fools would they have been if they didn't suspect him? In any crime of this nature, the husband, the lover, the ex-husband, is always a suspect, and Fuhrman had been to the house before when O.J. beat in the window of Nicole's Mercedes with a baseball bat."

"What about the DNA?" asked Nancy. "Isn't that supposed to put him away? Didn't you say it's better than fingerprints?"

"I've begun to think the DNA isn't going to have any effect in the long run," said Gus, shaking his head. "It's too difficult to understand. I figure that if I can't get it, they're not getting it in the jury box, either. The more information you give a jury, the more you confuse them. My take on Barry Scheck's strategy on DNA, about which he knows a great deal, is that he talks brilliantly over the heads of the jurors, knowing they're not understanding what he's talking about, so that in the long run they'll dismiss the importance of it."

"Gus is going on a rampage again about the trial," said Merv Griffin.

"I know. It's become my sole topic of conversation," said Gus. "Talk about something else."

"How was Diana?" asked Nancy.

"That's right, I forgot," said Gus. "You had her and Prince Charles at the White House, didn't you? I remember those pictures of her dancing with John Travolta."

"That was quite a party," said Nancy.

"I couldn't get over how friendly she was," said Gus. "She thinks O.J. is going to get acquitted."

Gus and Marcia Clark were at Suzanne Childs's house in upper Bel Air. "It's strictly an off-the-record night, Gus, just us," Suzanne had said when she asked him for dinner in court a few days before.

"Do you remember that night I met you at Ray Stark's before the trial began?" asked Gus.

"With Betsy Bloomingdale and all those fancy people. Of course I do. You and I were the only ones who sat all the way through *Legends of the Fall*," answered Marcia. "All those movie moguls tiptoed out during the picture. I couldn't get over that."

"There was a guy there that night named Alan Greisman, who used to be married to Sally Field," said Gus.

"And you read in the tabloids that I'm having an affair with him. Right?" said Marcia.

"Right."

"Listen, Gus, I had dinner with the guy exactly once. We had dinner at a little Italian restaurant in Beverly Hills, and we talked about our divorces, and that was it. And the tabs have built it up into a hot affair."

"Par for the course," said Gus.

"This is not exactly the time in my life for romance," said Marcia. "I happen to have other things on my mind, like O.J. Simpson."

"As they say, the price of fame," said Gus.

"Did you see that topless picture of me *The Enquirer* printed? Do you know how old that picture was?" asked Marcia. "That picture was taken in the south of France during my first marriage. I'd like to know who sold that to them."

"At least they had the good taste to put a bar over your nipples," said Gus.

All through dinner they dished the trial. Marcia Clark was sitting on the floor in front of the fireplace, a glass of red wine in her hands.

"Marcia, there's this guy who lives on Bristol Circle, about a block away from O.J.'s house on Rockingham," said Gus. "His trash barrels were out that night for a morning pickup. This guy claims that he found bloody sheets and towels in his trash barrels. But no one had heard about the murders yet, and the barrels were picked up. The guy goes to the bar at the Bel Air practically every afternoon and tells the story to anyone who will listen."

"Gus, do you have any idea how many cockamamy stories like that we've heard since the murders?" said Marcia.

"I suppose," said Gus.

"If there was anything to the story, Lange and Vannatter would have checked it out long before now," said Marcia. "There were dozens of bullshit stories like that."

"Then I guess I better not tell you about the guy who told me he had a call in Marbella, Spain, from someone, not O.J., who was *at* the crime scene before the police arrived on the night of the murders."

Marcia laughed. "No, Gus, don't tell me," she said.

"Or about the drug dealer who's taken two lie-detector tests who says he sold crystal meth to Kato Kaelin and O.J. at Burger King at twenty minutes of eight on the night of the murders?"

"No, Gus, please."

They all laughed.

Nate 'n Al's deli on Beverly Drive in Beverly Hills was a popular breakfast spot for people in the film-and-television industry. Gus entered on a Saturday morning to meet with Elaine Young, a well-known real-estate personality, about whom he had written in *Vanity Fair* during the halcyon days of the eighties, when the new wealth of the city began buying up the great mansions of Beverly Hills and Bel Air and then tearing them down in order to build larger mansions, which were out of proportion to the lots on which they stood. Even at eight in the morning on a week-end, the place was packed and there were people waiting in line for tables.

"Right this way, Gus," called out the hostess,

who was seating people. Since Gus had begun appearing on television every day and night, people he didn't know would call him by his first name in public places. He hadn't made a reservation that morning at Nate 'n Al's, but his recognition factor as a participant in the O. J. Simpson trial was such that customers who did have reservations didn't seem to mind that the hostess was seating him ahead of them.

"Is he gonna walk, Gus?" asked a man who was waiting in line for a table. No one had to say O.J.'s name anymore when they talked to Gus. They just used the pronoun *he*, and it was understood.

"I liked what you said on the news with Dan Rather last night," said the hostess as she led him to his table.

"What'd I say?" asked Gus.

"About Johnnie Cochran trying to turn the trial into the Fuhrman trial instead of the Simpson trial," said the hostess. "This is your table, Gus."

"Thanks," said Gus. He waved hello to the famed film figure Lew Wasserman, who was having breakfast with his grandson a few tables away.

"Coffee, Gus?" asked the waitress.

"Thanks, Addie," said Gus. "I'm waiting for somebody, so I'm not going to order yet. I'll have some grapefruit juice, too. I've stopped drinking orange juice because of the O.J. of it all."

"You're not going to believe who's been coming in here, Gus," said Addie.

"Who? Kato Kaelin?"

"Oh, not him," she said with a dismissive shudder. "None other than A. C. Cowlings, acting like he's as important as Mr. Wasserman over there. I said to the boss that I wouldn't wait on him, but the boss said that I had to—he had to be treated like he was any other customer—so I said I was going to say to him if I had to wait on him that I didn't want to wait on the man who was driving O.J. Simpson in the getaway car. And, if he gave me any lip, I've got the number for the *National Enquirer* taped to the pay phone in the kitchen."

"You tell 'em, Addie," said Gus.

"Hi, Gus, sorry to be late," said Elaine. Gus rose to greet her, and they kissed on both cheeks. Years before, Elaine had been married to the actor Gig Young, who was once a great friend of Gus's. Gig had later shot and killed his fourth wife and then himself on their honeymoon.

"I wanted to tell you about O.J.'s house on Rockingham. To give you a little background, I sold O.J. the house originally for six hundred and fifty thousand. I have to say this about him, the guy was the best client I ever had. I didn't even know who he was at the time. I wasn't into sports. Before he bought it, I'd rented the house to Carly Simon when she was married to James Taylor, and then to Tony Orlando. It's a good house. He's going to have to sell it at some point, even if he wins the case, which people are beginning to think he's going to do. Am I right?"

"I still think it's going to be a hung jury," said Gus.

"I heard you say that on the news," said Elaine. "Anyway, back to my story. If a normal person owned that house on Rockingham, it would go on the market today for two-point-eight or two-point-nine million."

"Doesn't all the publicity of the last year about the house decrease the value? I'd certainly never want to live there," said Gus.

"Are you kidding? Because it's O.J., a lot of wealthy guys want to buy it. I know for a fact they'd pay four-point-five or even five million for it," said Elaine.

"What is this telling us, Elaine?" asked Gus.

"Listen, Gus, what I want to know, do you think I'd get death threats if I were the real-estate person of record to sell it?"

By the time Gus got from downtown Los Angeles to the Church of the Good Shepherd in Beverly Hills, the 7:00 p.m. funeral mass of Eva Gabor had already started. When Gus had lived in Los Angeles, Good Shepherd was the church that he and Peach attended. His sons, Grafton and Zander, had gone to Sunday school there. His daughter, Becky, had been christened there as a baby and buried from there as an adult.

The church was packed. There was a roped-off area toward the front where the celebrated mourners were seated. Fans and members of the public were seated behind. Just as Gus ducked into a pew at the rear of the church, he was spotted by an usher who recognized him from the trial.

"Oh, Gus, no, no, not in there. We have a seat for you up in front in the reserved section," said the usher.

"This is okay here," said Gus.

"Oh, no, the family would want you in the reserved section," said the usher, as if he knew that to be true, which he did not.

As they walked side by side up the aisle, Gus was aware of the faces of people whom he hadn't seen for years. The usher escorting him began talking about the trial, leaning in toward Gus to speak in his ear as they walked forward. He didn't like Scheck, he told Gus. He couldn't stand Johnnie Cochran. He told Gus not to get him going on Shapiro, which Gus had no intention of doing.

"How far up are you taking me, for God sake?" asked Gus, stopping. "This is fine right here in this pew."

"No, no, we have a seat saved for you," said the usher, persisting in his mission.

"We are going too far forward for the degree of my friendship with Eva," said Gus.

"Right here," said the usher. "With Mrs. Reagan."

Gus, to his embarrassment, found himself being placed in the family section, in the same row with the former First Lady and Merv Griffin, the multimillionaire entertainer and real-estate tycoon, who was for years the very best friend of the deceased Eva. Gus saw that he was directly behind Eva's sisters, Zsa Zsa and Magda Gabor, who looked like glamorous grandes dames in black chiffon dresses with pearls at the neck and diamonds at the ears.

"I'm mortified that guy put me in here, Nancy," whispered Gus to the former First Lady. "He talked to me about O.J. all the way up the aisle, even when I didn't answer him. I just hope Zsa Zsa doesn't turn around and make a scene when she sees me in the family section."

"Oh, I don't think that's going to happen, Gus," said Nancy.

"I'd forgotten how pretty this church is," said Gus. The sunset was shining through the stained-glass windows behind the altar. "I haven't been in here since Becky's funeral."

Memories of that day began pouring into his consciousness as he went through the motions of participating in the funeral Mass he was attending. He could see Peach in her wheelchair, wearing her pearls, a lavender caftan, and a large straw hat. He could see the look of numbness on her face. That same look was on the faces of Grafton and Zander, who sat on either side of their mother. He could see Becky's casket, covered with lavender flowers, within touching distance.

"Hello!" shouted Gus into the telephone. He had already called downstairs to the garage for his car to be ready. He had collected his notes for the speech he was about to give. He was partway out the door when the telephone rang.

"Gus, it's Chata. I can tell by your voice I got you at a bad time." Chata was a childhood friend of Peach's who had been a bridesmaid when she married Gus. Now she worked part-time as Peach's secretary, paying her bills, answering her mail.

"Yes, I'm rushing," said Gus. "I'm giving an O.J. speech for Stop Cancer, and I'm already a little late. What's up?"

There was a moment's silence.

"Is something the matter?" asked Gus. "Has something happened to Peach?"

"No, it's not Peach. She's fine. This may not be anything at all, Gus, and I know you're so busy."

"What? Tell me, what?"

"Zander is missing," said Chata.

"Missing? What do you mean he's missing? I just talked to him yesterday."

"He went hiking yesterday, later, after you talked to him," said Chata.

"Oh God," said Gus. "But he's a good hiker. He goes hiking all the time."

"That's right. But he didn't come back, and he didn't take any water or food with him."

"Oh God. Does Peach know?"

"No. She's not having a good day."

"Then don't tell her. Have you talked to Grafton?"

"Grafton's coming from New York."

"Listen, I have to give this speech, and I'm late. It's too late to back out. People have paid for tickets to be there. Can you stay there at Peach's house? I'll call back as soon as my speech ends. If he's still missing, I'll fly over in the morning."

He called down to the desk. "Mario, it's Gus. Can you check for me and see what planes are flying to Tucson in the morning? Leave the information in my box. I'm going out to give a speech at the Beverly Wilshire, and I'll be right back afterward."

On his way to the Regent Beverly Wilshire Hotel, Gus decided to make a detour, even though he was already late. He drove west on Wilshire Boulevard. Just past the Avco Embassy Theater, he turned left and drove into the cemetery of the Westwood Mortuary. He drove his car around the circle and stopped. On Becky's grave was the yellow rose he had left on Saturday morning on his weekly visit. He knelt. When he leaned down to kiss the headstone, he whispered, "Becky, help Zander, wherever he is." In moments of stress, he often asked Becky for help.

"I'm not going to be able to stay for the dinner afterward," Gus whispered to Sherry Lansing, the head of Paramount Pictures, just before she went to the podium to introduce him.

"I have you at my table," said Sherry. "Next to me, as a matter of fact. Everyone wants to meet you."

"I have a family crisis, Sherry. I said I'd be by the telephone at the hotel right after the speech," said Gus.

"Is it Peach?" asked Sherry. Everyone knew that Peach was an invalid and had been bedridden for years.

Gus didn't answer.

When he was at the podium talking about the trial, he felt perfectly safe in expressing his opinions of Johnnie Cochran, Robert Shapiro, Barry Scheck, and F. Lee Bailey. He knew he was talking to a ball-room full of people who were of like mind concerning the matter of the guilt of O.J. Simpson. But he also acknowledged the flaws that he had begun to perceive in the prosecution.

"What the defense is doing so brilliantly is to keep repeating the word *contamination* over and over and over again, like a mantra, so that the jury becomes brainwashed by the cesspool smell of the word. They are convincing the jury that the police and the criminalists befouled the crime scene with their slipshod performance, their carelessness, their stupidity, rendering the blood at the scene of the crime virtually useless for DNA testing, so contaminated is it. This deceit is from Barry Scheck, who knows more about DNA than anyone in that courtroom, except Dr. Henry Lee, America's foremost forensic scientist. What neither Marcia Clark nor Chris Darden has ever explained to the jury, in the low-down manner in which it would have been understood, is that if the police had urinated, defecated, and then vomited into the blood at the crime scene, it would not have changed the fact that the blood belonged to O.J. Simpson."

"Is there any word?"

"None."

"Have the police been called?"

"Yes."

"I'll be there on the first plane out in the morning."

"What about the trial?"

"Fuck the trial."

21

In his "Letter from Los Angeles," Gus wrote:

From the very beginning, a reporter from the Philadelphia Inquirer *named Robin Clark won his way into the hearts of all of us covering the trial with his reporting talent, his writing style, and, most of all, his wit. He could do an off-the-top-of-his-head one-liner about any of the players in this trial—from Judge Ito to Deputy Jex, and all the lawyers in between—that would rock the media room with laughter. Friday, when we were breaking for the weekend, Robin introduced me to a cousin of his who was visiting from New York with a friend of hers, and he said he was going to take them for a spin up the Pacific Coast Highway in his convertible, with the top down. It sounded so wonderful, so fresh, after the week-long claustrophobic atmosphere of the courtroom. An hour and a half later, all three were killed in a head-on collision. Andrea Ford of the* Los Angeles Times *was the first to get the word. She called Shirley Perlman of* New York

Newsday, *who called me at the Chateau Marmont Hotel, as did Joseph Bosco, who is writing a book about the case. For the first time in the long months of the trial, we heard one another cry as word passed from one reporter to another, from one hotel to another. It made me realize how close we have all become, sharing this extraordinary experience that the trial has been. The following Monday in court, Judge Ito kept Robin's seat in the courtroom empty, and Deputy Jex hung Robin's press pass on the back of his seat. I missed Robin Clark's memorial service, which was held at the house that author Joe McGinniss, who is also writing a book about the case, has rented for the duration of the trial. All the media attended, as did members of both legal teams, as well as the sisters of O. J. Simpson. My son Zander had been reported missing in the Santa Rita Mountains of Arizona, and I had left for the Nogales home of my former wife, Peach, where, with our son Grafton, we waited out the agonizing, nerve-racking days.*

Years before, Gus and Peach had been married in Nogales at a posh wedding with many bridesmaids, many ushers, and many guests in attendance. Later, after their divorce, after Becky's murder and the trial that followed, Peach left Beverly Hills and moved back to Nogales, where she had been raised. Ever since, Gus had spent every Christmas and most Thanksgivings there with Peach and their sons.

"The nurses think we shouldn't tell Mom about Zander," said Grafton.

"She looks very fragile," replied Gus.

"They don't think she can handle it," said Grafton.

"I have a feeling she knows something's wrong," said Gus. "How could she not? The house is full of people. The telephone never stops ringing. People are sending over hams and casseroles and cakes and pies and baskets of flowers. The house feels like there's been a death in the family."

"The police chief wants to talk to you, Gus," said Sigrid Maitrejean, a cousin of Peach's, who was manning the telephones and keeping track of the messages. "He wants you to go on television and give the facts of the case."

"The search parties can't start the search until we find out where your son parked his car to go hiking," said Chief Lopez. "Once we locate that, the search parties can fan out in all directions. If you go on TV and talk, maybe some other hiker who saw him on one of the trails will remember him and come forth. People recognize you from the O. J. trial, and they'll pay attention. Will you do it?"

"Of course," said Gus.

"The Santa Cruz County Search and Rescue, the Pima County Search and Rescue, the Nogales Police Department, the Rangers, and the Air National Guard Reserve Unit are standing by," said the chief.

"Good God," said Gus, as if he was realizing for the first time the seriousness of his son's plight. He looked over at Grafton. They had looked at each other the same way fifteen years earlier, in the room where Gus was then living in Greenwich Village, after Detective Harold Johnston of the Los Angeles Homicide Bureau had called at five o'clock in the morning to say that Lefty Flynn had strangled Becky and that she was near death at Cedars-Sinai Medical Center. Gus had said to Grafton, "He killed her," and they had stared at each other until the words sank in.

"Three of the Tucson stations have crews outside your house," said the chief.

"It's Mrs. Bailey's house, not my house," said Gus.

"Mrs. Bailey's house," said the chief, correcting himself.

"Let's do it outside," said Gus. "There's too much going on in the house already. Zander's mother is not well, and she hasn't been told yet that he's missing."

"Gus, there's a guy here from the Associated Press who wants to interview you. He says Linda Deutsch of the AP told him to call you. There's also a reporter from the *New York Post,* Brendan Bourne, and there's someone from the Tucson paper."

"Good God," said Gus.

"All this press is because of you, you know that, don't you?" said Grafton, with a slight tone of accusation in his voice.

"This is the second time you've said that to me, Grafton, and I don't think it's fair," said Gus. "Don't turn on me now, just because we're all tense and upset."

"I don't see why you have to talk to these reporters," said Grafton. "We didn't ask them to come here."

"It's not because of *me* that this has become a news event," said Gus. "It's because I've become a noticeable figure at the O. J. Simpson murder trial that they're making Zander's disappearance a news event. Otherwise, it would have made the local paper in Nogales and nothing more."

"It's on CNN every hour on the hour," said Sigrid.

"I know. Mario, at the Chateau Marmont, just told me on the telephone that Mart Crowley sent a fax from Tuscany. He read about it in the Paris *International Herald Tribune*," said Gus. "I have to talk to these reporters."

"Why?" asked Grafton. "You don't *have* to talk to them."

"Yes, I do," replied Gus. "I'm in the same business they are. I do what they do for a living. Ask questions of people in distress. I can't pull a 'No Comment' act on these guys."

"A guy who saw you on television last night called the television station," said Chief Lopez. "He says he saw your son late Saturday afternoon on the Patagonia Trail of the Santa Rita mountain range. He said he didn't have any water. He said he was looking for a stream. This man told him where to go. He didn't have a map. But now we can start looking for the car. We have pinpointed on the map exactly where the man met up with Zander. The car will have to be within walking distance of that. There are two helicopters. What they do in search cases like this is paint the missing person's name on the bottom of the helicopter. Do you want it to say Zander or Alexander?"

There were volunteers from two counties, K-9 patrols, police, a sheriff, helicopters, and two planes, one of them from the television show *Entertainment Tonight,* joining in the search. The helplessness of sitting around waiting for news was unnerving for Gus. At the end of day four, he gave up on the possibility of a rescue.

"I don't see how he could possibly be alive," he said to Grafton.

"No, no, he's alive," said Grafton. "Believe me, Dad, I know my brother. He's going to show up."

"No food, no water, the guy on the mountain said," replied Gus.

"I just have a feeling he's going to reappear. We can't give up," said Grafton.

"No, you're right," said Gus. "I'm not giving up, but I'm feeling very pessimistic."

Then came the rains. Torrents of water.

"They've called off the search. They've brought everyone back down," said Sigrid. "It was just on the news."

"Dear God," said Gus. "I have to tell your mom, Grafton. It's not fair for her not to know, especially when she finds out this has been going on for five days."

"What are you going to say?" asked Grafton.

"I don't know."

Peach's house, under the supervision of Zander, had been built to the specifications of an invalid. The master suite, from which Peach rarely ventured, could have been in a big city hospital, so accommodating was it to the needs of a helpless person. No amount of yellow chintz on bed and chair coverings or family photographs in silver frames could disguise its medical purpose. At the bottom of her bed was a giant television set that was almost never turned off. The nurses who sat with her twenty-four hours a day switched channels each time a newsbreak came on, so Zander's disappearance was still unknown to her, or so they thought.

Gus, tentative, sat on the side of Peach's bed, as he often did when he came into her room to speak to her. He knew she liked to hear about the trial, which she watched religiously. For a while he watched with her. His reporter friends from the courtroom, Shoreen Maghame and Harvey Levin, called him each night to fill him in on what had gone on that day.

"That's Marta Weller, with the red hair, from Channel Five in Los Angeles," said Gus to Peach. "I'm surprised you get that here in Nogales. She's the anchorperson, and she keeps the commentary going all day. I've been on quite a few times with her. During breaks, Ron Olson, who's that reporter right there holding the microphone, grabs you and puts you on to tell what's just happened in the courtroom, and then Marta asks questions. Ron's camera setup is right outside the media room on the eleventh floor of the Criminal Courts Building. Right after I saw the autopsy photographs of Nicole and Ron, which made me feel faint they were so terrible, Ron grabbed me and I went on the air with him and Marta. Maybe you saw me, if this is the channel you watch; I was still white-faced from the faint feeling. Nothing had prepared me for the savagery of those murders. You can't even imagine what a slit throat really looks like. That afternoon back in court, I couldn't look at O.J. after seeing those pictures, Peach. I actually hated him. Only a monster could kill people that way. I still think he had to have been on drugs to have done it. Drugs are the dirty little secret of this case, but nobody wants to talk about drugs at the trial. The thing that upset me the most, looking at the pictures, was that Nicole's eyes were open, and so were Ron's, so they knew who it was who was killing them. In the novel I'm writing on the case, I'm going to go inside the heads of both Nicole and Ron at that final moment and tell the last thoughts of their lives. . . . Do you know who's at the trial? Judge Katz, or former Judge Katz, as they call him on *Larry King*. He's become a reporter for the *Malibu Times,* and he goes on TV every five minutes, doing legal analysis. Do you remember at our trial when he called the photographer from *People* magazine into chambers and asked him which pair of glasses made his eyes show up better in the pictures? I don't speak to him. I almost walked off *Larry King Live* one night when I found out he was going to be on it, too. Harvey Levin told me Katz is writing a book about his career on the bench. Apparently there's a section about our trial, explaining why he refused to allow that other woman to testify, whom Lefty beat up so terribly. I don't give a flying fuck what he has to say on the subject. I believe if a man who beats women kills a woman, the jury ought to hear about his past history of abuse against women. Listen, Peach, there's something I have to tell you. I'll, uh, wait until the nurse leaves the room. Oh, do you know who else I saw? Not at the trial but in the courthouse. Marv Pink, Lefty Flynn's lawyer. Remember him? As if we'd ever forget. Do you remember that day in court when he said to Katz, 'Your Honor, Zander Bailey has tears in his eyes,' as if it were an evil thing to be grieving for his sister, and they kicked Zander out of the courtroom? I didn't recognize him at first. He's stopped wearing that thirty-five-dollar rug he used to wear. Leslie Abramson, who's a friend of his, once told me, when we were still speaking, that I'd hurt his feelings when I wrote that his toupee looked like a veal chop pasted to the top of his head. Apparently Pink was under the impression everyone thought the rug was his real hair. They all think that, guys who wear rugs. Do you remember when you and I used to count toupees at all those Industry dinners we had to go to at the Beverly Hilton Hotel? The Directors Guild Dinner always had the most. I once suggested to Graydon Carter an article called 'The Top Ten Toupees in Tinseltown,' but he said it sounded cheap. The only rug that ever fooled me was Lyle Menendez's. . . . Oh, speaking of rugs, I saw Sinatra recently at Kirk and Anne Douglas's. Frank's stopped wearing his rug. He pretends he doesn't see me, and I do the same. Very subtle. No one notices. I never had it in me to forgive him, because he never had it in him to apologize to you for the way he spoke to you at Swifty and Mary Lazar's party in the upstairs room at the Bistro. It was me he disliked, not you."

But Gus was only half-involved with what he was saying, and Peach was only half-involved in listening. Their minds were on other things.

"See that guy talking to Marta and Ron? With the neck brace? That's Joe Bosco. He broke his neck diving into Joe McGinniss's swimming pool. He's writing a book on the case. So's Joe McGinniss. Joe rented Evie and Leslie Bricusse's house on Tower Road while he's here for the trial. He gives great media parties in that house. We've all been together so long, we've gotten very close. Joe's house is the only place we ever get to unwind. One of his parties ended up on Page Six of the *New York Post,* because David Margolick from the *New York Times* and Michelle Caruso of the *New York Daily News* had a romantic moment in the pool. You and I went to a party in that house once—you probably don't even remember—just before we broke up, for Joan Collins and Tony Newley, when they were married. By the way, their son, Sacha, wants to paint my portrait. He's pretty good. He already painted Gore Vidal and Billy Wilder. I told him I couldn't do it until after the trial's over. . . . You have no idea how much mail I have started to receive. Stacks of it. Like movie stars get. The magazine forwards it out to me every week. That's how strongly people feel about this case. I couldn't ever possibly answer all of it. But I also get quite a bit of hate mail. I never had that before. I seem to enrage some people when I talk about Simpson's guilt in all my 'Letters.' Some of it's sort of scary. A lady from Warren, Ohio, wrote that she wished I was lying in a pool of blood, like Nicole and Ron. That makes you feel great to read. I've become very close to the Goldmans, and I write about Kim and Fred and Patti a lot. These hate letters, especially the anonymous ones, are virulently anti-Semitic. They say things like 'How do you like sitting next to those big-nosed Goldmans?' There's another lady, in Portland, Maine, who wrote me that I deserve every tragedy that's happened to us in this family. She was talking about Becky, of course. Imagine writing that. I have this urge to answer the hate mail, but everyone tells me I'd just be asking for trouble if I do. These people take it as encouragement, and the next thing you know, they'd be showing up on my doorstep in Prud'homme with a gun in their hands. . . . You know I wasn't bragging about the fan mail, don't you? It's the sort of thing I have to discuss with someone, and you've known me the longest. It's a new experience for me, being recognized. People who read *Vanity Fair* were aware of me, and people who read my books. My lectures at clubs and hotel ballrooms always sell out, but I was never a name or a face to the people you pass on the street or see at the supermarket. Now I am. It's all over the television. I have a face now that people associate with O. J. Simpson. They see me, and O. J. Simpson jumps into their mind, and they want to talk about him. The stewardess on the plane flying over here from Los Angeles literally knelt by my side the whole flight so she could tell me her theory of what happened that night. She said O. J. went to Bundy to cut the tires of Nicole's car, because she hadn't saved him a seat at Sydney's recital, et cetera, et cetera. If you *knew* how many theories about what happened that night at Bundy I've listened to in checkout lines and at gas stations. People I see at Beverly Hills parties give me messages to give to Marcia Clark, like Bud Yorkin, who told me the other night at Tita Cahn's, 'Tell Marcia to introduce the freeway chase, for God sake.' By the way, Bud's second wife, Cynthia, was in Becky's acting class. They have tiny little kids, and Bud's my age. Women give me letters to Marcia offering her clothes to wear at the trial. Every butler in town knows me. So does every maître d'. They all ask me questions about O. J. 'Do you think he's going to walk?' is the most frequent. That's what everyone seems to think is going to happen. Not me. I still think it's going to be a hung jury. I'm counting on juror number three in the front row, a sixty-year-old blond woman, to hang the jury. People want to know if Marcia Clark and Chris Darden are having an affair. I don't know if they are or not, and I wouldn't tell if I did know. I was up in their office with them recently, after the trial, after everyone was gone. Just the three of us. I was telling them something I'd heard. Marcia keeps a bottle of scotch in her desk drawer. She knocked back a few straight shots. Chris had a beer. They acted cozy with each other. They've become very close. It's only natural when you spend that many hours a day together, working in tandem, passionately believing in the same thing, as they do, that O.J. killed these people. It's like when you're on location for a movie. The two leads usually fall in love, at least for the length of the picture. Like Loretta Young and Clark Gable. Ali McGraw and Steve McQueen. On and on. And when the picture's over, so's the romance. I don't think it's any more than that, and it may not even be that, for all I know, but I think so. The people all want to know why Marcia doesn't use the freeway chase. They tell me, as if I didn't already know it, that ninety-five million people watched the freeway chase. Oh, here's a scoop for you that you don't know. My mole on the defense team tells me O.J. failed a lie-detector test with a minus twenty-four the day after the murders. Shapiro and Kardashian set that up. I make sure to repeat it everywhere I go. I told it at Betsy Bloomingdale's the other night. She seems to have forgiven me for the book. She told me she liked Marcia Clark better with the curls than the Diane Sawyer look. A girl I met at Paul Jasmin's birthday party told me she'd once been in a threeway with O.J. and Paul Sabara. She gave me details, but I won't go into that. You never shared my interest in that sort of information, Peach. See? I got you to smile. I went to Eva Gabor's funeral, and the usher who walked me up the aisle asked me questions about O.J. all the way, until he put me in the same seat with Nancy Reagan and Merv Griffin, a row behind Zsa Zsa and Magda. Do you remember that time we went to one of Zsa Zsa's weddings? When she married that friend of your father's, Josh Congdon? I wish you could have seen them, Peach. They looked wonderful, like something out of Colette. On the altar, there was this huge photo blowup of Eva, very glamorous, in color. The frame was made out of pink roses. I hadn't been to Mass for quite some time, so I got right back into Catholic action and was doing all the sits and stands and kneels in the right places. During one of the kneels, Nancy Reagan leaned over and whispered to me, 'Gus, promise me at my funeral you won't let them put a photo blowup of me on the altar.' Naturally, I collapsed with laughter just as the consecration bell was ringing. . . . You know, Peach, it was the first time I'd been in Good Shepherd Church since Becky's funeral. It brought that whole day back to me. Do you remember when the chauffeur opened the door of the limousine outside the church the confetti from a wedding just before our funeral blew into the door?

And all those cameramen surrounding you as the boys were getting you into your wheelchair? Okay, I won't talk about it. I know you don't like to talk about it. I've been going to the cemetery every Saturday since the trial started. I always leave a yellow rose. I went there five nights ago, on my way to give a lecture for Sherry Lansing's charity at the Beverly Wilshire, and I said, 'Becky, help Zander.' Listen, Peach, this is what I've been leading up to. Zander's missing. I know it's painful even to think about, but it would be wrong for you not to know. You must have known something was going on here. You must have wondered what I'm doing here in Nogales in the middle of the trial of the century, and what Grafton's doing here in the middle of casting his movie. The house has been full of people for days, although no one comes back to this part where you are. Food's being delivered. Flowers are being delivered. There's a bouquet for you from Elizabeth Taylor that's nearly as big as your bed. The phones never stop ringing. The nurses have turned off the phones here in your room so you can't hear. The nurses turn off the news when it comes on, so you won't know. Sigrid is manning one phone line and Chata the other. He went off on an afternoon hike five days ago, and he hasn't come back. Calls are coming in from everywhere. All over the world, as a matter of fact. It's on CNN every half hour, apparently. I know you always said I was a terrible name-dropper when we were married, and I can anticipate that Miss Porter's School haughty look you used to get on your face when I'd say something crass like, 'Becky's godmother is Gary Cooper's daughter,' but name-drop or not, King Hussein and Queen Noor sent us a fax from Amman, saying they were praying for Zander. Everyone who calls or writes or faxes says that they're praying. There are crews from all the Tucson stations outside. Listen to this, if you would like to hear something utterly improbable. *Entertainment Tonight* has sent a plane to join in the search for Zander in the mountains. We were going to snub them, but they have the best plane and the best pilot who can fly the lowest over the mountains, so we accepted their generosity. I was in the plane a couple of days ago with Charlie Wessler. Charlie located Zander's car from their plane, so the search parties could start fanning out from there. It was such an odd feeling sitting in that plane with a cameraman holding a video camera pointed right at my face in case a discovery was made out the window. They painted Zander's name on the bottom of the helicopters, so if he's hurt and lying somewhere, he can look up and see his name and know that people are looking. I went to McDonald's and bought seventy-five hamburgers to take up to the battle station halfway up the mountain. Yesterday, when I was in the helicopter, Judge Ito called me from the trial. He said everyone was praying. I was so touched by that. He's been very kind to me on several occasions, and I feel guilty when I criticize him. Gil Garcetti called to see if there was anything his department could do. He's the D.A. in L.A. Marcia Clark called.

Oh, and Fred and Patti Goldman called. Can you imagine, with what they're going through, that they took the time to call? They're great people. You see, it's all because of O.J. that there's all this media hype. The other day Grafton practically turned on me and said, 'You know, this is all your fault,' meaning all the reporters and cameramen. I tried to explain to him that it's not Gus Bailey who's making this newsworthy. It's Gus Bailey of the O.J. Simpson trial. O.J.'s the key here. This new friend of mine, Robin Clark of the *Philadelphia Inquirer,* was killed on Friday in a car wreck on the Pacific Coast Highway, and Zander went missing the very next day, so they're working up some kind of O.J. jinx story, I suppose. Nancy Reagan called. She sent you her love. She's praying. Everyone's praying. Ronnie's in terrible shape, everyone says, but I never talk to her about that. Some of Zander's friends from school have arrived to join in the search. A lot of your L.A. friends have called. Connie Wald. Ann Petroni. Jill Cartter. . . . Gordon Miller called from Santa Fe. Oh, listen, Peach, when you dozed off, Tita Cahn told me David Begelman committed suicide at the Century Plaza Towers the same day Zander was reported missing. Shot himself. I called Annabelle. I don't think you knew Annabelle. The wife you knew was Gladyce. She died. David always married nice ladies. Annabelle said, 'I'm praying for you, Gus,' and I said, 'I'm praying for you, Annabelle.' I had dinner with David and Annabelle a couple of Sundays ago at Matteo's in Westwood. He wanted to talk

325

about the O.J. trial. I told him that he was responsible for my second career as a crime reporter. He seemed puzzled at first. Then I told him that when I was down and out I helped the two investigative reporters from the *Washington Post* break the story of his forging that check with Cliff Robertson's name. David was so perverse that he roared with laughter when I told him. I know I'm talking nonstop, Peach. I know I'm getting on your nerves. I can't bring myself to face the reality that Zander might be gone. If I keep talking, I can put it on the back burner for a few paragraphs at least. I drove by the old house on Walden Drive the other day. The new people, whoever they are, have kept it up nicely. They're not the same ones you sold it to. They sold it to whoever has it now. They took out the rose garden in the front. They moved the swimming pool from where we had it. Do you remember how we loved that house? So much happened there. There were some great parties in that house. I wish you could remember some of the good times we had and not just the bummers. Like Kate and Ivan's wedding. And the black-and-white ball. Can you remember all the talk that party caused? Can you believe we ever gave that black-and-white ball? Two orchestras. We must have been out of our minds to have given a party like that. I can't believe we ever lived like that. Do you remember? We emptied the house and had all the furniture put in storage! Do I see just the beginning of a smile on your lips?"

"And don't forget, we put the kids and the nanny

in the Beverly Crest Hotel," said Peach. They both began to laugh at the memory they were sharing.

"But it sure was pretty," said Gus.

"Gus, Gus, pick up the telephone," called in Sigrid. "It's Chief Lopez on the second line. Zander's alive. They found him. The rain saved him. He lay there where he fell and held his mouth open. You better talk to him."

"Oh, my God, Peach. He's alive. He's alive." Gus started to cry. He knelt down by her bed and dropped his head on her mattress. "I couldn't have gone through that a second time. I couldn't have gone through it again. I wouldn't have made it, Peach."

"Listen, Peach, I'm off. Grafton and I are driving up to Tucson to see Zander in the hospital. He's dehydrated, bruised all over, sprained ankle, but otherwise well. We're going to have to have a press conference, according to the hospital, because there are so many reporters there. I just said to Grafton, I wish he'd at least have broken his leg. It would have made the press conference easier. After that I'm going to head back to L.A. and the trial. Judge Ito's been very patient about my scat. Apparently I didn't miss much in the trial while I was here, except Gretchen Stockdale, the model O.J. Simpson left a cheap romantic message for a few hours before the murders. I just asked my friend Dan Abrams of Court TV if she was pretty, and he said, 'When Gretchen Stockdale walked off the stand, the defense table rose by six inches.' Well, I thought it was funny. I don't know when I'll be back, other than Thanksgiving and Christmas. This is a first for us in a long time, Peach. This is a story with a happy ending. Zander's safe. Thanks for letting me cry on your shoulder. You always were the class act, you know. I was the mongrel."

22

In his "Letter from Los Angeles," Gus wrote:

From hanging out at murder trials, as I do, I have grown despondent about the goodness of people. Whatever happened to truth? Truth has taken an ignominious decline in importance in the courtrooms of our land. Truth has become what you get the jury to believe. I'm sure there are several jurors on this panel—I could tell you which ones, but I won't—who actually believe that O.J. Simpson was chipping golf balls at his estate on Rockingham while a Colombian drug gang was murdering Nicole Brown Simpson over at her condo on Bundy, because that's what they've been told by some of the fanciest lawyers in the workplace. I remember saying to F. Lee Bailey, early on, before the trial started, when we were still speaking, words to this effect: "You can't really think anyone's going to buy that Colombian-drug-gang story, do you?" Lee was right: There are those who do buy into it, which is a form of untruth in itself, the way I look at it.

329

Truth doesn't matter. Freeing O. J. Simpson is what matters.

But I saw and felt goodness again in No-gales, Arizona, during the five-day search in the Santa Rita Mountains for my missing son. There were volunteers from two counties, K-9 patrols, police, a sheriff, helicopters, and a plane from Entertainment Tonight. *The telephones never stopped ringing. People from everywhere called to say they were praying. All those prayers were heard. My son reappeared, having fallen down a ravine and having survived. We experienced joy.*

Gus returned to Los Angeles from Arizona on Saturday. Everyone at the front desk at the Chateau Marmont told him how happy they were that his son had been found. Everyone said they had prayed for Zander. There were hugs all around. Phalaenopsis plants with gift cards filled his rooms. The entire sofa was covered with letters and cards. His desk was overflowing with faxes. Maria, the maid, whose son worked in the garage, gave him a Mass card.

"You must be exhausted," said his friend Judy Spreckels, whom he referred to as a "trial historian" when he wrote about her during the Menendez trial. When Gus talked to his friends about her, he always said, "Judy Spreckels knows more about murder trials than anyone I know, except possibly Theo Wilson, the great crime reporter." While he was gone, she had organized all his letters and cards and faxes. She had clipped every newspaper account of Zander's disappearance. She had made lists of all the people who had telephoned and had recorded the messages of each caller who said that he or she was praying.

"I'm overwhelmed at what you've done, Judy," said Gus, looking around the room. "You even have the letters alphabetized. I never could have pulled this together in such order."

"The least I could do," said Judy. "Mario and Frederica at the front desk were great. This hotel sure loves you."

"Business tripled here after I wrote in *Vanity Fair* that the night maids leave a gold-wrapped condom rather than a gold-wrapped chocolate mint on the pillow each night," said Gus.

Judy had once married into the very rich Spreckels family, of the sugar fortune, in San Francisco, but a variety of life circumstances had altered that way of being. She lived modestly in a little book-filled house in the San Fernando Valley. Like Gus, she had never believed for a second that the Menendez brothers were sexually abused by their father. Their certainty that the defense's claim was bogus was the beginning of their friendship.

"I don't know how I'm ever going to be able to answer all these letters," said Gus. "There must be a thousand there."

"One thousand two hundred and fourteen as of this morning's mail, and that doesn't include the faxes and the telephone messages," said Judy.

"Efficient, as always. I knew you'd know it right

down to the last one," said Gus. "How am I ever going to answer all these, Judy?"

"I've been thinking about that while you were gone," she replied. "Why don't you write up a thank-you note that would apply to everybody, talk about it being a story with a happy ending, like I heard you say on television, et cetera, et cetera. I'll have a couple of thousand xeroxed, and all you have to do is write 'Dear Marlo and Phil,' or 'Dear Howard and Lou,' or 'Dear Carolina and Reinaldo,' or 'Dear Freddie and Isabel,' or whoever and whoever, and sign it 'Gus Bailey,' and I'll do the envelopes and stamps."

"That's a lot of work for you, Judy," said Gus. "What did Marlo and Phil send?"

"Those white orchids in the basket. They came just before you got back. Card said, 'Dear Gus, We are overjoyed for you. Our prayers were answered. Love, Marlo and Phil.'"

"They're called phalaenopsis," said Gus. "Everyone's been so nice. There must be a dozen or more."

"Fourteen," said Judy.

"Take one home. Take two," said Gus. "I missed my deadline for my 'Letter from Los Angeles' when I was over in Nogales, so I have to write a double-length one for next month."

"Here's a loose-leaf notebook with all the newspaper accounts about Zander," said Judy.

"God, I didn't see some of these," said Gus, as he leafed through the clippings. "Look at this headline in the *New York Post*: NEW AGONY FOR AUGUSTUS BAI-

LEY. Is that cheap enough for you? Did I tell you they sent a plane from *Entertainment Tonight* to aid in the search?"

"Yes, I saw you in the plane on *Entertainment Tonight,*" said Judy.

"They had a guy with a video camera aimed right at my face, for a reaction shot in case something happened, like Zander was dead, for instance, which was on a lot of people's minds, myself included. There I'd be in close-up," said Gus, shaking his head at the memory. "I hope the time will come when this will strike me funny, but I'm not there yet. I'm still shaken by it. I'm still close to tears all the time. Before the O.J. trial, none of this would have happened. It might have been a story, but it would have been about this little on page forty-two of the Metro section and probably wouldn't have made the evening news on television."

"How's Peach?"

"I think she's had more than her share of being put to the test in life," replied Gus. "I think all the years of being as ill as she has been have put her in a different sphere of reasoning than those of us who are still involved in the day-to-day drama of life, like this damn trial that has taken over my life, that has even *become* my life."

"Where is Zander?"

"He's still in the hospital in Tucson, but he's okay. He's dumbfounded by all the publicity. Zander's the shy one in the family. He's the only one who never sought the limelight, and then he became the center of it. I'm sure in time he'll write about it. Grafton's gone back to his movie. He wrote it with a friend and he's directing it. I think it's about Peach, but I'm not sure. And Monday morning, I'm going back to the Criminal Courts Building and the O.J. Simpson trial."

"Are you exhausted?"

"I am," said Gus. "I held it together until after he was found, and then I fell apart. The only night I slept was when I took a Tylenol PM, but I felt groggy the next day."

"You're supposed to go to dinner at Charlie Wick's house in Malibu. I called earlier and said that you probably wouldn't be able to make it. I'm sure you'll have dinner on a tray in your room, watch television, and go to bed early," said Judy.

"Get real, Judy. I'm going to the Wicks' in Malibu," said Gus.

"Why don't you take a night off?" asked Judy.

"I might miss something."

The dinner at Charlie and Mary Jane Wick's beach house in Malibu was for Walter Annenberg, former ambassador to the Court of St. James. Annenberg and his wife, Lee, were spending August at their bungalow with its own swimming pool at the recently reopened Beverly Hills Hotel. Everyone at the party told Gus how happy they were that his son had been found. Everyone said they had prayed for Zander. There were hugs and kisses.

"Here's a note I wrote you," said Betsy Bloomingdale. "I hadn't had a chance to mail it yet, and then Mary Jane said on the telephone that you were coming. How's Peach?"

Charlie said the ambassador had a few questions he wanted to ask about the trial. Later, during dessert, when the champagne was being poured, Charlie asked if Gus would mind saying a few words. Charlie said that people were becoming concerned with the way the trial was going.

"I haven't been in the courtroom for the past week, but I've been watching the television coverage while I was in Arizona," said Gus when he rose to speak. "I was talking with the ambassador before dinner, and I hope you won't mind, sir, if I repeat myself. There is a feeling of despair in the town as to the way the trial is going. There is no question that the defense is superior to the prosecution. The prosecution is proving incompetent, and the defense is immoral. For them, there is only one thing that matters, and that is to win, and they are willing to do whatever it takes to win. Indeed, the Fuhrman tapes were devastating, but they really have nothing whatever to do with the murders. I don't think we should feel as bleak as we are feeling about the outcome of this trial."

When Gus spoke at the dinners he went to, he knew that the audience he spoke to was in complete accord with his own feelings. The possibility of an acquittal for a man who had murdered two people was a matter of repugnance to them all.

"I have great faith in juror number three," said Gus, continuing. "She is a sixty-year-old white woman, extremely attentive to what's going on in the courtroom. She watches. She listens. She takes notes. She seems to absorb. She never looks bored, the way some of them do. I don't know this, but I was watching her when F. Lee Bailey cross-examined Fuhrman, and my feeling was that she couldn't stand F. Lee. Her name is Anise Aschen-bach," said Gus. "My source on the defense team tells me Cochran refers to her as 'the Demon.' At another trial where she was a juror, she became the lone holdout, and during deliberation she managed to bring the minds of the other eleven jurors around to her way of thinking."

"How do you know her name?" asked Walter Annenberg. "I thought the jurors' names were protected."

"They are, but I had dinner at Drai's recently with one of the dismissed jurors, Michael Knox. He's going to write a book for Michael Viner of Dove Books, who arranged for me to meet with him. He was the juror who was kicked off the panel because he peered too long at the pictures in O.J.'s house when the jury went through. He told me the names of all the jurors. So say your prayers at night for juror number three."

"Maybe she'll save the day again," said Charlie Wick.

"She'll never turn these jurors around, the way

she did last time. There is no possibility in the world that there will ever be a conviction, but she could very easily hang the jury, which is the most that we can hope for."

"Why is there no possibility of a conviction, with all the evidence the prosecution has?" asked Charlie.

"Because the African-American jurors won't be welcome back in their neighborhoods if they send their hero to prison," said Gus. "It's as simple as that."

The next morning Gus attended the eleven o'clock A.A. meeting at Cedars-Sinai Hospital. Everyone told him how happy they were that his son had been found. Everyone told him they had prayed for Zander. There were hugs and kisses.

"I was praying every minute," said Faye Resnick when they met up at the coffee machine.

"I'm so happy for you, Gus," said Bernard Lafferty. "Elizabeth was very upset, too."

"She sent beautiful flowers to Peach," replied Gus.

"Would you like to come up to Falcon Lair for lunch after the meeting?" asked Bernard. "You've never seen the house. It's just the way it was when Doris was alive."

"I can't, Bernard. I'm going to a barbecue for some of the reporters at Larry Schiller's house out in the valley," replied Gus.

"Too bad. Andy will be disappointed."

"Andy?" asked Gus. "Who's Andy?"

"Andy Cunanan. He said he met you at a dinner for Marcia Clark. I introduced you to him at the opening of the Beverly Hills Hotel. Andy's been staying at Falcon Lair."

Then Gus went to the barbecue lunch that Larry Schiller and his fiancée, Kathy Amerman, gave for members of the media who were covering the trial. It was held at the house they were leasing from the German film star Maximilian Schell in the San Fernando Valley. Gus had been at Schiller's house several times before. It was there that he had listened to hours and hours of the Fuhrman tapes that Johnnie Cochran got from Laura Hart McKinny when Schiller, who was astute in technical matters, was cleaning them for courtroom clarity.

"I thought I was going to be listening to some monster of hate on these tapes," Gus had said. "He doesn't sound to me as bad as Cochran makes him out to be."

"If Cochran knew you had heard these . . ." said Larry.

"I know, I know. I won't tell anybody," said Gus.

Since the trial began, Gus had gone through a variety of feelings about Larry Schiller. In the beginning, even when he thought he didn't like him, he found him interesting. "He plays every side against the middle," he said to David Margolick. They liked to compare notes about him. Margolick called him "the Candyman," because he was always eating Snickers bars or bags of M & M's, even right after lunch, when he'd had a big piece of lemon meringue pie for dessert.

"He plays a dangerous game," Gus said another time to Margolick about Schiller. "He's going to be a wonderful character in my novel when I get around to writing it. I'm thinking of calling him Joel Zircon. The character is a sort of triple agent of the Simpson trial. Hanging out with the defense as he does, giving the appearance of being part of it, he is privy to things that no other reporter or journalist or novelist covering this case has access to, and I know for a fact he believes O.J. is guilty."

"I know," said Margolick.

"He's going to have one hell of a book when this is over, if he hasn't been mysteriously murdered first," said Gus.

"He asked me to write it with him," said Margolick.

"He asked me, too," replied Gus. They laughed.

"I'm still shaky, and I cry a lot, which is very embarrassing," said Gus to Larry Schiller when Larry embraced him in the hallway. The guests were outside by the pool.

"Everybody was saying their prayers for you," said Larry.

"I know. That's what saved him, you know— prayers," replied Gus.

"Come on outside," said Larry. "Kathy's going to want to give you a hug."

Outside, everyone told Gus how happy they were. Everyone told him they had prayed for Zander. There were hugs and kisses.

"At Robin Clark's memorial service, Linda Deutsch asked everyone to be quiet for a minute and say a prayer for your son," said Shoreen Maghame.

"Thank you, Linda," said Gus.

"Some of us thought Zander might have been kidnapped," said Linda.

"Good God," replied Gus. "You mean kidnapped because of me? Because of what I've written and said? I'm glad that thought never occurred to me during the five days."

"You didn't miss much at the trial," said Shoreen. "Except for Gretchen Stockdale. You would have loved her, Gus."

Back in court on Monday morning, Johnnie Cochran, who didn't like Gus, shook his hand and said he was glad his son had been found. Carl Douglas, who really didn't like Gus, did the same. Barry Scheck hugged him. Robert Shapiro hugged him. Robert Kardashian, whom Gus had often described as the man "who walked off the Rockingham property with Simpson's Louis Vuitton carry-on the day after the murders," sent a father-to-father letter to Gus that made him cry. "As a father of four," he wrote, "I can only imagine the grief and anguish which you have suffered over this past week." Judge

Ito began the day by saying from the bench, "Welcome back, Mr. Bailey."

"I was overwhelmed," said Gus over the telephone to his friend Karen Lerner in New York. "It was a lesson to me about good behavior. I mean, I've written very critically about these guys, and I've been pretty mean, too, and they all were so nice, even Cochran."

"How about F. Lee Bailey?" asked Karen. "Did he hug you, too?"

Gus laughed. He and F. Lee Bailey had long since stopped speaking. "Actually, he wasn't in the courtroom, but I think I have less chance of a hug from him than Bob Shapiro does."

23

In his "Letter from Los Angeles," Gus wrote:

Anthony Pellicano, the renowned Los Angeles private detective, whose name usually appears in every criminal case of consequence in the city, has been acting as Mark Fuhrman's adviser and spokesperson during the detective's current ordeal. Although he admits in the press to being as shocked as anyone else by the excessive use of the word nigger, *as mouthed by Fuhrman, in Laura Hart McKinny's "blockbuster" tapes, he continues to defend him. About the rest of the material on the tapes, he said, "Mark was trying to impress this McKinny woman. He was trying to be Macho Man and Supercop rolled into one, for her lousy screenplay. At that time of his life, Mark hated everybody. He was an equal-opportunity hater." I have known Anthony Pellicano for years. I once hired him to follow Lefty Flynn, the man who murdered my daughter, when he was released from prison after serving only two and a half years.*

"Gus, it's Bernice, from the New York office. You had a call here from a man in Florida that I thought you should know about. So many of the people who call you here at the magazine sound like nutcases, but this man sounded very intelligent. He said it concerned something that was in your last article that he had to talk to you about. He made it sound as if it was urgent. As I said, he was a nice man. He had nice manners. I hate to bother you when you're so busy at the trial, but I thought you should know. This is the number in Florida. Oh, by the way, his name is Goodhue. Albert Goodhue."

"Hello!" The man who answered sounded annoyed at the intrusion of the telephone.

"Mr. Goodhue?"

"Who is it?" The sound of annoyance continued.

"Augustus Bailey."

"Oh, Mr. Bailey, forgive me for the way I answered. I have been under the most terrible stress."

"Is your distress caused by something I have written?"

"By a name in your most recent article. I don't read *Vanity Fair.* It's not a magazine I have come in contact with. Two days ago I was in my dentist's office. Just as I was to go in for my appointment, an emergency came in, a little girl, and they took her ahead of me. I had to wait almost an hour. There on the table was a copy of *Vanity Fair.* I saw your name on the cover of the magazine. I've watched you on television, and I agree completely with your stand on this case, and so I read your article, the 'Letter from Los Angeles.'"

"Yes," said Gus.

"There is a name in the piece that interested me very much," said Mr. Goodhue.

"Who is that?" asked Gus.

"Lefty Flynn."

"Oh?" Gus was taken aback; it was the last name he had expected to hear. Whenever the name Lefty Flynn was mentioned, which was rarer and rarer as the years went by, he experienced a feeling like a stab wound. He had put in the reference to Flynn, the man who had murdered his daughter, in his description of Anthony Pellicano, the private detective, as an aside to his editor in New York. He fully expected it to be edited out, as it didn't relate to the story of O.J. Simpson, but Wayne Lawson had said, "Let's keep it. It roots you to the story."

"What about him?" asked Gus in a tentative voice.

"Does he live in Seattle?" asked Goodhue.

"I don't have any idea where he lives," answered Gus. "Will you tell me what this is about?"

"My daughter is engaged to be married to a man called Lefty Flynn," said Goodhue. "When I read that name in your article, I nearly fainted. I had to know if it was the same person."

"It's John Flynn," said Gus.

"John, yes. That's his name. There are fifty John Flynns in the book. You don't know if he lives in Seattle?"

"My sons and I let go years ago," said Gus. "None of us wanted our lives to be about revenge. I don't know where he lives. What does this guy do for a living?"

"He's a chef at a fancy restaurant in Seattle," said Goodhue.

"That's him," said Gus. "Have you spoken to your daughter?"

"I am going to call her now," he said. "What do you think I should tell her?"

"Tell her to get the hell out of there," said Gus. "Guys who beat up women don't stop doing it. Will you let me know what happens? I'm at the Chateau Marmont in Hollywood. I'll give you the number."

When Gus got out of the station wagon at Wyntoon, Veronica Hearst was waiting. Gus kissed her on both cheeks. "This is so beautiful, Veronica," he said, raising his voice over the roar of the river that twisted through the vast estate. He looked in all directions. There were four small castles built side by side in the Bavarian style, giving the appearance of a village of castles. Wyntoon was the little-known Hearst ranch. San Simeon was the famous Hearst ranch.

"It used to be much larger," said Veronica, "but during World War Two the Hearsts gave the government a hundred thousand acres, and they were never given back."

"What was left over seems ample," said Gus.

"We drove for over half an hour after we turned in your road off the highway, and Wayne, the driver, said it was all yours, as far as I could see in any direction. Tell me about these castles."

"Actually, they're all guest houses. You're going to be in that one," said Veronica. "It's called Angel Cottage."

"Which one is yours?"

"Oh, you can't see ours from here. Ours is miles away," said Veronica.

"Did old Mr. Hearst bring these castles over from Europe?" asked Gus.

"*Phoebe* Hearst, William Randolph Hearst's *mother,* built Wyntoon, *not* William Randolph, who was Randy's father. He rarely came here. He much preferred San Simeon, which he was still building at the time of his death, but Marion Davies liked it here. She liked to get away from San Simeon from time to time. By the way, we're taking the two planes and flying over to San Simeon for lunch on Sunday. How was the plane? I hope everything was comfortable for you. Isn't it glorious, landing right at the base of Mount Shasta like that? Who was the pilot? I think it was Pete, wasn't it? Randy thinks Pete's the best pilot around. Oh, no, no, Gus, the boys will do all that with the bags. Don't you worry about anything. We saw you on TV. You looked so tired. We just want you to rest and not even think about that awful trial. Wayne, or Bill, either one, take Mr. Bailey's bags to Angel Cottage. He's in the Tartan Room. Rose will unpack for you. I'm so glad your son is safe, Gus. Everyone I know was praying for you. Was it awful? Do you hate talking about it? Everyone's out swimming, or golfing, or playing tennis, or sailing, or hiking, or whatever. The rest of the house party flew out on the other plane from New York. I think you probably know everyone. Chessy Rayner. Duane and Mark Hampton, John Richardson, the Boardmans, Audrey Hepburn's ex-brother-in-law. And Betsy Bloomingdale. Is everything all right with you and Betsy? Mark Hampton said on the plane on the way out that there was a little trouble between you and Betsy after your book? Jerry Zipkin made a terrible fuss about you at the time, Mark said. But Chessy said it's all straightened out. Now here's the plan. The whole house party's meeting up for drinks at eight-thirty in Angel Cottage on the balcony overlooking the river. You'll see the sunset. It's so divine from there. Then the vans will take you up to the big house for dinner. That's where Randy and I live. There's a masseuse, Lisa, divine, absolutely divine. She's waiting for you. Don't be surprised if she walks on your back. I'll see you up at the big house. Jacket but no tie. That's the way Randy likes it. Dressy for the ladies. Oh, and tomorrow lunch. There's going to be a picnic deep deep in the forest by the side of the river, and the boys are going to catch the fish we have for lunch. By the way, Randy's dying to talk to you about the trial. Everybody is. Did you know that Randy hired F. Lee Bailey to represent Patty after she was kidnapped by the Symbionese Liberation

Army, and Bailey *lost* the case, and Patty had to go to prison?"

"Yeah, I knew that," said Gus.

At dinner in the Big House, which looked like one of Mad King Ludwig's Bavarian castles, the New York crowd discussed New York things. Everyone's favorite topic was the scandalous divorce of the very rich Frank Richardsons, whom everyone knew.

"Can you imagine why Nancy's giving out all those interviews to the magazines?" "Did you read the one where she was quoted as saying, 'We were never happy, but we were a perfect couple'?" "Do you remember when all that Astor furniture ended up in Texas?" "Anne Bass has been very loyal to her." "Frank must have been out of his mind to keep a diary." "Exactly how much is Frank worth?" "Does anyone here know Judge Kimba Wood?"

Gus knew Judge Kimba Wood, who had become known as "the other woman" in the Richardson divorce, and liked her, but he didn't reply. He had been away from New York for so long that New York social news was less interesting to him than it had been before the trial began.

John Richardson, the art historian and biographer of Picasso, who was not related to Frank Richardson of the divorcing Richardsons about whom everyone was talking, had not been friendly with Gus for years, ever since *People Like Us,* when offense had been taken and nasty things said. Although no words on the subject of Gus's book were spoken, the two began to speak in a friendly manner for the first time in years. Richardson was fascinated by the O.J. Simpson case, and Gus filled him in on the sort of stories about the trial that never got into the newspapers.

"I can't get a reading on the Brown family," said John.

"They're actually all quite nice, but it's a difficult family to categorize," replied Gus. "It's unusual when an innocent victim's family is so unsympathetic. They rarely come to court. When Tanya, the youngest sister, who couldn't be nicer, finally came, after a little prodding from me, she brought her fiancé, a hot number called Rico, and they *necked* in the courtroom, right in front of the jury."

"You can't be serious," said John, delighted.

"They couldn't keep their hands off each other," said Gus. "At one time, Rico had his legs spread apart like this, and Tanya, who was in a miniskirt up to here, placed one of her legs between his two legs, and Rico had his hand on Tanya's thigh. This is not a great look for the sister of the victim, when the African-American females on the jury don't have a very high opinion of Nicole in the first place."

"Unbelievable."

"What are those two talking about over there?" asked Veronica.

"Gus is probably telling O.J. stories," said Chessy.

"You can't get Gus for dinner in L.A., he's booked so far in advance," said Betsy. "Everyone wants to hear about O.J."

"Gus, you know my old editor, don't you? Verna Arkoff?" asked John Richardson.

"Yes, I know Verna," said Gus.

"Call her, and she'll tell you this story firsthand. She has a friend in New York who used to be a very high-class hooker in L.A. Very expensive. Good-looking. Great legs, all those things. Apparently, according to Verna, whom I've always found to be highly reliable with news of this kind, the friend used to do threeways with O.J. and Nicole on a fairly regular basis, and it was pleasant and agreeable for everyone. Then she said O.J. started to change. She was sure he was on some drug. She said she became afraid of him. She thought he went a little crazy when he was high, and she stopped seeing him. Call Verna. I'm sure she'd introduce you to her friend."

"That's the second threeway story I've heard about O.J.," said Gus, entering John's story in his green leather notebook.

Gus was having lunch in his favorite booth at the Polo Lounge of the Beverly Hills Hotel with his son Zander.

"You're looking pretty good, Zander," said Gus. "A lot better than when I saw you at the hospital in Tucson. How's the back?"

"Okay. Not perfect, but okay," said Zander. He looked around the room. "I don't think I've been in the Polo Lounge since my eighth-birthday party."

Gus smiled. "I remember that," he said. "We ran

a movie in the projection room first, *The Sound of Music,* I think it was. Then the ice cream-and-cake part for all the little boys was here in the Polo Lounge. Michael Lerner came. Brook Fuller. Little Tyrone Power the third. Somebody threw up. I have pictures of that in my scrapbooks in Prud'homme. That seems like another lifetime ago to me."

"It sure was," said Zander.

"It ain't been easy for you boys, I know," said Gus. "An invalid mother. A failure father, drunk and bankrupt. A murdered sister."

"We've managed," said Zander. "And you can't call yourself a failure anymore. Every time I turn on the television, there you are."

"Thank you, O. J. Simpson," replied Gus. "One of these days, I want to hear what it was like for you lying there for five days. Did you eat leaves? Did you think about dying? What was it like when you saw the helicopter with your name painted on it, and you couldn't move to signal it? You *have* to talk about it."

"I know," said Zander. "I only meant to go for the afternoon. I knew I didn't have any food or water, but I kept going on. I kept telling myself I should stop and turn back, but I had this desire to just reach the next peak, and when I got there, I'd say just one more and then I'll go back, and then it got dark, and that's when I fell."

"I really think that you should write about it," said Gus. "Describe it all. Even if you never show it to anybody. Maybe we all should, you and Grafton and I. Actually, I have. After the fourth day, I really thought you were dead. Grafton didn't, but I did. I was even wondering if you should be buried in Westwood next to Becky, or in Nogales, where your mother's family is. That's the state of mind I was in."

"God," said Zander.

"It's amazing what goes through your mind at a time like that," said Gus. "I kept thinking about when you were little kids and we lived in the house on Walden Drive. I kept wishing we'd stayed home more nights and had dinner with you kids instead of going out to a party every night the way we did. Your mother wanted to stay home more. I was the one who was always pushing. And lately, I've been so obsessed with this trial that I haven't checked in like I should. You're writing your first novel. Grafton's directing his first movie. These are all important things, and I haven't been there."

Just then, Kathryn Lethbridge from Old Prud'homme, Connecticut, stopped by Gus's table to say hello and to be introduced to Zander.

"Everyone in Prud'homme was praying," she said.

After she went on to her own table, Gus said to Zander, "Saved by the gong in that serious conversation we were starting to get into."

"Listen, Dad, Grafton and I were talking. You're not going to fall apart, are you, if O.J. gets acquitted?" asked Zander.

"He'll never be acquitted, Zander," replied Gus. "It'll be a hung jury. I'm sure of that."

"Grafton says that if you ever do another murder trial after this one, he's going to have an intervention," said Zander.

In his after-dinner talk that evening in the garden of Mrs. Murray Ward's house in Bel Air, Gus paid the proper compliments to his hostess on the beauty of the evening, acknowledged his old-time friends at the party, like Bob and Rosemary Stack, and then segued effortlessly into what he called his floor show.

"The alternate jurors are dwindling down to a precious few, as Judge Ito keeps dismissing jurors. I think this is very serious, what's happening. George Vernon, who is a mystery journalist among us, from a nonexistent newspaper—I for one happen to think he is planted in our midst by the defense—is spreading stories about the latest alternate juror who has ascended to the jury panel. He seems to have an inordinate amount of information about her, which is unusual, in that the identities of the jurors and alternate jurors are so carefully protected. This is the same guy some of you may have heard me talk about when I spoke downtown at the new Los Angeles library, which is fabulous by the way. He told me in what I thought was a mildly menacing manner that people in Chicago didn't like the way I was covering the trial. He says that the new juror, who is Caucasian, went to a Christmas party last year, before the trial started, and told people she was going to write a book about the trial and make a million dollars, and therefore she should be bumped from the panel. He had some other disqualifying stories about her, but I had tuned out of the conversation. There is no way George Vernon, with his no-credentials, could know that information. Either what he is spreading into every ear is totally bogus, or he is being fed information by the two private investigators for the defense, who have probably checked out the backgrounds and persuasions of all the jurors and alternates. I've known Pat McKenna since he was hired by the Kennedys for the William Kennedy Smith rape trial in Palm Beach. This guy could dig up dirt on Mother Teresa. The point is, this new juror, who is probably a prosecution juror, will probably be a nonjuror in a very short time. The campaign against her has started. The defense wants to get rid of her. This young lady is history. I find it interesting that the highly paid defense jury consultant Jo-Ellan Dimitrius continues to sit in court every day of the trial. Jo-Ellan, whom I like, is tall, blond, beautiful, and seems to have caught the eye of Larry King, who was recently seeing Suzanne Childs of the D.A.'s office, but that's another story. In effect, Jo-Ellan Dimitrius's job was completed when the jury was seated. Further, there are constant rumors that O.J. is having difficulty paying his lawyers. So why is she sitting there, being highly paid? My take is, Jo-Ellan's telling Johnnie Cochran which jurors aren't defense-friendly. Anyway, I've talked enough. Thank you very much, Peggy."

354

"Could I ask just one question, Gus. Just one?"

"Of course."

"Is there any truth to the rumor that Marcia Clark and Chris Darden are having an affair?"

The trial was coming to a conclusion. Tempers were frayed. The courtroom friendliness between Marcia Clark and Johnnie Cochran had come to an end. The looks exchanged between Chris Darden and Johnnie Cochran were filled with loathing. Lawyers on both sides openly despised one another. No one liked Judge Ito. In the corridor during breaks, the friends who surrounded the Simpson relatives and the friends who surrounded the Goldman family stared at one another with hostility and began to comment about one another in derisive tones. Most of the reporters couldn't stand Deputy Jex, and Gus couldn't stand either Jex or Deputy Browning, even though the imitation he did of her at Joe McGinniss's parties had been a great success. He had also developed an antipathy to a CNN legal analyst whom he had never met, named Greta Van Susteren.

"She's too pro-O.J. for me," said Gus, whenever Van Susteren's name came up in conversation. "She gives me Barry Scheck feelings when I watch her on CNN. I would *never* go on that show."

"There are a lot of people who think you're too pro-prosecution, Gus, both in the way you write and the way you speak on television," said Shoreen.

"That's different," said Gus. "I'm on the side of

355

the victim. I don't have to pretend I think O.J. didn't do it, like Greta does."

At every dinner Gus went to, when there were important members of the Industry present, he always brought up the name of O.J. Simpson's great friend Don Ohlmeyer.

"Don't you think it's odd that the president of NBC West Coast is a constant visitor to Simpson in jail while the trial is going on?" he asked. "Shouldn't the management of a network maintain an impartial stance during such a sensitive trial?"

"Gus, I heard from someone in the program department at NBC that the word is out that nothing Gus Bailey writes is to be bought by the network," said Douglas S. Cramer, the television producer and multimillionaire art collector. The last show Gus produced before he left the film-and-television business had been for Doug Cramer.

Deeper than that, long-simmering hatreds were coming to the surface. F. Lee Bailey's longtime friendship with Robert Shapiro had turned to sheer unadulterated hate early in the trial. It continued and worsened in the months that followed. They could not bear to be in each other's sight. They cringed with displeasure when circumstances required them to be in physical proximity of each other. Fred Goldman and Kim Goldman stared their hatred into O.J. Simpson's back, daring him to turn around and see the extent of the hatred they felt for him for Ron's slaughter.

Outside the courthouse, the crowds were growing in numbers each night. More people carried signs. More people were yelling that the L.A.P.D. had framed O.J. For security, all entrances to the courthouse were closed except the front entrance, making it necessary to walk through a battery of cameras in full view of the crowds when entering or leaving the building. For the first time, Gus heard himself booed. It sent a chill through him.

Several times Gus said to one of the African-American reporters, Dennis Schatzman, with whom he had become friendly, "Walk me to my car, will you, Dennis? I'm beginning to feel hostility from some of the people outside."

"No one's going to hurt you, Gus," said Dennis.

"I know, but—"

"Where're you parked?" asked Dennis.

Of late, the seeming civility between the Goldman and Simpson families that had been maintained for the first several months of the trial had deteriorated, and they began to show their deep dislike for each other. Over the months, Gus had formed a warm friendship with Kim. On several occasions during the trial, Gus had seen the Goldman family outside the courtroom.

"You're always talking to the killer's sisters, Gus, saying how nice they are," said Kim.

"They are," said Gus. "They didn't kill Ron. They're just related to the man who did kill Ron."

"Who's the one on the end, with the orange hair and the fancy hairdos every day?"

"That's Carmelita, and the hair's not orange," said Gus.

"Then neither is Johnnie Cochran's suit," said Kim.

Gus laughed. "What about Carmelita?" he asked.

"She gives me the middle finger when she's fixing her hair."

"Oh, I don't believe that, Kim. Carmelita wouldn't do that," said Gus.

"Watch, just watch," said Kim. "She pats her hair back, like she's fixing it, but she's only got the middle finger sticking up, and that's aimed at me."

"Why would she do that?"

"It's because we stare at the killer all the time. Even though he doesn't turn around, I know it freaks him out."

"Maybe you're getting to him," said Gus.

"Did you hate that guy who killed your daughter, Gus?"

"I did."

"Do you still?"

"I do."

"So you know how we feel?"

"Yes."

"Whatever happened to that guy?"

"I just heard he's in Seattle."

Mr. Goodhue from Florida had called Gus back. He had called his daughter in Seattle and told her to go out and buy the magazine and read Gus's "Letter from Los Angeles."

"And what happened?" asked Gus.

"My daughter showed Lefty the magazine open to the page where you wrote that he had murdered your daughter and asked, 'Is this you?'" said Goodhue.

"And what did Lefty say?" asked Gus.

"He grabbed the magazine from her and threw it on the floor without even reading it, as if he already knew what you had written about him, and he said, 'That was a long time ago, and I've been in therapy ever since.'"

"Yes?" asked Gus.

"Yes what?"

"Is that the end of the story? Did she leave him?"

"No. She wants to stay."

"Good God," said Gus. "How old is your daughter?"

"Twenty-one, almost twenty-two."

"I was talking to my son Grafton about your call. It made him absolutely furious. He said, 'Lefty Flynn hasn't learned a thing. He's the same con man he always was. He's engaged to be married to a young woman, and he hasn't even bothered to tell her he's murdered a girl and been in prison. What kind of marriage is that going to be with a little secret like that kept from the bride?' I don't wish to interfere in your affairs, Mr. Goodhue, but I don't think what my son said is out of line in the least."

Goodhue started to cry. "I don't know what to

say to her," he said. "He seemed perfectly nice when we met him."

"That's what the Browns say about O.J.," replied Gus. "Think that scenario through."

"What'll I tell her, Gus?" asked Goodhue, sobbing.

"You tell her that every time Lefty Flynn touches her to remember that the hands that are caressing her strangled a young woman exactly the same age as she is."

There was silence.

"Keep in touch," said Gus. "I want to know what happens."

The next day, the Simpson sisters went on television for the first time since the trial had begun. At a press conference called by the defense on the first floor of the Criminal Courts Building, Shirley and Carmelita denounced Fred Goldman for making disparaging remarks on television about Johnnie Cochran for bringing in bodyguards from the Nation of Islam.

In his rooms at the Chateau Marmont, Gus watched on television the press conference that he had attended several hours earlier in the courthouse. He kept switching from channel to channel to watch Shirley Baker. At first he said to himself, "She's being put up to this by Cochran," but he knew that Shirley was not being a reluctant performer thrust into the spotlight. He was stunned by the extent of her rage toward the Goldman family. It seemed to him that she was close to being out of control, as if months of suppressed rage were pouring out of her. At the same time, it shocked him to realize about himself that he had pompously expected Shirley and Carmelita to go on being benign and brave through defeat.

As he watched, he dialed Morton's, where he was expected for dinner, and said to his friend Todd Thurman, the maître d', who knew exactly where to seat everyone on any Monday night, the night to be seen there, "Todd, it's Gus Bailey. Scott Berg is expecting me for dinner. Will you tell Scott I'm running a little late and to start without me."

He turned back to the television set and listened to Shirley Baker again, as he began to pull himself together for dinner. As he looked at himself in the mirror to tie his tie, he knew that the moment had come when he had to declare himself, who he was and what he believed. To go on would be duplicitous. The end of the trial was at hand.

As the Simpson sisters and Benny started to move toward the courtroom door, which Deputy Jex was holding open, Gus quickly said to the three of them, "I have to talk to you for a minute before we go back into court. Okay?"

"Sure, Gus," said Benny.

They moved away from the people who were entering the courtroom until they came to a quiet place in the corridor.

"You know I'm deeply fond of you," said Gus. "You must have read what I've written about you."

"That goes both ways," said Shirley.

"For me, too, Gus," said Carmelita.

"I know, but I can't be false with you," said Gus. He looked at Benny. He knew that Benny knew what he was about to say. He didn't want to look at Shirley, but he forced himself to. "I realized that yesterday at your press conference. You know, we've always avoided the main topic of conversation between us. We've talked around the subject for almost a year, but we can't anymore. It's too close to the end. I think your brother killed Nicole and Ron. It pains me to say that, but it's what I think."

"He didn't, Gus," said Shirley.

"He didn't," said Carmelita.

"There's no way, Gus," said Benny.

"We can't play he-did, he-didn't," said Gus. "We've come to an impasse. There's no solution here. We've probably all known this was going to happen sometime."

"That's right," said Shirley.

"That doesn't mean that I'm going to end my affection for you," said Gus. "I would like to have stayed friends after the trial, but that can't be. We probably all knew that. You're doing what's right for your lives. I'm doing what's right for mine."

Everyone had gone in for the afternoon session. They were the last to enter. Deputy Jex was closing the doors. They walked toward the door of the courtroom in silence, all weighed down by the conversation they had just had. Jex scowled at Gus for being late. "It's a good thing for you Judge Ito hasn't entered yet, or you'd be out for the afternoon," he said, with the usual snarl in his voice. Gus, who despised him, walked past without replying. Then Jex smiled at the Simpson sisters and led them to their seats. "He's like an usher in the theater when he takes the Simpson ladies to their seats," said Gus to Shoreen.

The door to the holding room opened, and O.J. Simpson entered. He never failed, in all the months in that courtroom, to bring forth a hush as he walked in. His sisters strained forward with huge smiles on their faces to greet him, as they did every time he entered the courtroom, four times a day, every day. As he acknowledged his sisters with a nod of his head, his eyes cased the audience to see who was there.

"I never really knew O.J.," said Warren Beatty. "I'd see him around, at Hugh Hefner's, or the Daisy, or a closed-circuit fight, something like that, but I never really knew him. Once I had a long telephone conversation with him, though. It was about a maid who had worked for him whom I was thinking of hiring, at my old house on Mulholland that got ruined in the earthquake, and I called to get a rundown about her, and we had a nice talk, and we were going to get together and all that, but we never did."

Gus and Warren Beatty were having lunch in the dining room of another house on Mulholland that

Warren and Annette Bening, his wife, were renting while their own house was being rebuilt. Gus had known Warren at Fox before his fame, when he played a supporting role in an episode or two of the television series *Dobie Gillis,* which had starred Dwayne Hickman.

"After the murders, Bob Evans had a couple of parties I went to for Bob Shapiro, who was the hero of the hour at the time. I met F. Lee Bailey there one time," said Warren.

"I was in the courtroom during the Cotton Club murder trial when Bob Evans took the Fifth, with Shapiro standing beside him," said Gus. "As far as I'm concerned, you only take the Fifth when you've got stuff to hide."

Warren laughed. "You're very unforgiving, Gus."

"Only in matters of murder," replied Gus.

"That's kind of what I wanted to talk to you about. What would be a terrific book for you to write that could make a terrific picture—"

"Let me interrupt for a minute," said Gus. "There's the matter of an O.J. book, a novel, that has to be attended to before anything else."

"After that, I meant," said Warren. "This will hold. You should write the story of the Manson murders, Gus."

"My friend Vince Bugliosi already wrote that book, and wrote it wonderfully well," said Gus.

"But you know the other side of the story that Vince didn't know," said Warren. "He knew the bad guys. You knew the movie people, you and Peach.

You knew the life they lived. You were part of it. It was the crowd from the Daisy that went in and out of that house on Cielo Drive where the killings took place."

"Including you, and Jane Fonda, and quite a few others as I remember. I knew Sharon Tate and Roman Polanski. I knew Jay Sebring. I knew Abigail Folger, but I didn't know her boyfriend. The last time I saw Sharon before the murders was one night at dinner at Tony Curtis's when he was married to that German movie star, whose name I can't remember."

"Christine Kaufmann," said Warren.

"Right. They lived in a beautiful house, like a French château, right off Sunset, next to Jayne Mansfield's pink house, do you remember? There was a huge rose garden in the back, with gravel paths and boxwood hedges. After dinner I went walking in the garden, and Sharon was there. She looked so beautiful. Her pregnancy was beginning to show. I knew her from way back, before she married Roman Polanski, when she was Jay Sebring's girlfriend, and she'd sit in the room while Jay was cutting my hair. We just stood there in the garden and talked about old times and smoked a joint. Jay was so in love with Sharon. Dramatically, it's so extraordinary that he should have been murdered with her."

"That's what I mean, what you just said. Who else knows stuff like that?" said Warren. "Do you remember when Steve McQueen packed a gun at Jay Sebring's funeral?"

"Sure. Everyone was so afraid there were going to

be more movie-star murders," said Gus. "Peach and I sent our kids to her mother's ranch. Do you remember some of the people everyone was suspecting?"

"You have to write it, Gus," said Warren. "Roman's never really talked about it, but I know he'd talk to you. I could set that up. He took a lot of flak at the time, as if the kind of movies he directed set the scene for the murders that followed."

"It's an interesting idea, and I could write it, but I think I have to get away from murder for a while, Warren," said Gus. "It's beginning to deplete me. I get too emotionally involved. I can't keep that distance you're supposed to keep. I understand Fred Goldman's pain and rage totally. I admire him for exposing it. I have developed an unreasonable hatred for the kind of lawyers who would do anything, *anything,* to get a guilty man acquitted. This whole business of killers beating the rap is so repugnant to me that I stopped seeing my brother Malachy after he dedicated his last book to Leslie Abramson, whom I once called the patron saint of killers in an article I wrote. I shouldn't get into that. That's off the record, as people in my business say."

"Your estrangement from your brother is pretty well known on both coasts, Gus," said Warren.

"It is?"

Message left by Gus Bailey on Grafton's answering machine:

Hi, Grafton. It was great visiting you on the set yesterday. I'm glad you had to shoot Satur-

366

day, or I would have missed it. I wish my *Season in Purgatory* miniseries were shooting on Saturdays. I haven't been to the set once. It was really a wonderful experience for me, standing there and watching you direct a picture. I felt really proud of you. I was remembering the first time I took you to a set when you were a little boy. I was at Fox at the time, producing *Adventures in Paradise* with Gardner McKay. I almost fainted when I turned around and saw Steven Spielberg watching you direct yesterday. Obviously, he was there to see Kate Capshaw, but it was so unexpected to be face-to-face with him. I always remember how nice Steven was to Becky when she made *Poltergeist* for him. She always talked about him. I had a great chat with him, all about O.J. Simpson, of course. He reads all my O.J. articles in *Vanity Fair.* Do you know what he told me? He said he hates to walk onto other directors' sets, because it usually freaks out the director, but he said you just said, "Hi, Steven," and went back to work. I enjoy hearing my kid get compliments.

Listen, am I right in guessing that the plot of this movie you're making has to do with the night that your mother and I broke up? Charlie Wessler kind of hinted that to me the other night at Orso. I remember that party so well that you were shooting yesterday for your movie. Malachy and Edwina gave it when they lived in that huge falling-down house on Franklin Avenue. I think it was for Otto Preminger, the director. And Janis Joplin came, just like in your movie. They'd just written a picture for Preminger, who wore a Nehru jacket with a gold chain and a cross around his neck. You were too young by far to have been at that party, but you brought Mom, because we had split. It was a very sad night. I was very stoned, that much I remember. I'm rattling away, and your tape is probably about to run out.

One other thing. About Arizona. I still haven't recovered from what we went through those five days. I probably couldn't tell you this face-to-face, and you'd probably turn me off if I did, so it's nice we have tape machines to talk into. You were great over there, Grafton. You were commanding, in charge, calm during crises, and hilariously funny at the most inopportune times. Everything a brother can do for a brother you did. Your mother was proud of you, too. I had to laugh when you hugged me good-bye in Tucson and said, "See ya at the next family catastrophe."

Oh, by the way, I think Kate Capshaw will be wonderful as Peach.

24

In his "Letter from Los Angeles," Gus wrote:

Every day there are new and provocative stories about the principals in the case, which seem to appear with almost choreographed timing. Recently, in a story on Johnnie Cochran in the Los Angeles Times Magazine, *it was revealed, very deep in the article, that Cochran's first wife, Barbara, twice accused him of assaulting her, in 1967 and 1977. The 1967 declaration for a restraining order read, "My husband violently pushed me against the wall, held me there, and grabbed me by the chin. He has slapped me in the past, torn a dress off me, and threatened on numerous occasions to beat me up." With the prosecution opening its case on the issue of domestic violence, the timing could not have been worse. The first wife refused to deny the charges in the magazine, as Cochran had said she would, but she said that she was happy for Johnnie's success. Subsequently she announced that she is writing a tell-all book about their*

369

*stormy marriage. Then it appeared elsewhere, in
Cindy Adams's* New York Post *column and on
one of Geraldo Rivera's television shows, that
Cochran had a hitherto-unreported twenty-one-
year-old son from an affair he had with a Caucasian woman during the time he was married to
his first wife.*

*In one of the great tacky episodes of all time,
Cochran's first wife and his white mistress, who
goes by the name of Patricia Cochran, joined
forces on* Geraldo *to let Johnnie Cochran have it
on the day after he tried to convince the jury that
important evidence at the crime scene had been
moved or contaminated by the Los Angeles
Police Department. Patricia Cochran told Geraldo, "Before they selected the jury, I asked him,
'Johnnie, what are you going to do?' And he
said, 'Sweetheart . . . just give me one black person on that jury—that's all I ask, one,' and he
could get a hung jury."*

The portly and witty Prince Rupert Loewenstein, the
business manager for the Rolling Stones, leaned
across the luncheon table on the terrace of his house
in the Hollywood Hills and said, "Oh, Gus, do,
please, tell H.R.H. that *hilarious* story you told the
other night at Connie Wald's about Nicole Brown
Simpson's sister, the one who necked with her
boyfriend in the courtroom, in full view of the jury."

H.R.H. meant Her Royal Highness. To Rupert's
right was Princess Margaret, the sister of the Queen

of England, who was visiting Los Angeles to raise funds for the British Museum. To her right was Gore Vidal, the author. Then came Lady Anne Glenconner, a lady-in-waiting to Princess Margaret. Gus was seated next to her. On his other side was Lady Anne Lambton, who had recently come to Hollywood to seek a career in films. Then came Michael York, the film star, and, finally, Wendy Stark.

For thirty-two years, since a weekend party he and Peach had attended at Lord Plunkett's country house in Kent, England, Gus had been meeting Princess Margaret once a year or so at various lunches and dinners in New York, Los Angeles, and London. The chilliness he had felt from her on that initial weekend at Lord Plunkett's, when she was married to Lord Snowdon, had never dechilled in the subsequent years. Each meeting was a new beginning, with no references to past encounters. Each conversation was uphill and unrewarding. In the last several years, he had learned to say, on introduction, "Very nice to see you, Ma'am," and then scoot off to the other side of the room to chat with Lady Anne Glenconner, about whom Gus had once written in *Vanity Fair*, when she and her husband gave a costume ball on the island of Mustique.

The object of the lunch on the flower-filled terrace was to amuse the princess. Prince Rupert told a witty story. Gore Vidal told a wittier one. But the conversation kept coming back to O.J. Simpson, about whom the princess seemed to have no interest whatsoever, although everyone else at the table did.

Lady Anne Lambton said she and the British actor Rupert Everett watched the trial all day, every day on television and wouldn't miss Geraldo Rivera's nightly show on the trial for anything in the world. Michael York said that the guru at his wife's ashram in India was up to date on the trial in Los Angeles. Gus asked Rupert if the story was true that A. C. Cowlings had told Keith Richards backstage at the Rose Bowl exactly what had happened on the night of the murders.

"Good heavens, I haven't heard that, but I'll certainly check it out. Tell the story, Gus," prompted Rupert.

"You've sort of ruined it, Rupert," said Gus. "You've given away the punch line."

"Oh, no, no, tell it, Gus," insisted Rupert. "It's *such* a funny story." He turned to the princess. "You're going to love this story about the trial, Ma'am, the O.J. Simpson trial. As you can see, people over here talk of nothing else."

The princess's eyes rested on Gus as she waited to be amused. Reluctantly, Gus told the story. The princess didn't find it amusing, as Gus had known she wouldn't, and gave him no reaction. There was the usual moment of silence that follows a flop joke.

"What were you *doing* there?" asked the princess, in her snappish tone of voice, as if he had confessed to being in an improper place.

"Doing there, Ma'am?" asked Gus.

"At that trial," said the princess.

"That's how I make my living, Ma'am," said Gus.

"It's *such* a bore," she said, turning her head away from Gus, dismissing his topic, waiting for a new topic more to her liking to be introduced.

"It's not boring to me, Ma'am," said Gus quietly.

There was a brief silence. Other subjects were introduced, such as Princess Diana. "The only one who's behaved properly in the whole mess is Camilla Parker-Bowles," said one of the English ladies. "She's never said one single word to the press."

"Unlike a few others I could mention."

When Gus got up to leave, he ran into his friend Wendy Stark in the hallway. "You're not leaving, are you?" asked Wendy.

"I did my tap dance," said Gus.

"We're not supposed to leave until after H.R.H.," said Wendy. "Protocol, you know."

"Good luck. Do you think she was enough of a pain in the ass? '*Such* a bore,'" said Gus, imitating her vocal tone and facial gesture perfectly. He and Wendy laughed. "She could stand a few charm lessons from Princess Diana, if you ask me. I'm off. I have an interview."

"Where are you going?" asked Wendy.

"My friend Tom Murray, the sports announcer on Channel Eleven, has arranged for me to meet Anthony Davis," said Gus.

"Who's Anthony Davis?" asked Wendy.

"Anthony was a big football star at USC right after O.J.," replied Gus. "He even looks like O.J. He said he can't walk in Brentwood because people think he *is* O.J. The only thing is, he doesn't like

O.J. very much. He thinks he turned his back on his own people, and he wants to talk to me about him."

Gus was having dinner at Drai's with Michelle Caruso of the *New York Daily News* and Harvey Levin.

"I don't care what F. Lee Bailey said on David Frost's show about O.J. wanting to take the stand, Cochran will *never* let him take the stand," said Michelle.

"All of America would stop work to watch him," said Gus. "It would be a great moment in the history of television, watching him lie on the stand."

"They'll drop it in the press that he *wants* to take the stand, like F. Lee did on David Frost the other night, as if that shows the public that O.J. has nothing to hide. But it's all bullshit. Johnnie's too smart to ever put him on," said Harvey.

"The thing about it that's probably true is that O.J. does want to take the stand," said Gus. "It's in his nature. He's a showman. He's used to the cheers of the crowd. He understands the art of dazzling, whether it's making an eighty-yard run, or talking a police officer out of giving him a ticket, or hitting on the prettiest girl at the party. It's a performance he could play directly to the twelve people who count the most in his life at the moment."

"Schiller told me O.J. doesn't know how to give a simple answer," said Michelle. "You ask him a question and he'll talk for fifteen minutes without stopping."

"Marcia could make mincemeat out of him," said Gus.

"The defense brought down these two tough female prosecutors from San Francisco, who did practice cross-examinations at the county jail with O.J. over the past weekend," said Gus.

He was sitting at the dinner table of the television mogul Norman Lear and his wife, Lyn, high up in Mandeville Canyon, after watching a breathtaking sunset from their terrace. As always, when in posh circumstances, Gus noticed the beautiful details in the house, which had recently been completely rebuilt, after having suffered extensive damages in the earthquake. There were fourteen for dinner. Waiters in black jeans, white shirts, and black ties expertly passed the caviar pie, the crown roast, and the lemon soufflé. Other than paying compliments to the hostess on the delicious meal, they all talked of nothing but O.J. Simpson, and they were all of one mind. The bad guys were winning.

Gus was in a loquacious mood and held the floor for much of the meal. He told them about Truman Simpson's keeper who had tried to sell him a drug addict story. He told them that O.J.'s father had been a drag queen who had died of AIDS. He talked about the loyalty of O.J.'s sisters.

Howard Weitzman, who had been Simpson's first lawyer, and his wife, Margaret, were also at the dinner. Gus and Howard had seen each other a few days earlier on the ninth floor of the Criminal Courts Building, where Weitzman had been summoned by the defense team, who wanted to put him on the stand as a defense witness.

"Johnnie wanted me to testify that Vannatter wouldn't allow O.J. to have an attorney present at his taped interview, which was bullshit," said Howard. "After I left Gus in the corridor, I went into the empty courtroom, and there were Johnnie, and Shapiro, and the bunch, and I said to Johnnie, 'You guys are out of your minds if you put me on the stand with what I know.' Johnnie knew that I meant what I was implying."

"They would have been nuts to put Howard on," said Margaret Weitzman. "I still remember that first day after the murders, when Howard and I went over there to Rockingham to pay our condolence call, and there was blood right on the driveway."

"Oh, yes," said Howard, snapping his fingers, as if he had just remembered something he had forgotten in his story. "Johnnie also said they were pissed at some of the things that Margaret was saying around town about O.J. at all the parties."

Everyone at the dining table laughed.

Margaret, elaborately ignoring the laughter, asked, "What was that you were saying, Gus, about the two lady lawyers from San Francisco?"

"From what my mole on the defense tells me," said Gus, "the legal ladies got really rough with O.J., which is what they were being paid to do, to give him an example of what Marcia Clark would be like when she was cross-examining him. Nobody's supposed to know this took place, but I manage to work it into the conversation whenever I go out to dinner. From what I hear, O.J. didn't do so hot. He got angry a few times, which would be a disaster on the stand. That's what Marcia would try to make happen if she ever got him on the witness stand. She'd find a way to enrage him. He already hates her."

"It'll never happen, Gus," said Weitzman.

"I know it won't, but I wish he would take the stand, for the sake of my book. In the novel, I'm going to have the entire country stop work so they can watch O.J. Simpson testify, and I'm going to write it so that he lies and lies in response to every question that Marcia Clark asks him. But I'm going to have him look fabulous—wearing one of his great suits—while he's telling the lies. He's going to be confident and poised. I'm going to have him be a better liar than the Menendez brothers, and those guys could lie. I'm going to have him lie even when he's caught out in a lie. I'm going to have him lift lying to a new level."

"Has anybody optioned this book yet?" asked Norman Lear.

"Up for grabs, gentlemen," joked Gus. "Call Owen Laster at the William Morris Agency."

Gus was having lunch in the cafeteria with Larry Schiller, who had become Gus's authority on matters pertaining to Simpson.

"Before I came out here to the trial, I was talking to a lawyer in Connecticut I'd heard about who had been in Las Vegas on the weekend of the murders, staying at the Mirage Hotel," said Gus. "He freaked out when I called him. 'I don't want to get involved, Gus. Don't mention my name,' he said. There're so many guys who know stuff who don't want to get involved. You see him on Court TV from time to time, doing legal-pundit stuff on the trial. What he finally told me was that he got to talking to this beautiful young woman by the pool, where they just happened to be side by side on lounge chairs. She was in a bikini, dark glasses, covered in suntan oil. It was Paula Barbieri, but the name meant nothing to him at the time. In conversation, she told him about this guy in Los Angeles that she'd just broken up with the day before. He didn't know the guy she was talking about was O. J. Simpson. *But,* while he was there listening to the story of her break-up, she was paged over the public address system—there's a call for you, Miss Barbieri—and she went to take the call. When she came back, she said—words to this effect— 'Remember that guy I was telling you about, the one I just broke up with? His wife was just murdered.'"

Schiller nodded. "Paula was all through with O. J., after he wouldn't take her to Sydney's dance concert," he said. "I think Paula wanted Nicole to see her walk in there with O. J. So she broke up with him and went to Vegas."

"Did it ever occur to you that if Paula hadn't broken up with O.J. and gone to Vegas, Nicole and Ron might not have been murdered?" asked Gus.

"Many times," said Schiller.

"Paula rushed back to him from Las Vegas after the murders," said Gus. "Denice Halicki told me she stayed with O.J. in Kardashian's house right up to the freeway chase."

"True," said Schiller. "And she was always there when the lawyers talked to O. J., both at the house and in jail, reading her Bible and listening. She knows a lot."

"Have you heard the story that she doesn't wear underwear when she visits O.J. in jail?" asked Gus.

"Where do you hear all this stuff, Gus?" asked Schiller, laughing.

"It's jailhouse gossip from a guy I know who knows a guard in the sheriff's department," said Gus. "Like when O.J. confessed to the murders to Rosey Grier and the guard overheard. You're right. I could write a helluva sex scene in O.J.'s private visitors' room, without any touching. They'd be looking through the glass at each other talking over telephones. There's no guard, only a lawyer, Nicole Pulvers. It'll be a dirty-talk scene, with a climax, of course. The lawyer will read her law books all the way through it, oblivious to everything but the law, even screams of passion."

"I think this trial is getting to you, Gus," said Larry. "I think you're flipping out."

"Joe McGinniss thinks so, too. He told me that

the other night. He said I was too manic on television on Geraldo's show. I can't wait for this trial to end. I hope I'm not flipping out. Hey, look at the time. I have to get back up. Jex always tries to keep me out if I'm even ten seconds late."

"You go ahead, Gus," said Schiller. "I want to speak to Kardashian over there."

There were not enough elevators in the Criminal Courts Building for the number of people using them. Often, especially at peak times, such as after lunch, it was necessary to wait in line to get into an elevator. So it was a great bit of good luck for Gus when he entered an elevator that appeared empty just as the door closed. The only other passenger, who had not been visible from the corridor, was pushing the close button so that he could have the elevator to himself. The doors closed in the faces of the people waiting.

Gus turned. The passenger who wanted to be alone was Jason Simpson, O.J. Simpson's son from his first marriage. The two men looked at each other. Neither spoke. Jason Simpson had spoken to no one during the ten months that the trial had been going on, except for his sister Arnelle and his aunts Shirley and Carmelita. In one of his "Letters," Gus had described him as "surly and unfriendly, possessing none of the handsome looks of his father or sister."

Being alone with the son of such a famous defendant, who was thought to know things about the murders and the cleanup after the murders that no one else knew, was a reporter's dream, but Gus was not the type to reach in his pocket and pull out his notebook and pen and start asking questions. Instead, he looked straight ahead, ignoring Jason. "It always works," he said later to his friend Mart Crowley. "Invariably, they speak first."

In court, Gus had often watched as Simpson and Jason looked at each other. Unlike the loving looks exchanged between Simpson and Arnelle, Gus sensed in the looks of father and son a complicated relationship, sometimes bordering on dislike.

Gus suddenly realized that Jason had spoken to him.

"I'm sorry. What did you say?" asked Gus.

"I said, how was dinner at Norman Lear's the other night?"

Gus was dumbfounded by the question. "How in the world did you know that I had dinner at Norman Lear's?" he asked.

The elevator arrived at the ninth floor. The doors opened. As Jason stepped out of the elevator, he looked back for an instant, and his eyes connected unpleasantly with Gus's.

"I cooked," he said and walked away.

The implications of what Jason said so unnerved Gus that the elevator doors closed on him before he could get out, and the elevator continued going up. He quickly pushed the button for the eleventh floor, where the media room was, and got out when it stopped. Reporters at every desk were typing out their stories for the next morning's newspapers.

"David, I know you're on deadline, but I have to interrupt for a minute to tell you what just happened to me," said Gus to David Margolick.

"Unbelievable," said Margolick, after Gus told him the story.

"What are the odds of such a thing happening? The son of the defendant in this famous murder trial cooking for the catering service at a party where everyone's knocking his father and his father's lawyers. No one knocking him more than me, by the way. And what about the elevator? What are the odds that I should walk into an empty elevator for the first time in ten months and share it with Jason Simpson, who's never spoken to me before? If I hadn't stepped on that elevator, I would never have known. What do you think I should do?"

"Call the Lears. Tell them," said Margolick. "They probably didn't know Jason was the cook for the catering service. Use this phone."

"This is Gus Bailey," said Gus, when the Lears' phone was answered. "May I speak to Mrs. Lear?"

"The Lears left this morning for their house on Martha's Vineyard, Mr. Bailey," said the secretary who answered the phone. "I can't give out that number, but I'll be happy to pass on to them that you called when they check in."

"Thanks," said Gus. "I can be reached at the Chateau Marmont." When he hung up, he said, "They've gone to the Vineyard. I'll call Margaret

Weitzman and tell her. Jason must have heard everything we said last night. All those waiters passing the crown roast certainly heard, and they probably told him what we were saying. I wish I hadn't told the story about O.J.'s father being a drag queen. No wonder the guy looked at me that way."

Six members of the Fruit of Islam, the security arm of the Nation of Islam, patrolled the ninth-floor corridor of the Criminal Courts Building carrying walkie-talkies. Six feet tall, dark-suited, bow ties in place, they cast an ominous and menacing feeling in the already troubled atmosphere outside the courtroom. They had been brought in by Johnnie Cochran to be his personal bodyguards. Their presence was resented by almost everyone, including the sheriff's deputies who monitored the floor and courtroom. Male members of the media complained to Judge Ito that the Nation of Islam guards would not let them use the men's room when Cochran was inside. The judge put a stop to that. Blacks and whites who had been together for so long in the courtroom and had long since worked out an everyday truce began to look at each other in an uneasy fashion.

"In the novel, I think I'll have Cochran's bodyguards cause a riot," said Gus to Larry Schiller. "It'll go something like this: Chris Darden tries to walk into the men's room. But the Nation of Islam bodyguards won't let him in because Johnnie Cochran's inside talking to his favorite reporter from the *Los*

Angeles Times, who's going to write his book for him when the trial's over. Chris says to the guard, who's the same height he is, 'Get out of my way. I'm going into that bathroom.' He pushes past the guard and heads straight to the first urinal. The guard fires his gun, barely missing Chris at the urinal. From there, I'm going to build the novel into a *Day of the Locust* ending, with all of West L.A. on fire. Beverly Hills, Holmby Hills, Bel Air, Westwood, Brentwood, Pacific Palisades. All of it on fire."

"I think you're flipping out, Gus," said Schiller.

"You already told me that," said Gus.

No one found the presence of the Nation of Islam guards as repellent as Cochran's fellow defense attorney Robert Shapiro, who already disliked him for having assumed the leadership of the defense team that Shapiro had built up so carefully. After Gus left David Margolick in the media room, he returned to the ninth floor twenty minutes before the afternoon session to use the pay phone to call Wayne Lawson, his editor at *Vanity Fair,* to see if he could insert a few paragraphs in his next "Letter" about the encounter with Jason Simpson that he had just had in the elevator. It was too late, said Wayne. The issue was closed, gone to the printer.

"Damn," said Gus.

"Save it for your novel," said Wayne.

At the far end of the corridor, all alone, stood Robert Shapiro, looking downcast and unhappy.

Such solitude was uncharacteristic of him; he was usually schmoozing and joking with the reporters. Gus had gone through a variety of feelings about Shapiro since they first met at the Marvin Davises' ball a year before. He hadn't admired Shapiro for introducing the race card before the trial began and then distancing himself from it when the criticism began. But with time, and after meeting his wife, Linell, Gus had started to like him.

Gus watched Shapiro from the phone booth and realized he was in distress. His early popularity with the public had evaporated. Recently he had been booed at several sporting events, which had devastated him. Even worse, members of the congregation at the Stephen S. Wise Temple hissed at him when he held the Torah during Rosh Hashanah services. When Gus hung up, he walked down the long corridor.

"Is something the matter, Bob?" he asked.

"How *could* he bring in those fucking anti-Semitic Nation of Islam guards?" Shapiro asked. "How *could* he?"

He was enraged at Johnnie Cochran. For him, it was the ultimate affront.

"Sneaking them in here on us like this," said Shapiro. "I wonder how Scheck feels. I wonder how Neufeld feels. He says he's in danger? Bull fucking shit! I have bodyguards, too. If you're in danger of being shot, your bodyguards don't strut around like that. They make themselves invisible."

"Everybody's angry," said Gus. "They wouldn't let anyone in the men's room when he was in there."

Shapiro leaned toward Gus. "I hate Cochran. I hate him, I hate him, I hate him," he said over and over. He twisted his body as if he were in pain. "This is all off the record. Right, Gus?"

"Sure, but it's not exactly the surprise of the year," said Gus.

"It's very nice of you to call me back, Mr. Bailey. I didn't know when I called your magazine in New York if they would ever get the message through to you that I had called, and then I didn't know if you'd ever answer it, you probably get so many calls," said Wanda Perlini, when Gus returned her call in Seattle. "I was afraid you might think I was some sort of crackpot."

"No, no, go on," said Gus. "The operator at the magazine indicated it was important."

"Is it all right if I call you Gus? Everyone calls you Gus on TV. Mr. Bailey sounds so formal."

"Yes, by all means call me Gus."

"I watch every minute of the trial, and I'd like you to know I agree with you one hundred percent about Mr. O.J. Simpson. Guilty, guilty, guilty is what we say in my family. And I just can't stand that Barry Scheck. But I'd like you to know that my heart breaks for the Goldman family. My daughter and I love Kim. But that's not why I'm calling, Mr. Bailey, I mean Gus. I know you're busy, and I won't take up much of your time. I'm calling because my daughter works for Lefty Flynn here in Seattle."

"Oh?"

"She's a sous-chef at the Boromeo Bistro, where Lefty's the head chef. Are you with me?"

"Go on, Wanda."

"Recently, Lefty's fiancée, Alison Goodhue, who was a friend of my daughter's, broke up with Lefty. Moved away. She told my daughter she'd just learned that Lefty had once killed a girl and done time, which he had never bothered to tell her about. *No one* here in town knew he'd ever killed a girl. It was a terrible shock to everyone at the restaurant. A couple of the waitresses quit when they found out. They said they didn't feel safe working for a man who had committed a murder, even if he had done time. After Alison left town, Lefty told my daughter that the writer Gus Bailey was responsible for her leaving him. He said that Gus Bailey was harassing him."

"Lefty Flynn said I was harassing him?" repeated Gus.

"That was the first time that anyone here realized that it was your daughter Lefty had murdered. I had read about your story in some interview, and I'd seen your biography on the Arts and Entertainment channel, but I never put the two together until now, and I just thought that you ought to know about this."

"Thank you very much, Wanda," said Gus. "I'm deeply appreciative."

"Just in case you're in danger or anything," said Wanda.

"Oh, I think Lefty Flynn's done all the damage in our family that he's ever going to do."

"One other thing, Gus."

"Yes?"

"He's just changed his name."

"Oh?"

"He's no longer John Flynn. He's taken his mother's first name for his last name."

"Siobhan," said Gus quietly.

"Yes, Siobhan. How in the world did you ever know that?"

"I remember his mother from the trial," said Gus.

"My daughter received a fax from him today about his name change. He sent it to all the employees at the Boromeo. Would you like me to read it to you?"

"Yes."

"It says, 'Greetings to all employees. As I believe myself to be a victim of harassment in the media, I have decided to legally change my name. From this time forward I will now be known as John Siobhan. I have adopted my mother's name, Siobhan, as my surname. The name of Lefty Flynn is never to be used again.'"

"I see."

"It has his home address and phone and the number and address of the restaurant. Would you like me to fax it to you?"

"Please."

25

In his "Letter from Los Angeles," Gus wrote:

A reporter I know who's a friend of a deputy who's a friend of another deputy who's connected to the jury of the Simpson trial called me at the Chateau Marmont early on the morning of October second, the first day of jury deliberation on the fate of O. J. Simpson, to tell me that some of the jurors had already packed their bags in the Inter-Continental Hotel, where they have been sequestered for nearly a year, before leaving for court. At that time, that bit of information seemed too far-fetched for me to pay serious attention to. I had told both Dan Rather and Larry King on television that I believed there would be a hung jury. But it turned out to be true. Some of the jurors had packed their bags and belongings. Apparently, they had also already made up their minds. The deputy who told the deputy who told my friend said three of the jurors had made plans to fly to Las Vegas for the weekend. The night before, a person I know had vis-

ited Simpson in the county jail. He reported him to be upbeat, making plans for his future, looking forward to being with his kids. He said he was a man without a negative thought on his mind.

Because of the pressures of time, Gus was being photographed by the pool of the Chateau Marmont as he was being interviewed by Austine Brophy of *TV Guide.* Shooting on the miniseries of his last novel, *A Season in Purgatory,* had just been completed, and *TV Guide* was doing an article on Gus and his upcoming miniseries. Gus and Austine Brophy had known each other for years.

"Where are you cutting me off, Herb?" Gus asked the photographer.

"Waist," replied Herb.

"Make it tighter. Make it a chest shot. My waist is widening. I've been going to too damn many parties. Where were we, Austine?"

"You just said you didn't go to the set once," said Austine, checking her notes. "Why, for heaven's sake? It was shooting right here on the Sony lot in Culver City."

"I still call it MGM," said Gus. "Sounds better to my ear. The reason I didn't go, Austine, is that I've been so involved in the trial I never had the time to watch any of the shooting, which is quite unlike me. I'm usually a pain in the ass when they make changes in my books."

"I remember all those fights you had on *People*

Like Us," said Austine. "Remember, I interviewed you then, too."

"I remember well. I think I said something in your article that pissed off the producer," said Gus. "So I don't have much to say about the miniseries except that my agent says the network is pleased, but they always say that. Other than Brian Keith, I'm not even sure I know who's cast in it."

"It's not Brian Keith. It's Brian Dennehy," said Austine.

"Don't ask me anything about Whitewater, either, because I don't know," said Gus. "I haven't read a word about it. The only thing I can talk about anymore is O. J. Simpson."

"At least tell me the plot of *Purgatory,*" said Austine.

"You mean you haven't read it?" asked Gus.

"Yes, I've read it, but I need to quote you on something," said Austine.

"It's about a rich kid in Connecticut who killed the girl next door and got away with it," said Gus. "It's about how rich and powerful people can circumvent the law, even in matters of murder."

"Isn't this book and miniseries of yours actually based on a real unsolved murder?" asked Austine.

"The girl was called Martha Moxley. She was fifteen years old. It happened twenty years ago. In real life, the two main suspects are Ethel Kennedy's nephews, the Skakel brothers. If you use that in your article, don't quote me as saying it. It's a known fact.

It's been in the papers. You could have heard it from anyone."

"Are you still going to meetings, Gus?" asked Austine, unexpectedly. "Off the record, of course." She leaned forward in her lounge chair and switched off her tape recorder.

For a second Gus didn't answer. "The same way I go to Mass," he replied. "Not enough."

"You should, you know. This trial must be a terrible strain day after day, especially after Becky, and then Zander getting lost, and your wife so sick."

"I did a double whammy after Zander: Mass *and* A.A. on the same Sunday morning," said Gus. "By the way, it's ex-wife."

"People still say Gus and Peach, or Peach and Gus, you know," said Austine. "How are things with you and your brother?"

"I thought we were talking about *A Season in Purgatory*."

"The tape recorder's still off. I'm curious," said Austine. "People are talking about it. I know you both. Why not ask? Wouldn't you have asked if you were me?"

"I would have asked sooner," said Gus.

"Well?"

"Things ain't so hot," said Gus.

"You're carrying around a lot of baggage, Gus," said Austine.

"You don't know the half of it, Austine," replied Gus. "Lefty Flynn's back in the picture. One of the

greatest fears of my life has been that I would some-
day run into him."

"Have you?"

"No, but I understand that he is claiming in Seattle, where he now lives, that I am harassing him,"
said Gus.

"Are you?"

"I wrote something about him that apparently
caused his fiancée to leave him."

"Good. Maybe you saved her life," said Austine.

"That's what Grafton says."

"Gus, it's Judy Hilsinger. Do you know anything
about a two-hour documentary the E! channel is
making on your daughter's murder?"

"No. You have to be mistaken," said Gus. "I
would have heard if there was such a thing in the
works and put a stop to it."

"I'm not. I just had a call from the producer. She
knew I publicized your books. She said they'd like
to interview you for the documentary. Are you
interested?"

"Absolutely not."

"I said already that I didn't think you would be.
What will I tell her?"

"Tell her I am absolutely not interested. Tell her I
am speaking for my two sons also, as well as their
mother. Tell her the family will not cooperate," said
Gus.

"She wants to buy the rights to the article you wrote about Becky's trial," said Hilsinger.

"Not for sale. And she may not quote from it," said Gus.

"I'm just the middleman here, Gus," said Hilsinger.

"I understand that, Judy. I'm sorry if I'm sounding testy. It enrages me for them to be doing a documentary on Becky's death fifteen years after it happened. Why? You know as well as I do why they want to do it now. It's the O.J. connection. Men who beat women. O.J. Simpson and Lefty Flynn. Men who stalk women. O.J. Simpson and Lefty Flynn. Men who kill women. O.J. Simpson and Lefty Flynn. The parallels are strong."

"Then why don't you cooperate?" asked Judy.

"Because they're doing it for the wrong reason," said Gus. "They sneaked into this project. They didn't come and ask my family if they could do it. They're doing it because of the name value. I'm on TV every day at the O.J. Simpson trial. You can't pick up a newspaper without reading about Grafton. Malachy and Edwina have new books out. Known names all. And Zander, the one member of the family who wants nothing to do with the spotlight, has just been right in the brightest glare of it. I can see why they want to do it, but my family's not going to play ball."

"Judge Katz is going to be in it," said Hilsinger.

"If I ever had a doubt, that cinched it, Judy," said Gus.

"He told them he wouldn't be in it if you were going to be in it," said Judy. "Naturally, they would have preferred you."

"Well, now they have Katz for marquee value."

Within days people who had been involved in Lefty Flynn's trial began to call Gus to tell him they had been contacted by the E! channel to appear in the documentary about Becky's murder and the trial that followed. Grafton and Zander had received similar calls from people they knew. They all wanted to know whether or not they should appear.

"Tell anyone who asks that the family is not going to cooperate, but we have no objection if any witnesses or friends want to appear," said Gus.

"They're going to make it anyway, whether you cooperate or not," said Charlie Wessler, Grafton's friend. "Flynn's lawyer, Marv Pink, is going to appear in it. It might be good to have someone who could speak for the family. I'd be happy to do that."

"By all means, Charlie," said Gus.

Gus said to Grafton on the telephone, "I can't deal with this documentary they're going to make on Becky. Don't you think there's enough going on in our lives without this? It's so close to the end of the trial, and I don't want to have my attention diverted. I told Owen Laster to tell the people at the E! channel that I don't want to hear any more about it. I couldn't believe they'd go forward with it if we didn't cooperate, but they are."

For his appearances on *Good Morning America,* Gus had to get up at three in the morning. A car and driver picked him up at the Chateau Marmont at three-thirty to drive him to the ABC studio. When he was delivered back to his hotel at five in the morning, after his segment with Charlie Gibson or Joan Lunden, he was never able to get back to sleep before his regular six o'clock wake-up call. He found he slept less and less, but his social life continued unabated each night after court and after appearing on the evening news. More and more he preferred to be only with people who shared his obsession about the Simpson case. He had dinner at Morton's with Bill Whitaker of CBS, who reported on the trial with Dan Rather every night. He enjoyed introducing his media friends to his movie friends, and his movie friends enjoyed talking to his media friends about the trial. "Barry Diller, this is Bill Whitaker of CBS," Gus said. He attended a dinner at Eclipse that Dan Abrams gave for his father, Floyd Abrams, the constitutional lawyer. Cynthia McFadden of ABC, Jeffrey Toobin of *The New Yorker,* David Margolick of the *New York Times,* and Jack Ford of NBC were the other guests. They talked about O. J. Simpson until the restaurant closed. So engrossed was Gus in a conversation that he failed to notice that the film star Sharon Stone, whom he had recently met for the first time at one of Roddy McDowall's parties, was seated at the next table. He addressed a group of Catholic reporters at St. Paul the Apostle Church in Westwood, arranged by Kitty Feld, who was covering the trial for National Public Radio. He had lunch with Nancy Reagan and Marje Everett to discuss the trial. He spoke at a meeting of Justice for Homicide Victims, the group that Peach had started in Los Angeles, for which she had received a medal from President Bush. He visited Elizabeth Taylor to discuss the trial. He spoke about the trial for Cheryl Reventlow's charity, Haven House, a home for battered women, in the garden of an estate in Brentwood. He read them a letter that Nicole Brown Simpson had sent to O. J. Simpson detailing the beatings and humiliations she had endured during their marriage. He attended a party Joe McGinniss gave for the media at the house he had rented in Beverly Hills. He had dinner at Drai's with Shirley Perlman, who was covering the trial for *Newsday*. He had dinner at Morton's with Art Harris of CNN to talk about Mark Fuhrman. He went to Linda Deutsch's birthday party at a restaurant in the San Fernando Valley and sat in a corner with Shoreen Maghame of *City News* and Mary Jane Stevenson of Court TV, talking about Marcia Clark. He had dinner with former Los Angeles district attorney Ira Reiner, who commentated on the trial each night with Tom Brokaw on NBC, and his wife, Judge Diane Wayne. He appeared on Tom Snyder's show. He appeared on the *George and Alana* show. He appeared on *Larry King*

Live. He appeared on Geraldo Rivera's show. He appeared on Charles Grodin's show. He did his Friday segment with Dan Rather. He did his Sunday segment with Harvey Levin. He talked of only one thing. The subject never changed. As the days of the trial dwindled down, and the closing arguments were at hand, his anxiety reached a fever pitch.

He wrote in his journal, "Why does this matter so much to me?"

Marcia Clark looked drawn, tired, tense, thin. "She eats nothing, she smokes too much," Suzanne Childs said about her to Gus. Watching her, Gus remembered the night he met her, in the drawing room of Ray Stark's house, when the whole world was smiling on her. She had walked in that night like an actress who had just been given the starring role in the biggest picture of the year. Now she had dark circles under her eyes, as she stood for a moment looking at the jurors before saying good morning. The jury had not liked her. By now she knew it. The race issue had taken over the trial. To pretend that was not the case was foolhardy. Over and over again people had said to her about the African-American jurors, "They can't go back to their neighborhoods if they convict him." She knew by then that most of the twelve in front of her had to answer to other people for the way they voted. She had gone into the trial confident of winning a conviction. She knew now that her maximum hope was a hung jury. The nine black jurors were lost to her. The Hispanic was unknown to her. Of the two white jurors, she could be sure of only one. Only in the eyes of Anise Aschenbach had she seen revulsion at the horror of the murders.

Gus, in the front row, watched. In his thoughts, he urged her on, as if his thoughts could be implanted in Marcia's head. *Play to Anise. Play to Anise,* he said over and over in his mind. *She is your only hope of hanging this jury.*

But it went wrong from the beginning. Marcia began with a negative. She began with an apology to the jury for Mark Fuhrman. It fed right into the racism of the trial. It took precedent over the two murdered people.

Looking at the jurors apologetically, distancing herself from the witness she had presented to them, she said, "Did Mark Fuhrman lie when he testified here in this courtroom saying that he did not use racial epithets in the last ten years? Yes. Is he a racist? Yes. Is he the worst the L.A.P.D. has to offer? Yes. Do we wish that this person was never hired by the L.A.P.D.? Yes. Should the L.A.P.D. have ever hired him? No. In fact, do we wish there were no such person on the planet? Yes. But the fact that Mark Fuhrman is a racist and lied about it on the witness stand does not mean that we haven't proven the defendant guilty beyond a reasonable doubt, and it would be a tragedy if, with such overwhelming evidence, ladies and gentlemen, as we have presented to you, you found the defendant not guilty in spite of all that, because of the racist attitude of one police officer."

Why isn't this better? thought Gus. Why is she falling into the defense trap of turning this murder trial into the trial of Mark Fuhrman? *There are two murdered people, Marcia. Get to them. Start talking about slit throats, Marcia. Why are you speaking in such apologetic tones when you tell the jurors that Simpson is guilty? Why don't you point at Simpson and say, "There is a* killer *in this courtroom."*

"Are you okay, Gus?" whispered Shoreen Maghame.

"Sure. Why?"

"You seem like you're going to jump out of your skin."

"Sorry."

"How do you think Marcia did, Gus?" asked Art Harris of CNN, as he left the courtroom.

"Oh, I thought she was great," Gus heard himself saying, but it was loyalty, not belief, that dictated his words.

That night at Harry Evans and Tina Brown's dinner for Gore Vidal at L'Orangerie, to celebrate the publication of his memoir, *Palimpsest,* Gus arrived late, after appearing on *Larry King Live.* He said to his old friend Tina Brown, whom he hadn't seen for ten months, "If I act peculiar, tell me, Tina. I feel like I'm flipping out. I've become a zealot over this trial. I can't think of anything else. I even *dream* about O.J. One night, I *reenacted* the fucking murders at Nicole's condo on Bundy, with Robert Altman directing. That's how nuts I've gotten. I look over there at that table, and I see Gil Garcetti, the district attorney of the City of Los Angeles, holding court for all the movie stars and famous people you have here, discussing the case, and I want to go over and scream in a loud voice, 'What are you doing here at a glamorous party for Christ-fucking-sake, when you're losing the case? Why aren't you down at the Criminal Courts Building helping Marcia and Chris with their closing arguments, which did not get off to a rousing start today.'"

"Don't, please, you'll ruin the seating if he leaves," said Tina, laughing as they hugged. "You know Gore."

"Only since I was twenty," said Gus. "I think I already told you."

"I was already famous way back then," said Gore. "Gus is only a Johnny-come-lately."

"True, true, an upstart. The story of my life," said Gus. "I haven't read your book yet, Gore. I bought it at Book Soup, and I'll read it right after the verdict, which should be very soon."

"You're in my book," said Gore. "Twice. Once with Anaïs, of course, and another time with Jackie Kennedy."

"That ain't bad company. I'll settle for that," said Gus. "In the meantime, I can't pronounce the title and don't know what it means."

"Harry is going to explain that in his speech," said Gore.

"I'm thinking of writing a memoir myself, when I finish my Simpson novel," said Gus. "I have this disturbing feeling of not being able to visualize myself very far in the future anymore, whatever that means, so I want to get it all down before it's too late."

"If you're going to write a memoir, you have to be ready to tell all," said Gore. "It can't be selective memory, you know."

"Oh, believe me, I'm ready," said Gus.

"We're sitting down," said Tina. "Gore, you're next to Roseanne. I can't remember whom you're next to, Gus. We've changed the *placement* so many times, because of last-minute dropouts and additions. Madonna backed out this afternoon at four."

"Movie stars always back out at the last minute," said Gus.

When Gus found his place, he was seated next to Lady Anne Lambton. "I apologize for the rudeness of H.R.H. at Rupert Loewenstein's lunch," she said. "I couldn't *believe* her when she said O.J. Simpson was such a bore."

"*Such* a bore," said Gus, imitating the princess's snub.

"All I want to talk about is O.J. Simpson. I am riveted, and you have to meet my friend Rupert

Everett, who's as hooked as I am, and he's dying to meet you. Come to lunch Sunday. What did you think of Marcia's closing argument? Did you think she was wonderful?"

"I learned something from Leslie Abramson during her closing argument in the Menendez trial. She knew that the men on the jury hated her, so she made no attempt to win them over. She played her whole closing to the women of the jury, who admired her, and it worked for her. She got a hung jury for a couple of cold-blooded killers. Marcia should have played her entire closing argument to juror number three, Anise Aschenbach, who's the only one on that jury who could save her from defeat. There was no way she was going to win over the others. It's a given that she's lost them. She never had them. She needed only one juror to hang the jury, and that one juror was number three."

When Gus returned to the Chateau Marmont after the party, there was a message for him to call Norman Carby in Hawaii. The telephone operator had written on the message sheet "He said call tonight, no matter how late you get in." Carby, a painter, used to live in West Hollywood. Two weeks before Lefty Flynn killed Becky, he had beaten her up, and she had taken refuge in the bungalow of Norman Carby, who took Polaroid shots of the bruises on her face and the purple marks on her neck. The photographs were used as exhibits in the trial.

"Hi, Norman, it's Gus," Gus said when he called from his room.

"I saw you on TV tonight," said Norman. "You look worn-out."

"I am. I have to go to bed in a minute, so I can't talk long. What's up?"

"Did you know that the E! channel is making a documentary about Becky?"

"Yes."

"They want to fly me over to Los Angeles to be in it," said Norman.

"Yeah, I'm sure. They seem to be going after everybody who was involved. Our family is not cooperating, but it's okay with us if you appear in it. You were an important witness."

"The producer told me you weren't cooperating," said Norman.

"If I weren't at this O.J. trial, they wouldn't be doing this documentary," said Gus. "That's what pisses me off."

"I have to say, she seemed nice, but I said I wouldn't appear," said Norman. "They're trying to find Lefty Flynn, but they can't locate him anywhere. They want to get a shot of him on camera. Nobody knows where he is, and Marv Pink, who is going to appear, won't tell them where Lefty lives."

"I just happen to know exactly where he is," said Gus. "The reason they can't find him is that he's changed his name. He lives in Seattle. He's the head chef at a restaurant called the Boromeo Bistro. Now, listen, Norman, and listen carefully. This is very important. Do you have a fax machine?"

"No."

"Do you know anyone who lives near you who has?"

"Yes."

"I'm going to fax you where he can be reached. A woman in Seattle recently got hold of me to say her daughter worked for him. I don't want this traced to me. I don't want the E! channel to know that I provided you with this. But *you* can send this on to the producer of the show. You can make up some cockamamy story about how you happened to get it. I'd like to see them catch Lefty on camera. To warn off any other girl he happens to be with."

Gus raged as Cochran spoke to the jury about the twins of deception, although he was not completely sure he understood the implications of what Cochran was saying. During the break he talked about it with Schiller, whispering in a corner.

"The twins-of-deception remark was intended to evoke the devil to the jury," said Schiller.

"Explain that to me," said Gus.

"In the jargon of the Nation of Islam, *devil* meant white. Vannatter and Fuhrman are twin devils of deception."

"White devils," said Gus.

"You got it."

"And the jury gets it, too, I suppose."

"That's the idea."

"Johnnie looks ridiculous in that knit cap, but goddamnit, it works. It's theater. He's got those jurors on the edge of their seats," said Gus. "I hate the kind of lawyer he is, but I have to admit he's putting on a show. He makes Marcia and Chris look pathetic. They should have pointed right at O.J.'s face and said to the jury, This man is a *killer*! They're still treating him like a fucking football star. They apologized to the jury for having to say that their hero is a killer. That's not the way to do it."

"Your verdict goes far beyond the doors of this courtroom," said Cochran. "That's not to put any pressure on you."

"Oh, no?" whispered Gus.

"*Shhh*," whispered Shoreen.

"Just to tell you what is really happening out there," Cochran continued.

Gus wrote in his notebook, "Vote the party line, or don't bother to go home."

"Stop this cover-up. Stop this cover-up," said Cochran, his voice taking on preacher cadences. Several times he called Mark Fuhrman a genocidal racist. "If you don't stop it, then *who*? Do you think the police department is going to stop it? Do you think the D.A.'s office is going to stop it? Do you think we can stop it by ourselves? It has to be stopped by *you*. . . . Who, then, polices the police?

You police the police. You police them by your verdict. You are the ones to send the message."

"Dear God," whispered Gus. "He's becoming Louis Farrakhan before our eyes. He's telling them to send a message. He's telling them it doesn't matter whether or not O.J. did it."

"*Shhh,* Gus," whispered Shoreen. "Jex is looking at you."

"There was another man not too long ago in the world who had the same views," said Cochran. "This man, this scourge, became one of the worst people in the history of the world, Adolf Hitler, because people didn't care or didn't try to stop him. He had the power over his racism and his anti-religion."

"O.J. got his money's worth out of Johnnie today. He was disgusting," said Gus during the break. "And fascinating, I have to admit that. His closing argument made me realize how different we are, blacks and whites. He wouldn't have dared give that closing to a white jury, likening Mark Fuhrman to *Hitler.* He didn't consider how offensive that appalling parallel must have been to the Jewish members of his own Dream Team. He knew as he was saying it that they had pinned a bad rap on Mark Fuhrman when they accused him of moving or planting evidence. He told them to send a message to the Los Angeles Police Department. He gave them their marching orders as black people. He said some people just don't want to face the truth, and he looked over at Fred Goldman as he said it, the father of the man he knows his client murdered. I felt hatred for Johnnie at that moment, when I realized just how low they are willing to go to save this rich killer."

That night at dinner, Gus said to Marje Everett, "Fuhrman's life has become disposable. They've turned him into the most reviled man in America. They have ruined him."

"If I still had Hollywood Park, I'd hire Mark Fuhrman in a second to head up security," said Marje.

Gus attended the opera with Annabelle Begelman, whose husband had recently committed suicide, but he spent the entire performance of *The Flying Dutchman* writing notes about the trial in his green leather notebook for his "Letter from Los Angeles," which was due the following day. At intermission, he remained in his seat when Annabelle went to the ladies' room.

"Hi, Gus."

Gus looked up and saw Bernard Lafferty. "Oh, Bernard, hello," said Gus, standing up and shaking hands. "You look very smart, very proper. I can remember when everyone in New York wore black-tie to the opera. The only thing missing on you are those beautiful diamond studs you were wearing the last time I saw you all dressed up."

"Oh, yes," said Bernard.

"I told Elizabeth the diamonds were so big they looked like Doris Duke's earrings," said Gus.

"They were," said Bernard. "Miss Duke gave them to me before she died. It was Miss Duke who said they'd be beautiful studs."

"And where are they, Bernard?" asked Gus.

Tears filled his eyes. "Do you remember Andrew?"

"Andrew?"

"Andrew Cunanan."

"The one I met at the Starks'?" asked Gus.

"And the reopening of the Beverly Hills Hotel," replied Bernard. "He always said you never recognized him."

"What about him?" asked Gus.

"He skipped town. He was staying at Falcon Lair for a couple of weeks," said Bernard.

"He skipped town with the earrings?" asked Gus.

"Studs," corrected Bernard.

"I mean studs," said Gus.

"Yes. There were so many things he could have taken that I wouldn't have minded losing, or missed so much, but Miss Duke gave me those herself. It was at the house in Newport. She was in bed, and she had all her jewels out in front of her, and she said, 'I want Oatsie to have this,' and 'I want C.Z. to have this,' and 'I want you to have my earrings, Bernard. They'll make the most divine studs.'"

"And the trick walked off with them, huh?" said Gus.

"If you want to know the truth, Gus, I'm glad he's gone. He was beginning to make me nervous. This is probably not a very nice thing to say, but I really don't think Andrew is a very nice person. I mean, some of the things he said."

"I could have told you that the first time I saw the guy," said Gus. "There was something peculiar about the way he was looking at Ray Stark's Monet. He wasn't responding to the beauty of the water lilies, or the brush strokes, or the blue of the water. He was responding to the worth of it. His face had a covetous look."

"*Covetous* is a good word to describe Andrew," said Bernard. "He wants things, and if he doesn't get them, he could become very nasty."

"Now that you're so rich, Bernard, you have to be careful who you hang out with," said Gus. "It's been in all the papers that the Duke estate paid you five million dollars outright and a half-a-million-a-year income for life. Get real, Bernard. You're a sitting target for guys like Andrew Cunanan."

26

In his "Letter from Los Angeles," Gus wrote:

I never thought it would end this way for O. J. Simpson, winning and losing concurrently, with the loss somehow exceeding the win. I had always thought it would be a hung jury. My jaw dropped—in case anyone didn't notice it on television—when the verdict was read. There were hosannas to my left, where the Simpson supporters sat; there were tears to my right, where the Goldman and Brown families sat. Simpson was a free man. When he arrived back at the gates of his Brentwood estate to restart his life, a party was in preparation. Crates of champagne were delivered. His mother, Eunice, pretty in pink, arrived in a Rolls-Royce. The crowds cheered. It was all on television, like a premiere. Women in pink pantsuits waved champagne toasts to the media. Everyone hugged. The ever-loyal Al Cowlings was there. The ever-loyal Don Ohlmeyer, the president of NBC West Coast, was there. The ever loyal Robert Kardashian was there. As was Larry Schiller, the coauthor of Simpson's best-selling jailhouse book, I Want to Tell You. *Jubilation reigned.*

No one in the courtroom was more stunned by the acquittal of O.J. Simpson than Gus Bailey. The day before, when word came that the jury had arrived at a verdict after less than four hours of deliberation, Gus, who had always predicted a hung jury, said to his editor, Wayne Lawson, "They're going to convict, I know. I know." Even when he watched his friends Ira Reiner and Jack Ford on NBC predict an acquittal, he was sure they were wrong. The next morning in court, when he watched Jason Simpson lose total control of himself as he sobbed lying on the floor in front of his mother and sister, Gus was even more certain that the jurors were going to convict. "There's no way they can acquit him," whispered Gus to Shoreen. Shoreen didn't answer. They sat next to each other, as they had for the entire trial, speaking in whispers, like people in church waiting for the service to begin.

"Look at Jason," said Gus. "I never saw a guy cry that hard. He must know something we don't know. I bet he knows the verdict. I bet Jex told him the verdict. Jex would know. That's why he's crying like that. His rich daddy's going to go to prison for life."

"You can never predict a jury, Gus," said Shoreen.

"I know. They fool you every time," said Gus.

"Steve Barshop told me that once. He was the prosecutor in Lefty Flynn's trial."

"I'm worried about Kim," said Shoreen, looking past Gus to the Goldman family on his other side.

"So am I," said Gus.

"I hope she doesn't scream out or anything."

"Jex will throw her out of the courtroom if she does, sister of the victim or not," said Gus.

"She has to get away after this, or she's going to have a breakdown," said Shoreen. "The strain is too much."

"Fred, too," said Gus. "I'm worried about Fred, that he might do something crazy."

At one minute before ten o'clock, the deputies escorted Simpson from the holding room into the courtroom. For an instant, he looked at his daughter, his son, his first wife, his mother, his sisters, and his brother-in-law, who were all looking back at him.

"Everybody stand," said Jex.

Judge Ito entered the courtroom and took his place.

The moment was at hand. Gus reached over and squeezed Kim Goldman's hand.

"I'm panicked," she whispered.

"So am I," whispered Gus.

"Counsel, is there anything else we need to take up before we invite the jury to join us?" asked Ito.

The answer was no.

The jury entered. Everyone stared at them. They looked straight ahead, revealing nothing. "None of them looked over at O.J.," Gus whispered to no one.

"Madam Foreperson, would you please open the envelope and check the condition of the verdict forms," instructed Ito.

She did so.

"Are they the same forms you signed, and are they in order?"

"Yes, they are."

"If there is any disruption during the reading of the verdicts, the bailiffs will have the obligation to remove any persons disrupting these proceedings," said Ito, looking out at the spectators in the courtroom.

"Mr. Simpson," said Judge Ito, "would you please stand and face the jury."

"Mrs. Robertson," said Ito to Deirdre Robertson, the court clerk, cuing her to read. As if she was shocked by what she was about to read, Robertson stumbled in her pronunciation of the name Orenthal. "Orenfal," she said, and then corrected herself.

"We the jury in the above-entitled action find the defendant, Orenthal James Simpson, not guilty of the crime of murder in violation of Penal Code Section one eighty-seven A, a felony, upon Nicole Brown Simpson, a human being, as charged in count one of the information," read Deirdre Robertson.

A gasp sounded in the courtroom.

Mrs. Robertson continued to read. "We the jury find the defendant, Orenthal James Simpson, not guilty of the crime of murder . . . upon Ronald Lyle Goldman, a human being."

Later, for weeks, even months, people Gus knew

said to him, "I'll never forget the look on your face at the time of the verdict." Strangers on the street said to him, "Your face was how we felt." He looked to the right at Fred Goldman and Kim, who had become his friends. Their faces were twisted in agony, their bodies racked with pain. It was a moment so private and personal to them that he had to look away. He turned to his left, to Shoreen Maghame. "What did she say?" he whispered to her, as if he might have misheard the clerk, with his partially deaf ear.

"Not guilty, both counts," said Shoreen.

"I can't believe it," he said.

"Are you all right, Gus? You're not having a heart attack, are you?" asked Shoreen.

"No." He looked over at the defense table at O. J. Simpson, who had fulfilled his slain wife's prophecy. "He is going to kill me, and he is going to get away with it because he is O. J. Simpson," Nicole had said to her mother, to her sisters, to her friends, to nearly everyone she knew. To no avail. Gus interpreted the look on the acquitted man's face as a smirk, another game won. Johnnie Cochran embraced him from behind. In front of him, Robert Kardashian's face seemed to register blatant disbelief that such a thing could have happened, while F. Lee Bailey glowed with victorious pleasure as he stamped his cowboy boots on the floor of the courtroom. Gus felt revulsion at what he was watching.

Simpson looked over at the Goldman family and smiled.

"You fucking murderer," said Kim, as people around her tried to calm her down.

"The defendant," said Ito, "having been acquitted of both charges . . . is ordered . . . released forthwith."

Gus looked over at juror number three, on whom he had counted so heavily for a hung jury. Then he watched juror number six raise his hand in the black-power salute as he left the courtroom. Without looking down at his pad, he wrote on it, "That's all this trial was ever about. That juror, Lon Cryer, a former Black Panther, just said it all with that gesture in this courtroom."

Still numb with disbelief, Gus stood up to leave the courtroom. The Goldmans had already been escorted out by members of the prosecution team, as had the Browns. The aisles were full of people. The entrance was clogged. The movement toward the exit was slow. As he neared the door, he turned back to look for the last time at the courtroom where he had sat each day for nearly a year. I won't miss this place, he thought. There, standing at their seats watching people leave the courtroom, were Shirley and Benny Baker and Carmelita Durio. Of late, since their conversation in the corridor the week before, they had all dropped their eyes when they passed one another. Gus turned around and walked back into the courtroom.

"Where are you going?" asked Jex.

Gus pushed past him without speaking and walked over to where the Simpson sisters were standing. They looked at one another. Unlike Johnnie Cochran and F. Lee Bailey, they had the class not to gloat in their victory. He shook hands with each.

"I know this is a very joyous moment for you," said Gus.

"Thank you, Gus," said Shirley.

For an instant they looked at one another. They would probably never see one another again. They all knew that.

"Well, good-bye, and good luck," said Gus.

"Good luck to you, Gus," said Benny.

Outside the courtroom, Art Harris of CNN said, "Gus, let me grab you for a minute to go on CNN. Susan Rooks is on live."

"No," said Gus. "I want to go to Gil Garcetti's press conference. I want to hear what Marcia and Chris have to say."

"It's not going to start for fifteen minutes," said Art. "You'll be back in time."

"It's not a good idea, Art," said Gus. "I'm not myself. I haven't quite absorbed this yet, what just happened in there. I still can't believe he's been acquitted."

"It's just across the way at Camp O.J. It's all set up and ready to go. We'll just have the soundman put the mike on you," said Art, as he led Gus. They went down in the elevator in silence, out the door of the courthouse. The crowds outside were cheering at the verdict.

"I don't think I can do this, Art," said Gus. "Look at these people. They're ecstatic."

"There he is, there's the writer!" shouted a woman in the crowd. Gus turned and looked at her. She was African-American, past middle age, and her eyes were filled with loathing as she met Gus's look. "Hey, Gus, what do you think now?"

"This is not a good idea, Art," said Gus.

Art took hold of Gus's arm and propelled him through the crowds to the CNN platform.

"There's no monitor here on the CNN platform," said Art. "You won't be able to see Susan Rooks. She's in Washington. Greta Van Susteren and Roger Cossack are on with her at the moment."

"Greta Van Susteren!" exclaimed Gus. "She must be thrilled with the news."

"Joining us from Los Angeles, where he has just been in the courtroom, is writer Augustus Bailey, the special correspondent for *Vanity Fair* magazine. Can you hear me, Gus?"

"Yes, Susan."

"What do you think? Tell us firsthand."

"What I think is that the jury is a disgrace, an absolute disgrace," said Gus. His voice was strident. "They just gave the middle finger to justice. They did not even bother to deliberate. They ignored ten months' worth of testimony. They have just acquitted a guilty man. *That's* what I think, Susan."

"How do you account for it?" asked Susan.

418

"I think the Fuhrman tapes had a great deal to do with it," said Gus. "Those *N* words on Laura Hart McKinny's tapes were manna from heaven for the defense. But those tapes had nothing whatever to do with the murders of Nicole Brown and Ronald Goldman, which this trial was supposed to have been about."

"I don't think the tapes were manna from heaven," said Roger Cossack in Washington. He began to elaborate his theory about the tapes, but Gus had stopped listening. I don't give a flying fuck what you think, thought Gus, but he said nothing.

Then Gus heard Greta Van Susteren. She spoke in a complacent tone, clearly indicating her belief that the jury had arrived at the correct verdict. "The jury has spoken," she said. "The jury has given its message to the L.A.P.D."

The rage that Gus had felt since the acquittal erupted. "Giving a message to the L.A.P.D. was *not* what the jury's job was in this courtroom!" he shouted from Los Angeles. "There are two dead people here who seem to have been forgotten." He could hear the anger in his voice and feel rage building up inside him. He looked over at Art Harris, who was watching him nervously.

Just then roars of derision went up from the crowds on the street behind Gus. He turned to watch a cadre of a hundred police officers march in front of the courthouse to keep order in the crowds. Shouts of booing and jeering from the crowds on the sidewalk filled the air and momentarily drowned out the audio

419

on the television hookup with Susan Rooks in Washington. There was unadulterated hatred for the police in the ugly booing.

Gus pointed at the scene on the street behind him and shouted into the camera at Van Susteren, "That's what your message from the jury to the L.A.P.D. is all about."

"This man is an anarchist," said Van Susteren.

"I don't have to take this crap," said Gus. When she used the word *anarchist* the second time, he pulled the microphone off his striped tie and yanked the hearing device out of his ear and threw them at the camera, as if he was throwing it in Van Susteren's face.

"I'm sorry, Art, if I let you down, but I can't stand that mealy-mouthed talk of Greta's about the jury giving its message to the police, like it's a wonderful thing they've done," said Gus. "They have acquitted a guilty man. That's all they've done. I'm going back to Garcetti's press conference. I wish I hadn't come here."

"Do you want me to go with you, Gus?" said Art. "The crowd is sort of hostile out there."

"They're just booing the police still," replied Gus. "No, I'm okay. I have this terrible desire to cry. I had no idea this verdict would affect me so much. You know what, Art? This is my swan song. This is my last trial. I can't do this anymore. The bad guys always win."

Gus moved away from the CNN platform and headed across the street back to the courthouse. As he got to the steps leading to the courthouse, the same woman who had shouted at him before began to shout at him again. "We heard what you said. We heard what you said on CNN," she screamed at him.

"Just keep walking, Gus. Don't answer her," said one of the television cameramen whom Gus knew only by sight. "There's a TV set over there by the steps that they were watching you on just now."

"Thanks," said Gus.

The woman kept up her shouting at Gus. "There's the writer. There's the writer. There's Gus Bailey, the special correspondent for *Vanity Fair.* Oh, how fancy!" She pronounced every word distinctly.

"She's very good at mockery," said Gus, making his way through the crowd. He saw Dennis Schatzman, the African-American reporter.

"I'm scared, Dennis," he said.

"Don't answer her, Gus. Just keep walking," said Dennis.

"You deserve to be dead!" she screamed, walking next to him. "You deserve to be dead!"

"Dear God," said Gus.

"Just keep walking."

"I am. Did you hear what she said? She said I deserve to be dead."

"She wants you to turn around and yell back at her. They want to catch you on camera," said Dennis. "Keep moving."

"You must be happy, Dennis," said Gus. "You always believed in him."

"You have to look at it this way, Gus: Marcia and

Chris, they didn't prove it beyond a reasonable doubt," said Dennis, walking next to him. "The jury had no other choice but to acquit."

"I can't handle that conversation now," said Gus.

Again the woman shouted at him. Others joined in. The woman seemed to be the leader of a group. That Gus did not react to their taunts angered them more.

"Look at him. He's little!" screamed the woman in his face as she kept pace with him. "He's *little.*"

The women cupped their hands around their mouths and began to shout, *"Little! He's little! Little! Little man!"*

Gus showed his press pass to the guard at the door of the courthouse and walked in.

"Thanks, Dennis," he said. "That was one of the worst moments I've ever lived through."

"You okay, Gus?"

"A little hurt, Dennis. All my life I hated being little, but I never got taunted like that before."

Outside the district attorney's office on the eighteenth floor of the Criminal Courts Building sat a deputy named Frances, with whom Gus had had pleasant relations during the trial. At her request, he had once autographed one of his books for her. Breathless, Gus rushed out of the elevator.

"I'm here for the press conference," he said.

"The press conference has started," said Frances.

"I know. I had to go on CNN, and then it took a

few minutes to get on an elevator to get up here," said Gus.

"You can't go in," she said.

"What do you mean, I can't go in?"

"Just what I said."

"Frances, what's the matter with you?" asked Gus.

"The press conference has started. You can't go in," she repeated. There was a harsh tone to her voice.

"Gil Garcetti would want me to be in there," said Gus. "So would Marcia and Chris. Where's Suzanne Childs? She'll tell you it's all right for me to go in."

Frances returned to her reading, ignoring Gus.

"I thought you were different from Jex," said Gus. "I guess not. I'm sorry I wasted a book on you."

"I'd be careful if I were you," she said.

"The trial's over," replied Gus. "This press conference is the last jurisdiction you will ever have over me." Gus walked toward the elevator.

He called the Chateau Marmont from the media room on the eleventh floor. Judy Spreckels was in his room handling messages.

"I just saw you on CNN with Greta," said Judy.

"Did I make an asshole out of myself?" asked Gus.

"I didn't think you went far enough before you threw the microphone at her," said Judy.

Gus laughed. "This is my first light moment of the day," he said.

"I liked your saying the jury gave the middle finger to justice," said Judy.

"Oh, good. Then I'll use it again on *Geraldo*," said Gus.

"Are you all right, Gus?" asked Judy. "I worry about you sometimes."

"I had no idea this would affect me so deeply," said Gus. "I feel sort of the way I felt when Jack Kennedy was assassinated. A terrible evil had been done. There was this ghastly feeling of emptiness everywhere. People just stared at one another, not knowing what to do. That's the way I feel now about this verdict. Empty. Violated even." He paused for a moment. "Any calls?"

"Larry King wants you on tonight. Charlie Rose wants you on. *GMA* wants you on tomorrow morning. Charles Grodin wants you on. So does Geraldo. Michael Jackson. More, more, more. What will I tell all these people?"

"Tell everybody yes," said Gus.

Later, on television, Gus said, "This jury could have watched a videotape of Simpson, knife in hand, slitting the throats of Nicole and Ron, and the verdict would have been the same. O.J. could have saved himself a lot of money. He never needed Shapiro, or Scheck, or Neufeld, or F. Lee Bailey, or Dr. Michael Baden, or Dr. Henry Lee. He didn't need any of them. Johnnie Cochran could have gotten this same verdict all alone with the help of Jo-Ellan Dimitrius, the jury consultant. Race is Johnnie's area of expertise. It's what he's good at. It's what made him rich. It's what got Simpson acquitted."

"Be careful, Gus," warned a few of his media friends.

"Who do you think is the most responsible on the defense for the acquittal?" asked Larry King that night on the air.

"Jo-Ellan Dimitrius," replied Gus.

King, who sometimes took Jo-Ellan Dimitrius to dinner at Morton's and Drai's, looked surprised by Gus's answer. "Jo-Ellan Dimitrius?"

"She understood the brilliance of stupidity," said Gus.

Katie Spikes was waiting outside the studio when Gus left the set. "There have been some call-ins," she said. "Some people seem to be upset at what you said about the jury."

"I meant every word I said," replied Gus.

"I just wanted to warn you, Gus."

"Thanks, Katie," said Gus. "At least I didn't tell that their bags were packed before deliberation even started."

"Is that truc?"

"And I also didn't tell that three of the ladies are on their way to Las Vegas, all expenses paid at the Bally Hotel," said Gus.

"If it's true, why didn't you tell it?"

"I'm saving it for my last 'Letter from Los Angeles,'" said Gus.

At the stoplight at La Cienega and Santa Monica Boulevard, a red car with two African-American men in it pulled up in the lane next to Gus. The three men looked at one another. Gus felt uneasy. As soon as the light changed, he put his foot on the gas and sped forward. He looked through his rearview mirror and saw that the car had moved into his lane and was now following him. He remembered Marlene Schlessinger telling him not to stop if a person in another car hit him from behind. A block later, there was another stoplight. The red car pulled out from behind him and came up next to him. This time Gus looked straight ahead.

"You still think O.J.'s guilty?" one of the men asked.

Gus looked over at them and said good-naturedly, slipping into what he called his absent-minded-professor routine, "Oh, I was hoping you wouldn't ask me that." Surprised, the two men looked at him for a moment and then laughed, as did Gus. As they pulled ahead of him, the driver of the car waved good-bye.

That night, verdict night, Gus dined at Betsy Bloomingdale's house in Holmby Hills. There were fourteen at dinner in the dining room. The conversation never veered from the subject of the day.

"I'll never forget the look on your face, Gus, when they announced the verdict," said Betsy.

"Everyone tells me my mouth was hanging open," said Gus.

"I had to turn off the TV," said Natalie Robinson. "I couldn't stand looking at that victory party over at Simpson's house on Rockingham. Did you see those ladies in pink pantsuits waving champagne glasses at the cameras?"

"Everybody's forgotten there are two dead people," said Gus.

"What happened to that sixty-year-old white woman you told us at the Wicks' was going to hang the jury, Gus?" asked Betsy.

"She buckled under, I guess," said Gus. "She didn't put up a fight at all. I guess I expected too much of her."

"Were you surprised?"

"When I saw juror number six give the black-power salute, that told me a lot. You wait and see. Within a matter of days, weeks, or months, she's going to say she regrets that she voted for acquittal. She's going to say she realizes he was guilty. Too fucking late, Anise. Excuse my language, Betsy."

"What do you think Simpson will do now?"

"At the moment, his victory party is being photographed by Larry Schiller and his fiancée, Kathy Amerman, for one of the tabloid papers, *The Star*, for which Simpson and the photographers are rumored to be splitting two hundred thousand dollars. Then O.J.'s people, like Robert Kardashian and Skip Taft, are planning a Pay-Per-View television appearance of O.J., his kids from both marriages, his mother and sisters, and the Dream Team, which they expect is going to give him something like ten or twenty million dollars."

For a moment, there was silence at the table.

"It's very simple," said Mrs. Jerry Perenchio. "We'll arrange to boycott it."

When Gus got back to the Chateau Marmont that night, he returned a call from Graydon Carter in New York.

"Graydon, I must have woken you," said Gus.

"It's all right. I said call tonight, no matter how late. You have received six death threats over the telephone at the magazine," said Graydon. "Are you all right?"

"Yes. I know I sort of flipped out on CNN today—you probably heard," said Gus. "It was too soon after the acquittal for me to have gone on the air."

"Would you like a bodyguard? We'll get Gavin de Becker to set up a bodyguard for you," said Graydon. "One of the threats came from the L.A. Crips."

"That's *big time*," said Gus. "No, no, I don't want a bodyguard, Graydon. That seems so Hollywood mogul to me."

"We checked the Chateau for you," said Graydon. "They're going to have the night guard check on your room every hour."

"Nothing's going to happen, Graydon. Everyone's a little hysterical out here, myself included. It'll calm down in a few days."

"Stay off television, for God sake."

"I have a few more shows. Then I will."

"Then what are you going to do?"

"I'm going home to Prud'homme. It's time to leave. I want to write all this down."

27

In his "Letter from Los Angeles," Gus wrote:

The elation of the victory party at the mansion on Rockingham didn't last long. The participants having such a swell time began to get the idea that the city and the country weren't cheering and partying along with them. A sign went up on Sunset Boulevard at the entrance to Brentwood saying WELCOME TO BRENTWOOD, HOME OF THE BRENTWOOD BUTCHER. *Another read,* MURDER LOOSE IN BRENTWOOD. *A neighbor stated that Simpson gave new meaning to the phrase "There goes the neighborhood." The exclusive Riviera Country Club, where Simpson was a member, let it be known that he was no longer welcome there. Further, his much-heralded Pay-Per-View TV deal collapsed with a resounding thud, and along with it the $20 million he had assumed he would make. ICM, the talent agency that had represented him for twenty years, and Jack Gilardi, his personal agent, dropped him as a client, after protests from some of their most*

*powerful Hollywood star clients. Polls showed
that more than half of the country was outraged
by the verdict.*

*Nicole was right. Everything happened just
as she had predicted it would. What Nicole had
not anticipated, however, was the rage of the
white citizenry across the country over Simpson's
acquittal by a mostly black jury. Dream Team
member Peter Neufeld was quoted in the* Los
Angeles Times *as saying, "O.J. is entitled to
enjoy the fruits of his liberty the way the rest of
us are. I think it's unconscionable that people are
trying to deny him that." Get real, Neufeld. I
think it's unconscionable to be a participant in
the acquittal of a man who killed two people
while his kids were asleep upstairs.*

"What's it like being in Simpson's house?" asked
Gus over the telephone.

"I can't really talk here," replied Schiller.

"Is the killer sitting right there with you?"

"I wouldn't be on the phone with you if he was,
Gus."

"Does he know?"

"Know what?"

"That he is despised?"

"Yes."

"Does he give a shit?"

"Very much."

"Good," said Gus. "I was just watching Johnnie
Cochran doing his cock-of-the-walk act on Larry

King's show, like he thinks he's the new Clarence Darrow. Which he's not."

"I saw him."

"He told Larry that O.J. was angry. What the fuck does O.J. have to be angry about? He should be down on his knees thanking God that he's not doing life without parole."

"He's angry because Gil Garcetti said on television after the acquittal that the L.A.P.D. was not going to look for the real killer."

"What? The real killer? Tell him to look in the fucking mirror and he'll see the real killer!" screamed Gus.

"Stop yelling at me, Gus, or I'm not going to talk to you anymore," said Schiller. "I know you're unhappy about the verdict, but it's not *my* fault. You asked me a question, and I gave you an answer."

"I'm sorry to yell, but you sound like you're buying into his crapola about the real killer, Larry. It was bad enough when he had poor Jason read that ludicrous statement at Johnnie Cochran's press conference, that a priority of his father's life was going to be to find the real killer. That's the joke of the week. Did you notice Jason's body language when he was reading the statement? Did you think he looked embarrassed enough by the lie he was reading to the nation?"

Schiller didn't reply.

"All right, I'll calm down. Tell me this, is he freaking out with all those camera crews and reporters and crowds outside his house full-time?

There's some justice that he's a prisoner in his own house. Not as good as a cell, mind you, but there's some satisfaction that he can't go anywhere to enjoy his freedom."

"If I tell you something, Gus, will you promise you won't repeat it?"

"I promise."

"Swear?"

"Swear."

"He's not even here at Rockingham."

"He's not?"

"We got him out of here last night. A diversionary tactic. They called a press conference to be held outside the gates. While the camera crews were setting up, he sneaked out lying on the floor of a van, one of three cars in a caravan. Once he was gone, the press conference was canceled," said Schiller.

"Where's he staying if he's not at Rockingham?" asked Gus.

"You swear you won't use this?"

"I swear."

"At Don Ohlmeyer's house off Doheny."

"The president of NBC West Coast," said Gus. "It's perfect."

"Just to make it more perfect—I know you like this sort of thing, you're always talking about overlaps—Ohlmeyer bought the house from Kardashian three weeks before the murders," said Schiller.

"You couldn't make this stuff up," said Gus.

"I went to the movies with him last night," said Schiller.

"Did I hear you say you went to the movies with O.J. Simpson last night? Larry, this is the best conversation I've had in a long time. Keep talkin'."

"O.J. wanted to see *Showgirls*," said Schiller.

"Of course, he wanted to see *Showgirls*," said Gus. "I saw it at Arnie Kopelson's the other night. Tits, tits, and more tits. A perfect choice for his first movie in a year. But wait a minute, Larry. How could he be seen at a movie theater and not cause a riot?"

"I can't tell you that," said Schiller.

"Oh, yes, you can, Larry. Come on. You're in this deep."

"You swear?"

"I swear."

"They had the makeup woman who did his makeup on the pilot he made just before the murders come over to Ohlmeyer's house and give him a disguise," said Schiller.

"I have this desire to laugh, Larry," said Gus. "O.J. Simpson's in disguise?"

"He went to the Palm for dinner, with one of his golfing buddies from New York—whose wife, incidentally, picked out the horn-rimmed glasses at Oliver Peoples on the Sunset Strip that are part of the disguise—and *no one* recognized him," said Schiller.

"What did the makeup lady make him up *as,* for God sake?"

"She gave him a Hispanic look. A little mustache, neatly trimmed, a little goatee, neatly trimmed—and she taught him how to put them on himself—and the new glasses from Oliver Peoples on the Strip. It's amazing, Gus. He looked like he could have been a diplomat from Cuba or Haiti, or someplace like that. I've been looking at the guy close up every day for over a year, and even I didn't recognize him."

"Wouldn't you think a guy who's just been acquitted of a double murder three days ago and has just been released from jail after a year and a half of incarceration would have better things to do than getting into disguise and going out to see *Showgirls* and have dinner at the Palm, where he fooled all the people? Like he fooled the jury. Next to football, pretense is what he's good at. I think that's why he doesn't feel anything for the murders he's committed. I think he still thinks it's going to be like old times. But it's not. It's never going to be. His friends are going to drop by the wayside. You wait and see. If the guy has any sense, he'll leave this town."

"You know Kathy and I took the photographs at the victory party, don't you?" asked Schiller.

"I saw the pictures in the *Star* today," said Gus. "I read all those tabs every Monday. A reporter friend of mine at the *Star* told me you got two hundred thousand to split with O.J. and another unnamed person for those pictures."

"Shall I go on, or do you want to make cracks?" asked Schiller.

"Go on."

"A lot of his golfing buddies who came to the victory party didn't want to have their pictures taken with him," said Schiller. "They kept moving out of the way when Kathy or I went in for a picture."

"Hi, Gus, this is Lauren Nadler from *Day and Date*. We want you to come on the show today."

"Hi, Lauren. I can't. I'm packing. I'm getting ready to leave town in a couple of days. I've got a mountain of stuff I've collected during the last year. Besides, my magazine wants me to stay off television," said Gus.

"Why? You didn't have any death threats, did you?" asked Lauren.

"That isn't it. It's just that I've been on TV so much on all the shows, and I always get worked up and go overboard and say too much, and then there are calls to the stations to complain about me."

"That's what we love about you, Gus," said Lauren.

"That's what they all say, but I'm the one who gets in trouble, not the show," said Gus. "When I was on *Larry King* last night, some lady from Maine called in and said I was a racist. I said, 'Are you saying that because I think O.J. Simpson is guilty of the murders of which he was acquitted I am a racist?'"

"I saw you on Larry's show," said Lauren.

"If that is going to be the new criterion for racism, there are going to be an awful lot of racists out there," said Gus.

"How about today? Come on, Gus. It's sort of an interesting dilemma that O.J.'s in. He's virtually a prisoner inside his own house. He's free, but he can't go anywhere."

"*Hmmmm.*"

"He can't go to a restaurant. He can't go to the movies."

"What time's the show?" asked Gus.

"You'd have to be here at Television City by two for makeup."

"Will you send a car and driver for me?"

"Gus, it's David Margolick. Are you aware that Schiller's livid with you? Aren't you supposed to have breakfast with him tomorrow morning at the Beverly Hills Hotel before you leave? Forget it. He's not going to show up. I never saw him so mad. What did you say on television yesterday?"

"Oh, shit, did he see it?" asked Gus. "Three o'clock in the afternoon, I didn't think anyone would be watching."

"Apparently O.J. sits in front of six television sets all day long listening to what people say about him," said Margolick.

"You mean O.J. saw me, too?" asked Gus.

"The way I heard it from Schiller was that O.J. was sitting there watching the show with Schiller and Kardashian. The segment was called 'A Prisoner in His Own Home,' and you came on and said he'd been sneaked out of the house on Rockingham with a diversionary tactic to fool the media and that he went to see the movie *Showgirls*."

437

"Thank God I didn't say anything about the disguise, or that he went to the Palm for dinner," said Gus. "Go on. What happened?"

"So O.J. says, 'Only two people know I went to see *Showgirls,* you, Kardashian, and you, Schiller. Which one of you told Gus Bailey?' So Larry had to admit that he had, and O.J.'s really pissed at him."

"Oh, Larry, come off it," said Gus to Larry Schiller over the telephone. "It wasn't like I said that he confessed to the murders. All that I said was that he went to see *Showgirls.* Oh, yeah, I told about the three-car caravan getting him out of there, and the fake press conference. All those experts were saying how trapped he was in his house, and something came over me, and I couldn't resist telling it."

"I'm never going to tell you anything again, Gus," said Schiller.

"I'll worm it out of you," said Gus.

"O.J. was really pissed at me," said Schiller.

"It'll make a great scene in my novel, Larry," said Gus. "You and Kardashian and O.J. sitting in Ohlmeyer's house watching me spill the beans about him on television. I think in the book I'll have him in the Hispanic-diplomat drag with the goatee and the fake glasses while he's berating you."

"Your novel's starting to sound like a comedy," said Schiller.

"That's occurred to me," replied Gus.

"O.J. drove his Bentley to the Beverly Hills

Hotel today to have lunch with this New York golfing buddy who was staying in a bungalow," said Schiller. "He was making a right turn on Crescent Drive to park his car by the side of the hotel, and who do you think pulled up in the next lane?"

"Tell me."

"Kim Goldman."

"Kim! Did she recognize him?"

"They looked at each other, but she didn't recognize him."

"I bet he got off on it," said Gus. "I bet it's a story he'll tell to his golfing buddies. 'You won't believe who pulled up in the next lane at the stoplight on Sunset and Crescent. Kim Goldman, and she didn't even recognize me.' And there'll be a lot of macho laughter at poor Kim. I'll use it in the book."

"Kathy wants to have dinner before you go," said Schiller.

"I can't. I'm taking Kim Goldman to Drai's tonight with Shoreen Maghame and Cynthia McFadden, and tomorrow night my friend Wendy Stark's having a farewell dinner for me, and the next day I'm off for New York. I'm going to miss you, Larry. Next to me, you gave the best murder gossip at the trial. I expect to be invited to your wedding at the Elvis Chapel in Las Vegas. And you're going to make a great character in my novel. Give my love to Kathy."

The time was approaching for Gus to leave Los Angeles and return to his life in New York and Con-

439

necticut, where he planned to write his novel on the Simpson saga. He found to his surprise, as his departure day grew closer, that he was sad to leave, although he understood that it was time. The show was over. He had felt spiritless since the acquittal. He almost decided to stop watching television after he heard the juror named Brenda Moran loudly declare to the cameras that domestic violence had no place in the murder trial and should have been tried in another court.

"If I had had a rock, I would have smashed the television screen," he said to Harvey Levin when he called to say good-bye.

He did stop watching when he saw a clip of Johnnie Cochran telling the congregation at the Brookins Community A.M.E. Church in South Central that the defense had won because God was on their side.

"Then there must be more than one God," Gus said to Mart Crowley, when he called to say goodbye. "The God I believe in would never have been on the side of a man who killed two people and got away with it."

Sacha Newley painted his portrait for the book jacket of the novel he had not yet started to write, *Another City, Not My Own,* while he wrote his final "Letter from Los Angeles" for *Vanity Fair:*

What I have suspected since I became involved with the Los Angeles murder trials of the Menendez brothers and O. J. Simpson is that winning is everything, no matter what you have to do to win. If lies have to be told, if defenses have to be created, if juries have to be tampered with in order to weed out those who appear to be unsympathetic to the defendant, then so be it. The name of the game is to beat the system and let the guilty walk free. If you can get away with it.

The stench of O.J. Simpson's acquittal grows stronger by the week as allegations of jury tampering abound, and reports surface concerning a flunked polygraph test taken by Simpson two days after the murders, in the company of two of his attorneys. Although the results are thought to have been destroyed, I am told that a copy exists.

Gus had a farewell lunch with Nancy Reagan and Marje Everett at the Bistro Garden, which was shortly to close. Nancy had just returned from New York, where she had been at the time of the acquittal.

"I was at the opera that night," said Nancy. "At the intermission, I came out of the box, and Jeannie Williams of *USA Today* came up and told me they'd reached a verdict on the first day. I could think of nothing else. We went back in for Act Two. It was *Otello*. Plácido."

"I still can't believe it," said Gus. "Listen, I'm going to miss our Saturday-lunch club."

He made good-bye calls to his friends, old and new. He made farewell calls to the houses where he had regularly gone for dinner:

He left a message on Roddy McDowall's

answering machine. "Roddy, thanks for everything. You give the best dinners in town. Where else could I sit between Jennifer Jones and Sharon Stone at dinner and discuss O.J. Simpson on each side?"

He left a message on Sue Mengers's answering machine. "Sue, thanks for everything. You give the best dinners in town. Where else could I sit in a corner and talk to Jack Nicholson for an hour about O.J. Simpson? Love to Jean Claude."

He left a message on Tita Cahn's answering machine. "Tita, thanks for everything. You give the best dinners in town. Where else could I sit on a bar stool between Sean Connery and Sidney Poitier and talk about O.J. Simpson?"

He left a message on Mrs. Marvin Davis's answering machine. "Barbara, thanks for everything. You give the best dinners in town. Where else could I sit in such utter splendor with Plácido Domingo and Kevin Costner and talk about O.J. Simpson?"

He went down to the Criminal Courts Building to say good-bye to Suzanne Childs and Gil Garcetti. While he was waiting with Suzanne to go into Gil's office, he nodded his head in the direction of Frances and said, "I missed seeing Chris Darden break down and cry in the press conference because she wouldn't let me in."

"Come on in, Gus," said Garcetti, opening his door.

"Do you remember when Judge Ito sealed the

testimony of the jailhouse guard who heard O.J. confess to the Reverend Roosevelt Grier that he'd killed Nicole and Ron?" asked Gus.

"Yes," said Garcetti.

"I think you ought to figure a way to leak that sealed testimony to the media," said Gus.

"You know I can't do that, Gus," said Garcetti.

"I can't *stand* it when people get away with murder," said Gus. "Have I told you O.J.'s furious with you because you called off the search for the real killer?"

He left messages of farewell for Marcia Clark and Chris Darden. He gave his New York and Connecticut telephone numbers to his friends in the media. He called the Goldmans to say good-bye. "I'll never forget Ron," he said. He left a message for Denise Brown. "I'll never forget Nicole," he said. He went to the cemetery and left a bouquet of yellow roses on Becky's grave.

Later that night, Gus stood in the doorway of Wendy Stark's house saying good-bye to Howard and Margaret Weitzman, who were the last guests to leave Wendy's farewell party for him.

"This wasn't just a shipboard romance, you know," said Gus. "Just because the trial's over doesn't mean the friendship ends."

"Oh, don't worry. We'll let you know when we come to New York, Gus," said Margaret.

"Dinner at 'Twenty-one,'" said Gus.

"I hate good-byes," said Margaret.

"Me too. Good-bye."

"The help quit," said Wendy, when he walked back into the living room.

"What do you mean, the help quit?"

"The caterers. They didn't like the way you talked about O.J., calling him guilty after the jury found him innocent," said Wendy.

"The jury *didn't* find him innocent. They found him not guilty," said Gus. "There's a big difference."

"Don't start on me," said Wendy.

"And they walked out?"

"Yes."

"Not Wilbur, too?"

"Yes."

"I'm sick about Wilbur. That's really upsetting," said Gus. "I've been having long talks with Wilbur for years. You know what, Wendy? This is going to be the O.J. Simpson legacy. He's divided the races. We're back to where we were before Rosa Parks wouldn't sit in the back of the bus anymore in 1955, and the civil-rights movement started. All this because of a black guy who turned his back on blacks after he became rich and famous. He only liked white women, white neighborhoods, and white country clubs."

"I'm glad you left *that* out of your speech," said Wendy.

"Right," said Gus. "They might have dumped the crème brûlée they were passing right on my bald spot. I was wondering if I should modify my remarks. I thought to myself, Do I say what I believe to be true about the trial, or do I adjust my statements so that his supporters are not offended? I think it's important to say that an acquittal should not be confused with innocence. You know what, Wendy?"

"What?"

"It's a good thing I didn't speak *before* dinner."

"At least we finished dessert and coffee before they left," said Wendy. "Everybody got fed before you drove them out of my house."

"I'll help you do the dishes or load the dishwasher, or whatever has to be done," said Gus.

"Screw the dishes. Gracie comes tomorrow. Let's talk," said Wendy.

"I'm going to miss you, Wendy. I've gotten used to chatting every day again, like we used to when I still lived here."

"Are you sad about leaving?"

"I am, yes. When I stopped living here in 1979 and moved to New York, I left hating Los Angeles. I don't anymore. L.A. is a part of me just as much as New York is. I reunited with old friends here and made a lot of new ones. But it's time for me to go. I've been away for a long time. I have to get away from murder. I have to stop talking about murder, all day every day."

"You have to write your book first," said Wendy.

"Oh, yes, the book. That's the dark cloud hovering over me. Can I get it finished in time, that's what I keep wondering," said Gus.

"In time for what?"

"It's late. I have to go. I'm on the eight o'clock plane in the morning."

They walked to the door and hugged.

"That was nice, what you said about me in your toast, Gus," said Wendy.

"I meant every word. You always stuck by me, kiddo, even when I was down and out, and a lot of people let go. I'll always remember that, you know," said Gus.

"Gus, you sound like you're saying good-bye forever."

"That's what I feel like at this moment. Don't ask me to explain it. I don't have an answer," said Gus.

"You're not sick or anything, are you?" she asked.

"You mean cancer, AIDS, heart trouble? No, none of the above. I'm in good health. God knows why I'm in good health. I never take care of myself. But I am."

"You're just depressed about the verdict," said Wendy.

"I suppose," said Gus. "I'm also depressed the help walked out of here tonight when they heard me talk. It's probably because I said Simpson had no remorse, no scruples, and no ethics. That'll do it every time, I guess. So long, honey. Kiss-kiss, as they all say in New York society."

28

On Gus's first night back in New York after a year in Los Angeles, his driver, Dov Ehrenfeld, met him at the airport, dealt with the excess baggage, drove him to his apartment in Turtle Bay, and waited downstairs while he went up to his penthouse, where he showered, changed into black-tie, glanced at the list of calls his secretary, Arthur Gorton, had left for him, and read the cards on several "Welcome Home" phalaenopsis plants that had been sent to him. When he reappeared in the lobby, Dov drove him up Park Avenue and across Central Park to the Dakota on West Seventy-second Street, where he arrived just as the twenty-six guests were sitting down to a birthday dinner his old friend Gil Shiva was giving for Princess Firyal of Jordan.

As birthday parties go, it was a very swell affair. Unlike the casual look at most of the dinners in Los Angeles that Gus had attended over the last year, the New York look was more formal: Ladies wore long dresses and jewels. The waiters wore white gloves, and the guest list consisted of all the names that regularly appeared in Aileen Mehle's society column in

W, the same crowd Gus had written about in *People Like Us.* These were all people Gus knew, some for years, but he called only a few of them his friends. Still, he moved effortlessly among them, greeting this one, kissing that one, being greeted in return on his return to the city.

"Hi, darling. Kiss-kiss," said Kay Kay Somerset. "Was it awful out there? Was it ghastly? Did you just hate being there? I don't know how you stood it, every day in that awful courtroom. Oh, I hate that O.J. Simpson man. I just hate him. I had to let our cook go, Gus. She was so happy about the verdict, she was jumping up and down with joy in the kitchen, like those law students at Howard University. I was so damn mad at her I fired her right on the spot. Naturally, I forgot about the dinner I was giving the next night, so we had to have Chinese takeout, because I couldn't get anyone to cater at the last minute. Actually, it turned out to be a great success. We called it our Dennis Fung dinner. Darling, did you see Gus? He's back."

"You're over there, Gus, next to Nan Kempner," said Gil, pointing across the table. "Have you said hello to Firyal?"

"Sorry to be late," said Gus. "Hello, Firyal. Happy birthday."

"I'm sitting on your other side, and I intend to grill you about the trial," said the princess as they kissed on each cheek.

"I had such a nice fax from the palace in Amman when my son was missing," said Gus.

"Noor's so good about things like that. It's so American," said Firyal. "You know Jason Epstein, don't you?"

"Jason, I didn't see you," said Gus. Jason Epstein was one of the great editors of the publishing business. He and Gus were more used to running into each other at literary parties than at social ones.

"Gus, I can't believe you're here," said Jason. "I was thinking about you today. There's something I want to talk to you about. I didn't know you were back from the trial."

"I just got back an hour or so ago," said Gus.

"It seemed like you were gone forever," said Jason.

"A year. What did you want to talk to me about?" asked Gus.

"This party isn't exactly the right place to talk," said Jason, looking around. "Are you going to be in your apartment tomorrow morning? I'll call you there."

After dinner, Marvin Hamlisch, the composer, sat down at the piano, after being introduced by the host, and played and sang a birthday song he had composed especially for Firyal's party. The guests moved in around the piano to listen. Everyone laughed merrily and clapped enthusiastically at the charming song.

"You must sing it again, Marvin, all the way through, from beginning to end, so we can listen to the lyrics, they're *divine,*" said the princess, clapping her hands.

"He's caught you, darling, he's absolutely caught you," called out Ormolu Webb to the Jordanian princess, in her thrilling society voice. Everyone laughed. Ormolu was holding hands with her very rich husband, Percy.

When Hamlisch started to sing the birthday song a second time, Gus nudged Jason to follow him down the hall into the library, where they were alone.

"I've been going to a lot of this same kind of evening in Los Angeles," said Gus. "Amazing how different the two cities are."

"I thought you hated it out there," said Jason.

"I did. I don't anymore. What did you want to tell me?"

"Not here, Gus. I'll call you tomorrow morning."

"Oh, come on, Jason. Tell me now," said Gus, standing in the entrance looking down the hall. "No one can hear. They're two rooms away. Everybody's singing. Ahmet and Mica Ertegün have just arrived from some other party. Jamie Niven's lighting up a cigar. The French guy is talking about a ball he just gave in Paris. John Richardson's in deep conversation with Chessy Rayner, and Ormolu Webb and Firyal are checking out each other's rings and bracelets. What can I tell you, Jason? It's just another night out in New York society. Oops. What's this? Do you see that young guy in the Versace dinner jacket who just walked in with old Bertie de Lessops?"

"What about him?"

"Those diamond studs he's wearing used to be Doris Duke's earrings," said Gus. "Top that for unimportant information."

"You sound like Aileen Mehle, Gus," said Jason. "You should be doing social commentary."

"I used to write that kind of stuff—about the ladies of Palm Beach, that sort of thing—but now I'm into more serious things, like crime, like guys who get away with murder, like Mr. O.J. Simpson of Brentwood, California, and the kind of lawyers who make up the stories who get killers acquitted, for instance that Detective Mark Fuhrman planted the glove at the house on Rockingham."

"I know, I read your trial coverage in *Vanity Fair*," said Jason, holding up his hand as if to forestall a ten-minute tirade on the subject of O.J. Simpson's acquittal.

"I wasn't about to do a seminar on the subject," said Gus, laughing. "I'm more interested in hearing what you have to say."

"You know Larry Schiller, don't you?" asked Jason.

"Of course."

"What do you think of him? I've met him before, with Norman Mailer, but I don't really know him," said Jason.

"A fascinating character," replied Gus. "What about him?"

Jason thought for a moment before answering. "My company really wanted Marcia Clark's book. We met with her right after the trial. We liked her.

You should have seen the commotion she caused when she came to the office. Every person from Alberto Vitale and Harry Evans down to the kids in the mailroom came out in the halls to get a look at her."

"She's a major star at the moment," said Gus.

"We thought she had a great book in her, but the bidding got way out of hand. We dropped out at four-point-one million. Viking got her for four-point-three million," said Jason. "An absurd amount of money."

"I don't blame Marcia for taking the four-point-three million," said Gus. "I blame you guys in publishing for offering that amount of money for the latest celebrity's book."

"Let me finish here. Then Schiller appeared out of left field with a book proposal," said Jason.

"Really?" said Gus, surprised.

"If even half of what Schiller tells me checks out, he's got an incredible story," said Jason.

"Schiller played a very dangerous game during the trial," said Gus. "He ingratiated himself with Johnnie Cochran and Bob Shapiro when he put together O.J.'s book, *I Want to Tell You*. It was a brilliant public-relations bonanza for O.J. He could tell the public that he never, ever could have killed Nicole, that he loved her, that he loved his kids and missed them, and that he loved God. And he didn't have to answer any embarrassing questions—like what was his blood doing at the scene of the crime. The only money that most of the Dream Team got paid was from Schiller's book, so Johnnie Cochran arranged with Judge Ito to give him a seat in the courtroom with Shirley and Benny Baker, O.J.'s sister and brother-in-law. He heard everything."

"So you know all that?"

"I was there, Jason. I watched the whole thing. All that stuff I wrote in the magazine each month about O.J. being a part of planning the defense strategy, talking on a speakerphone from his jail cell to Cochran's office—I got all that from Schiller. He always had fantastic information."

"I'm considering making a deal with Schiller today, for a lot of money," said Jason.

"I assumed that was what you were leading up to—the deal, that is, not the amount of money," said Gus. "That should be some book. He knows backstage stuff about the defense team that no one else in the media knows. Sometimes he tends to embellish reality a bit. I'd have a very good fact checker, if I were you."

Jason leaned back on the green damask sofa and changed his position, putting his right leg over his left. "That's one thing I don't have to worry about. He has a source who was there from the get-go, with firsthand knowledge."

"Who could that be?" asked Gus.

"*That* I won't tell you."

"Oh, come on, Jason, we're in this deep, and the socialites in the drawing room are all being sociable."

"Off the record?"

"Off the record."

"Robert Kardashian."

"Robert Kardashian?" repeated Gus, his voice registering his surprise. "It takes a lot to stun me these days, but you've just stunned me, Jason. I would think he would be afraid if he betrays O.J."

"His name is never going to appear," replied Jason. "Schiller will split his fee with him."

"It'll leak, Jason. You must know that," said Gus. "Everything does leak in this story, except where O.J. stashed the murder weapon and the bloody clothes."

"Harvey, it's Gus. Have I got a scoop for you. I had to call someone or I couldn't have gone to sleep. The only thing is, it's off the record, because it could only have come from me, so you have to promise you won't tell anyone. Schiller just made a book deal for a lot of bucks. But that's not the scoop. *Whom* do you think is Schiller's secret collaborator on the book? Kardashian! The killer's best friend. No, I'm not kidding. It's absolutely true. Wouldn't you like to be in the media room at the house on Rockingham when O.J. hears that bit of information?"

Gus quickly discovered that he was unable to write his novel in New York, where he was invited out to dinner every night, and went. He was frequently commenting on television on the justice system in the wake of the unpopular acquittal of the former football star, or giving lectures, or speaking in tandem with Fred Goldman at the National Victim Center lunch in Fort Worth, or receiving the key to the city of Providence, Rhode Island, from Mayor Vincent A. Cianci, Jr., at a dinner where he received a standing ovation for his defense of the police in his trial coverage. He found that being a popular authority on O.J. Simpson was a delightful thing to be, but it took up almost all of his time. There was no time left for work. Everyone in the world seemed to have his unlisted telephone number.

"Gus, do you remember my sister, Sass? You met her at the Stephaich-Guiness wedding reception. From Hobe Sound? Sass Buffington. She's coming to New York, and she's your number-one fan of all time—she's read *everything* you've written about the O.J. Simpson trial—and it's her birthday, the big four-oh, and could you have lunch with us at Mortimer's, please, just this once, Gus, it would be so wonderful, please. Sass will die happy."

"I just couldn't *stand* that Johnnie Cochran," said Sass Buffington at lunch at Mortimer's. "Didn't you think he looked *hilarious* when he put on O.J.'s knit cap during the closing argument? Froggie and I couldn't stop laughing. All that fire-and-brimstone preacher routine, and the part about poor Mark Fuhrman being like Adolf Hitler. We couldn't believe he'd say that. Now, listen, tell me, Gus, I promise I won't tell anyone, I swear, but were Marcia Clark and Christopher Darden really having an affair?"

The next day Gus left New York for his house in Prud'homme.

Later, some people said that Gus had been hiding out in Prud'homme, but that wasn't true. He made no secret of his whereabouts; Gayle King of WFSB in Hartford came to Prud'homme with a television crew to interview him before the miniseries of his last novel, *A Season in Purgatory,* about the Bradley family and an unsolved murder in Greenwich, Connecticut, went on the air. He even agreed to walk up the long driveway with Gayle in an establishing shot, in which the exterior of his house was shown very distinctly in the background. Inside, during the interview, his living room was so identifiable on television that Gus's friend Mario Buatta, the decorator, called from New York to tell him the chintz on his living-room sofa was the same chintz that Mrs. Astor had in her library. It made Gus laugh. Finally, at this stage of his life, he was comfortably circumstanced.

As usual whenever he was interviewed about his upcoming miniseries, the interviewer talked more about the Simpson trial than about the miniseries of his book, or the case on which it was based, which was supposed to be the purpose of the interview.

"I'll never forget the look on your face at the time of the verdict, when the camera panned to you," said Gayle. It was a line that had been said to Gus over and over since the verdict. "We have a clip of it here as a matter of fact," said Gayle King. The video of the moment of acquittal appeared on the monitor, and Gayle's cameraman photographed Gus watching himself on the screen, at the shot he must have seen fifty times by then, of his mouth hanging open in disbelief after Deidre Robertson, the court clerk, read that Orenthal James Simpson was not guilty of the murders of Nicole Brown Simpson and Ronald Lyle Goldman.

Each time he saw it, he relived that moment. There, in his own living room, he could feel again his disbelief, his shock, and then the aching in his heart.

"Can you explain what you were feeling at that moment?" asked Gayle King.

"Shouldn't we be talking about my miniseries on Sunday and Tuesday nights on CBS?" asked Gus, not wanting to relive the moment.

"But you were there, Gus. You were in the room at the moment," said Gayle, pressing on.

Then, slowly, he began to speak. "I felt permeated by evil. I thought of the millions of dollars that had been spent, the lies that had been told, the cheating, the blackmail, the payoffs, the forgery, all that it took to make that moment of acquittal happen. Outrage seems to have gone out of fashion. I'm an old-fashioned kind of guy, Gayle. I still believe that killers should be locked up for life. They shouldn't be walking around among us."

To the surprise of some of his country friends, who were aware of his concern for safety after the death threats, Gus had even allowed his house to be open to the public for the annual Prud'homme Garden Club tour.

"It would help so much if you did, Gus," said Tom Rose, who owned the antiques shop in Prud'homme. "The garden-club ladies could sell a lot more tickets if your house were on the tour."

"Oh, all right," he finally agreed, although the reason he had gone to his house in Prud'homme was to get away from distractions that kept him from doing what he should be doing, writing his novel about the Simpson trial. Two thousand people went through his house in Prud'homme on the day of the tour, and many of them signed his guest book on the hall table, which he had forgotten to put away.

Gus was not unfamiliar with death threats. Several years before, after the first of the two trials of the Menendez brothers ended in a mistrial, he had called the young killers world-class liars in a *Vanity Fair* article, and had mocked the women of the jury for falling for what he believed were false claims of sexual molestation made by the defense. The threatening call he had received was from a poor relation of the rich brothers named Otto Santoro, making Gus aware that the possibility of vengeful murder existed. The viciousness of the call astonished and frightened him, and he was momentarily silenced, although he had the presence of mind to switch on the tape recorder attached to the telephone in his media room, a device that he sometimes used when interviewing people on the telephone. Although he later claimed to his friends and his sons that he hadn't taken Santoro's call seriously, he had. He sent the tape to Judy Spreckels, who was an authority on the Menendez case, telling her to give it to the police in case anything untoward ever happened to him.

"Has there been any attempt by the Skakel family in Greenwich to stop the miniseries of your book?" asked Howard Erskine a week before the show went on the air. Howard was Gus's oldest friend, from the time they had been roommates at Williams.

"Not that I know of," replied Gus.

"You didn't hear from their lawyer or anything?"

"I'm sure I would have heard from the network or my agent if such a thing had happened," said Gus. "CBS has been publicizing it for weeks, every hour on the hour practically, announcing my name about five times on each commercial and saying it was based on a true story that happened in a prominent Connecticut Catholic family."

"Amazing that you keep getting away with what you write, Gus," said Howard. "I used to worry about you after the way you wrote about Claus von Bülow. Then I used to worry about you after the way you wrote about the Kennedys at the Willie Smith rape trial. You told me yourself about that nut cousin who threatened you after what you wrote about the Menendez brothers being such liars. And now you have all these death threats for saying a guilty man has been acquitted in the Simpson trial."

"Do you have security in this house, Gus?" asked Colette Harron, a friend of Gus's in Prud'homme.

"I have an alarm system, yes," replied Gus.

"I mean, is there anyone who comes here and checks up on you?"

"The Bagwells and the Wagners both come by a couple of times a week. Why?" The Bagwells took care of the inside of Gus's house, and the Wagners took care of the outside, and both couples had become his friends.

"You annoy a lot of people, Gus," said Colette. "Your house is out in the open here. No neighbors. No dogs to bark. And your doors are always wide open. Anyone could walk in here."

"From nightfall on, I always close all the doors," said Gus. "I'm really quite careful. I barricade and bolt myself in nights."

"Do you close your gates at night?" she asked.

"No. Too much trouble to walk down there at night, especially in winter."

"You should get your gates electrified, Gus, and close them from the front hall without having to go outside. Push a button, that's all. That's what we did," said Colette. "There's a lot of nuts out there, and we all live at the end of long driveways."

"I'll look into that," said Gus.

"Do you ever get scared, Gus?"

"I never used to."

"But you do now?"

"Sometimes. I've been getting hang-ups lately," said Gus. "You're right about what you said. A lot of people do get angry at me. Last night there was a car parked down at the bottom of the driveway."

"That could just have been some fan who found out where you lived on the garden-club tour," said Colette.

"Probably. But it wasn't the first time I saw it there."

"Do you know anyone on the police up here?"

"Yes, I do, as a matter of fact. There's a state trooper named Conrad Winalski who lives right here in Prud'homme," said Gus. "I met him when I spoke about the trial at a fund-raiser for battered women at the governor's mansion in Hartford last week. He told me he's a big fan of Mark Fuhrman's."

"You ought to tell him about that car," said Colette.

"I will. I promise."

29

In his journal, which he kept daily for years, Gus seemed to accept the inevitability that what was going to happen was going to happen. He even seemed to understand the logic and the perfection of it as a final exit for him in the story of his life, which he fully expected someone would write after his death. Privately, he had picked the one, but no overture had ever been made.

The first time he met the biographer A. Scott Berg, at Nancy Livingstone's dinner for Sir Andrew Lloyd Webber before the opening of *Sunset Boulevard,* Gus said, "When I lectured at the Santa Barbara Writers Conference, I told all the fledgling writers to read your biography of Max Perkins if they wanted to know what writing was all about."

"Thank you, Gus," said Scott.

"When you described Perkins's understanding of the young Fitzgerald's talent before Fitzgerald understood it himself, I wanted to weep it was so beautiful," said Gus. Subsequently, they sometimes met to talk.

"It used to be that out here movie people only

talked about movies. Now they only want to talk about O.J.," said Gus. "I never knew until I read in your biography of Sam Goldwyn that Frances Goldwyn and George Cukor were buried together."

Following Gus's return from the Simpson trial in Los Angeles, his friend Jimmy Davison said to him, "You should write your memoirs, Gus, like Gore Vidal did. If you don't do it, someone else will, and whoever it is will probably concentrate on all the wrong things."

Gus nodded. He knew what the wrong things were.

"I never knew about that Oregon part of your life until I saw it on the BBC documentary they played on the Arts and Entertainment channel the other night," said Jimmy.

"I know, you're right," said Gus. "There was a time when I wouldn't have told the truth, or the whole truth, I should say, but I've passed that stage long since."

"Then do it," said Jimmy.

"I'll get to it. I have to write this O.J. novel first."

"Do you ever get sick of O.J. in your life, Gus?" asked the columnist Liz Smith when Gus had Sunday-night supper with her in the kitchen of her house in Prud'homme.

"Yes, I get sick of him. Deeply sick," replied

463

Gus. "He's taken up too much time in my life. But I can't give him up yet. I think about him all day long while I write my book. I talk about him at parties, or with whomever I'm having dinner, the way we're doing now. I talk about him to Deb at the gas station when she puts gas in my car. I talk about him to the train conductor on MetroNorth. I talk about him on the telephone to all my reporter friends, who always know I'm good for an over-the-top quote about him. I still read—two years later—every word that is written about him. I never miss Geraldo or Chuck Grodin or Larry King, in case they're talking about him, which they always are. My magazine gets me tapes of any show I might have missed. He's vented his anger at me on radio station KJLH-FM in Los Angeles, calling in from home, speaking in the patronizing voice of a man recently acquitted of two murders. He said I had only one perspective from day one. On that, he's absolutely right. I knew he was guilty from day one, and nothing has happened that has made me veer from that position. He singled me out in his speech at the Oxford Union in England, along with Tom Brokaw—I loved being grouped with Tom, climber that I still am—and also at the Scripture Cathedral in Washington just the other night. Did you see that show? It was terrifying— they practically put a death warrant on Geraldo Rivera, because Geraldo makes no bones about the fact that he believes O.J. is guilty of the crimes of which he was acquitted. Bravo, Geraldo. You'd think he'd know enough to go quietly into the night, to that ranch in Montana, or Wyoming, or wherever it was, that Schiller said he planned to go to for a few years if he was acquitted. But no such luck. He keeps pushing himself in our faces, waving from golf carts, as if he hadn't a care in the world. The sick part of it is, Liz, that it excites me to know that I have angered him enough to be singled out by him. Do you think I'm losing my mind?"

On the days leading up to the two nights that his miniseries was on the air, CBS played excerpts of his interview with Gayle to promote the show. Sitting in his media room, Gus watched. He saw his long driveway, his yellow house, his dock, and gazebo.

"I wonder why the hell I let them shoot the outside of the house," he said, talking to himself, which he sometimes did when he was alone at the house in Prud'homme.

Then the promo cut to his living room, where he was sitting on a chintz-covered sofa, saying about the acquittal, in reply to Gayle King's question, "I felt permeated by evil. I thought of the millions of dollars that had been spent, the lies that had been told, the cheating, the blackmail, the payoffs, the forgery, all that it took to make that moment of acquittal happen."

"That's about the seventh time today they've played that same sound bite," Gus said to himself, watching himself. "I'm beginning to sound like a nutcase."

The telephone rang.

"Gus, you've been on television all day long," said Colette Harron.

"I was just saying to myself I've begun to sound like a nutcase, they've run that sound bite so many times," said Gus.

"Why don't you come over tonight and watch your miniseries with us?" said Colette. "We'll have dinner on trays in front of the television. Just us. No party."

"Thanks, but I like to be alone when I watch my miniseries," said Gus. "I want to be near the telephone. I'm sure the boys will call when it's over."

"And some of your fans," said Colette.

"Hardly. My luster is dimming. I was in the A and P today, and not one person came up to me to talk about O.J."

"Do you want company?" asked Colette. "I hate to think of you there all alone. Peter and I will come over, if you'd like."

"No, really, this is the way I always watch my shows," said Gus. "I get nervous when I'm with other people, wondering about their reactions rather than concentrating on the movie. Oh, God, I just realized I was taping this conversation. Let me turn this damn thing off."

"Why?" asked Colette.

"I had this amazing telephone call from O.J. Simpson's niece today, and I recorded it, like I sometimes do when I interview people over the phone. But I didn't tell Terri I taped it."

"O.J.'s niece? What did she want?"

"She called about the miniseries. She read the book during the trial. She's a very nice young woman. Then she told me that she had told her mother she thought Uncle O.J. *might* have been guilty, and her mother hit her. She said, 'That's how great my mother's denial is.' It must be tough living like that, the whole family in denial. Is your TV on? They've got another sound bite of me about the miniseries tonight."

On the screen, Gus was saying, "The miniseries is based on an actual unsolved murder in Greenwich, Connecticut, where a fifteen-year-old girl was savagely and brutally beaten to death by a wealthy young man whose powerful family has been able to hold off the police."

"I wonder if the Skakels are watching," said Gus.

Gus Bailey's body was discovered by Jackie Bagwell, the owner of the Bagwell Cleaning Service in Prud'homme, when she arrived the next morning for her regular day at Gus's house. Standing in the front hall, she called out, "Hello," to let him know she had arrived. His tweed jacket hung on the newel post at the bottom of the stairway, where he always hung it, along with his blue baseball cap with *CBS Evening News* embroidered on it in white. When he didn't answer, she assumed that he was already at work in his office, which was outside the house in what had once been a caretaker's apartment attached to the garage. Jackie was forty and pretty. She and her husband, Dana, had a married daughter who lived in Honolulu and a teenage son who played football at Old Prud'homme High School and worked nights at the A & P. Jackie read Gus's books and articles and watched all his television appearances.

"You were great on *Sixty Minutes,*" she said one time. "Do you think Steve Kroft will be able to prove there was jury tampering?"

"Oh, I hope so," Gus replied.

"What I can't understand is how Judge Ito could kick Francine whatever-her-last-name-is off the jury on the basis of an anonymous letter," said Jackie. She was up on every detail of the case, and she accepted Gus's version of things as gospel.

"In my day, Jackie, they flushed anonymous letters down the toilet; they didn't act on them. Francine Florio-Bunten was the only juror who understood the relevance of DNA, and she would have hung the jury. She wouldn't have capitulated to the pressure and voted for acquittal like the other one did. The defense wanted to get rid of her from the beginning. Don't get me going, Jackie, or I'll get all worked up again over Simpson's acquittal, and I won't get any work done."

Today Jackie was eager to discuss Part Two of the miniseries, which had been on the air the night before. Keeping to her regular routine, Jackie went upstairs first to Gus's bathroom and gathered up his dirty laundry to put in the washing machine in the basement. That his bed had not been slept in did not

468

concern her. He was fastidious about making his own bed as soon as he arose each morning, and she assumed that he had forgotten that it was her day to change the sheets. She stripped the bed, emptied his laundry basket, and carried the pile down to the basement. When the washing machine was going, she went up to the cleaning closet on the first floor, next to the lavatory, and got out the vacuum cleaner, broom, mop, and her pails of sprays, soaps, and polishes. She noticed that the light in the lavatory was on. Then she saw that one of the framed Robert Risko caricatures of Gus that hung on the lavatory wall was awry, the one of him with Faye Resnick, Cici Shahian, and Robin Greer, which had appeared in *Vanity Fair* during the Simpson trial.

Jackie put down her utensils to straighten it. She knew that Gus hated pictures that were awry. Then she saw that the toilet paper with the picture of O.J. Simpson on every sheet, which the Marburgs had given him for Christmas, had been yanked off the roll and was lying on the floor. As she leaned down to pick it up, she recoiled at the sight of blood, for it looked as if a bloody hand had been wiped on it.

"Gus? Gus?" she called out. There was no answer. Stifling the panic she was beginning to feel, she opened the front door and ran outside to his office. The door was locked. The light was not turned on inside. He had not been there. Then she thought that maybe he had gone to New York unexpectedly, as he often did, without telling anybody. She looked through the garage window. His Volvo station wagon and his green convertible Jaguar were both there. She ran back into the house. In the front hallway, she turned left to the living room. Gus was a stickler for order, for having everything in its right place.

She saw with her expert eye that everything *was* in its right place in the huge room: the orchid plants, the Chinese export porcelain, the leather-bound first editions of Anthony Trollope and Edith Wharton, the silver-framed photographs of his children and his former wife, Peach, of whom he always spoke with affection. Surprisingly, however, the door to the terrace off the living room was open. Then she walked slowly, as if anticipating something dreadful, into the smaller room beyond, which he had insisted on calling his media room, although it was in fact merely a library with a large-screen television set, a few hundred videos of old movies, a vast collection of CD's, framed book jackets of his novels and collections of essays, and photographs of some of the famous people he had interviewed or written about over the years. Imelda Marcos. Elizabeth Taylor. Audrey Hepburn. Mrs. Jacqueline Kennedy Onassis. The Collins sisters, Joan and Jackie. Queen Noor of Jordan. The Glenconners from England with their friend Princess Margaret. Claus von Bülow and his mistress at the time of his second trial, Andrea Reynolds. And others. It was in this small room that the two thousand people who had gone through his house on the Prud'homme Garden Club tour had lingered to look at the glamorous figures in the photographs.

"Is that Princess Diana talking to Gus Bailey?" was the most frequent question asked of the docent on duty in that room on the day of the tour. Others asked, "Could you possibly read me the inscription that Nancy Reagan wrote to Gus Bailey on that picture in the silver frame?" Or, "Isn't that a shot of Claudette Colbert and Ann-Margret from the miniseries of one of his books?"

"I'm going to have to ask you to keep moving on to the next room," the docent said over and over. "There are others waiting."

Gus had often told his friends that his house in Prud'homme would be his last house; he wanted to have all the things that mattered to him in one place. The tables in the media room were filled with the memorabilia of his life: the leather box that held his Bronze Star from the Battle of the Bulge, where he had saved a man's life; the lucite clock with the insignia of the Los Angeles County Sheriff's Department, which the deputies at the trial of the Menendez brothers had given him; a cheap watch on the face of which a police car followed a white Bronco in a battery-operated unending freeway chase, a memento of the Simpson trial given to him by a reporter friend named Dennis Schatzman; and the key to the city of Providence, Rhode Island. Sacha Newley's portrait of him, which was to be the book jacket of his next novel, *Another City, Not My Own*, hung on the Chinese-red wall. In the portrait, he is writing his novel with a maroon Mont Blanc pen in a green leather notebook with gold-tipped pages, one of the dozen from Smythson's in London that Graydon Carter, the editor of his magazine, gave him for Christmas each year. There, in front of the bay window, on the Chinese-red sofa, its vivid color on first sight absorbing the enormous amount of blood that had spilled on it, lay the dead body of Gus Bailey. It was faceless.

Jackie Bagwell screamed and screamed, but there was no one to hear her. Afraid to be in the house, she ran out the front door and over to Gus's office. She knew where the key was kept, under the eave of the garage. She unlocked the office and went in to use the telephone. Crying, verging on hysteria, she told her husband, Dana, "He has no face. They shot off Gus's face! Call the police."

In his left hand was the clicker for the VCR. In time it would come to light that he had stopped the VCR as he was expiring, possibly to give a clue to the police as to the time of his death. The video showed that he had clicked it off during the scene in which the bloody clothes of Constant Bradley are found by boys fishing on the dock, found after Constant has been acquitted of Winifred Utley's savage murder, clothes that were valueless now as evidence against him, since he cannot be tried twice for the same murder. In his green leather notebook, while watching that scene in his miniseries, Gus wrote the last words that he would ever write: "This same thing is going to happen in the Simpson case; the bloody clothes are going to be found. Too late, of course."

The time of death, according to the video, was 10:46 P.M.

Zander Bailey made the arrangements for a three-way conference call between the cabin where he was living in northern California, the George V in Paris, where Grafton was casting his next movie, and their mother's house in Nogales, Arizona. The brothers wanted to break the news to their mother together. Zander, who was meticulous in his preparations, had instructed the nurses to keep the television set off until they had finished telling their mother.

"Mom, Dad's dead," said Grafton from Paris.

There was no reply.

"Did you hear me, Mom?" asked Grafton.

"Yes." Her name was Rebecca, but she had been called Peach all her life.

"Mom, it's Zander," said Zander from northern California. "Someone shot him dead in his house in Prud'homme."

There was no reply.

"Did you hear me, Mom?"

"Yes."

"They don't know who did it," said Grafton.

It was not the first time the three people had played this scene.

As word of the murder spread, a constant stream of people from Prud'homme, Old Prud'homme, Chester, and East Prud'homme, where the old opera house was, walked, bicycled, or drove slowly by the house, staring and whispering. Nothing so exciting had ever happened in Prud'homme. In the milling crowd, conspicuously alone, was a woman named Zara Soames, a newcomer to the area. Her eyes were red from crying. She pushed her bike from group to group, listening to all the latest bits of news. "I knew him," she said aloud on several occasions, overcoming her shyness, but her voice was meek and did not carry.

"There is a woman who has developed an obsession about me," Gus had said to his friend Alexandra Isles on the day of the garden-club tour of his house. "She moved to Prud'homme because I am here. She sends me flowers. She writes me poems. She cooks me muffins. Once I found her in my house. She is driving me crazy. I don't know how to deal with it."

"Are you afraid of her, Gus?" asked Alexandra.

"No. It's not like that, I don't think," Gus replied.

That night Gus Bailey's death was on every newscast. Dan Rather opened his *CBS Evening News* with the story, even though reports of Hillary Clinton's alleged séance with Eleanor Roosevelt were the main topic of the day on the other networks.

"Augustus Bailey, the novelist, journalist, and special correspondent for *Vanity Fair* magazine, who appeared on this program each Friday night from Los Angeles during the O.J. Simpson trial, was shot to death last night at his house in Prud'homme, Connecticut, where he was writing a novel set in Los Angeles during the Simpson trial. As of this moment, details of Bailey's murder are sketchy, and there are apparently no suspects. Three shots were fired into Bailey's face. Local police investigating the case say there is little doubt the killing was a carefully planned professional job. Correspondent Bill Whitaker, who became a personal friend of Gus Bailey's during the Simpson trial, reports from Prud'homme, Connecticut."

Bill Whitaker stood by the closed white wooden gates at the bottom of Gus's driveway. In the background, at a higher level, could be seen his yellow frame house with the gambrel roof. Police walked in and out of the front door.

"In this lovely, quiet town on the Connecticut River, violence has always been an unknown thing, unknown, at least, until now. Sometime in the half hour between ten-thirty and eleven o'clock last night, a person or persons entered this house behind me, belonging to the writer Augustus Bailey, through a terrace door opening off the living room. There are unconfirmed reports that the perpetrator may have arrived by a small motor boat, coming off the river into Whalebone Cove behind the house, and tied up at the small dock at the bottom of Bailey's garden. I have with me Police Chief Charles Olin of Westbrook, Connecticut."

"Do I look at you or straight into the camera?" asked Chief Olin.

"To me," said Whitaker. "Go on, sir."

"This sort of thing is new up here for us, you know," said the chief. "Things like this don't happen here, but a lot of celebrities have moved into the area in the last few years and bought up the old places, and I guess things change."

"Were there any signs of struggle?" asked Whitaker.

"None. Mr. Bailey was sitting on the sofa in his media room watching television. He had the VCR clicker in his left hand, taping the show he was watching. It is our feeling that the perpetrator entered the house through the terrace doors, which were open. There seems to be little doubt that the killing was a carefully planned professional job. You're going to have to excuse me, Mr. Whitaker. I see one of my boys calling me."

"Thank you, Chief Olin," said Whitaker.

Rather turned directly to the camera. "We'll keep you up to date on this story. Beleaguered First Lady Hillary Clinton denied emphatically today that she was involved in a séance with Eleanor Roosevelt. 'It's politics,' she said in New York."

News crews from Hartford, Boston, Providence, and New York were posted outside the gates, leaning on the fence. John Wagner and his wife, Kathy, who took care of the grounds at Gus's house, had made themselves known to the police and were helping out with crowd control and the protection of Gus's property. "No sitting on that fence, mister," Wagner called out to one reporter, who promptly removed himself. "No trampling on his roses," Wagner called out to another, as if Gus himself might appear from the house to complain of the desecration of his rose garden.

"It was on his mind that something like this was going to happen," said Wagner to State Trooper Conrad Winalski. "Kathy and I do his yard work, take care of his roses, take his trash to the dump, and I fix things for him that need to get fixed, paint the screen doors, stuff like that. I also take care of his cars and drive the Jag over to Hartford every couple of months for checkups. So I saw a lot of Gus, almost every day, and we always had talks, and I got to know him really well. A while back, he called me to come over. He seemed upset when I got here to the house—kind of like a disturbed look in his eyes. He took me into the living room and pointed to the floor, over where that stone eagle is by the terrace door. There were shards of glass from a broken window, and above, in the glass door leading out to the terrace, the outer edges of a smashed windowpane. He asked me, 'Do you think that was a shot? Do you think someone fired in here from the terrace?'"

"What was it?" asked Winalski.

"There had been a terrible storm the night before, one of those thunder–lightning–high wind kind of storms. It had lifted a large umbrella on Gus's terrace out of its base, and the umbrella flew toward the window like a guided missile and smashed it. I can understand how he could have thought it was a shot. When I told him what it was, he laughed. He said, 'I had myself believing I even heard the shot.'"

"But it was nothing," said Winalski.

"The point of the story is that he *really* thought someone had taken a shot at him in his house. When they had that garden-club tour—like about two thousand strangers walking through his house—Kathy and I were there keeping an eye on everything. Gus had a lot of little stuff on every table, and anybody could pick up something, like a souvenir from Gus Bailey's house. There could have been someone going through his house that day to get the lay of the land."

The limousine pulled up to the closed white gates of Gus Bailey's house. A policeman held up his hand. "No one, *no one,* can get through," he said to the driver. The members of the media started to crowd around the limousine, trying to see inside, but the darkened windows proved impenetrable. The driver's window came down. The driver had a beard and spoke with an Israeli accent. "I have here in the back the two sons of Gus Bailey," he said to the policeman. "We have just driven up from New York."

"My orders are that no one can go through these gates," repeated the policeman.

The back window came down. "I am Grafton

Bailey, and this is my brother, Zander. We are Augustus Bailey's sons. I have just flown in from Paris, and I am going into my father's house, whether you like it or not. We'd both appreciate it if you'd open the gate, or we'll drive through."

Grafton Bailey, now a film director, used to be an actor, and Officer Winalski recognized him from *An American Werewolf in London,* one of his favorite cult movies, the video of which he had borrowed from Gus several times. "Yes, yes, Mr. Bailey. I just have to check with Chief Olin and tell him who you are. You'll be in the house in a minute. Let me tell you how sorry I am about your father."

"Thank you," said Grafton.

"You were great in *Werewolf.*"

"Thanks."

"I'll get the chief."

"Thanks."

Grafton sat back and rolled up the window.

"Hey, Grafton, give us a picture," yelled out one of the photographers who had gathered around the car. "Roll down the window. Listen, we're sorry about your father. He always stopped when we asked him."

"Later, guys, not now," Grafton called back through the darkened window. "Okay, Dov, let's go. The gate's open."

Months passed. There were no breaks in the case. Gus's murder went unsolved. There had been endless speculation in the media immediately after the murder. Liz Smith, the gossip columnist, quoted friends who had come forward to talk about the hang-up telephone calls, the mysterious car at the bottom of the driveway, and other strange things they could remember. Then the media glare dimmed. Even in Prud'homme, Gus's death ceased to be a main topic of conversation. Like the unsolved Moxley murder in Greenwich, about which Gus had written so passionately, time passed on his own murder. Other things happened to divert the attention of people. Bernard Lafferty, who had inherited his fortune from Doris Duke's estate, died suddenly in Los Angeles. JonBenet Ramsey was murdered in Boulder. Ennis Crosby was murdered in Los Angeles.

It was only later, when Scott Berg, who was writing Gus's biography and who had been given access to the house in Prud'homme by Grafton and Zander before it was dismantled and sold, discovered quite by accident a pocket-size tape recorder far back in the drawer of the coffee table that sat in front of the Chinese-red sofa where Gus's body had been found. A wire with a rubber suction device used for recording telephone conversations was still inserted into the recorder. The bloodstained sofa had been removed and burned at the local dump after the police had finished with it, so Berg took the recorder out to the office where Gus had been writing his book. There he sat in Gus's chair in front of his computer. On the bulletin board, just as Gus had left them, were pushpinned the color photographs of Nicole Brown Simpson and Ronald Goldman dead, lying in pools of blood in the patio of Nicole's condo on Bundy, which Julie Coolidge had brought to him from the photo lab where Simpson's private investigators had taken them to be developed.

"Why do you keep those terrible photographs up there in front of you, Gus?" Cynthia McFadden had once asked when she came by for a visit.

"I'm so afraid Nicole and Ron are going to be forgotten as O.J.'s publicity machine starts its campaign for his reacceptance into society," said Gus.

The batteries in the tape recorder were dead, but Gus kept a well-stocked office, and Scott Berg soon found fresh ones. He rewound the tape and played it from the beginning:

"Gus, I don't know who to talk to, and my family always respected you, so I called Shoreen for your number, but she wouldn't give it to me because it's unlisted, and so on and so on, and I hope you don't mind that I'm calling you at your house in Connecticut."

"No, no, fine."

"I know you're working on your novel."

"That's okay, Terri. What's up? Are your parents okay?"

"It's hard being a member of this family, Gus, what we've gone through, what we're going through still."

481

"The last time I saw your mother, the day of the verdict, she looked so much older than when I first saw her before the trial."

"I know. My father, too."

"Benny's hair turned white during the trial."

"I know, my poor father. This is all we've talked about since Nicole was killed. This is what our life became. We pulled up stakes and became part of Uncle O.J.'s support group. My parents hardly ever missed a day in court. Every time Uncle O.J. entered the court, they smiled at him. Nights we either went down to the jail, to keep him company, or we sat around the table at Rockingham and talked about what had happened in court that day. Our lives didn't matter. Our lives became about his life. I couldn't take it after awhile. I started to drink during the trial. Did you know that? I couldn't go to sleep if I didn't take a six-pack to bed with me. My parents sent me to a rehab. I'm all right again. I'm in the program. I go to meetings. I have a sponsor. I'm back at my job again."

"Good girl, Terri. I'm in the program, too. Did you know that?"

"I kind of suspected it. In one of your books I read, the one about the mistress of Pauline Mendelson's husband, who was the friend of the President of the United States."

"I know the plot."

"You talked about the seven A.M. Log Cabin Meeting on Robertson Boulevard, and that's the

meeting I go to. So I kind of figured you probably were."

"What's up?"

"I wanted to wish you good luck on the show
tonight on television. I read the book, you
know."

"I remember. I felt very flattered when you
did."

"I need to talk to you, Gus. I need some
advice."

"First, tell me one thing, Terri. I never had
the nerve to ask Shirley and Benny this, and I've
often wondered. Do all of you really think O.J.
didn't do it? Or is that the family party line, as
directed by Shapiro and Cochran?"

"Listen to me, Gus. Once I told my parents in
the car when we were going to church that I
thought Uncle O.J. may have done what they
said he did. I didn't even say I thought he did it, I
said that I thought he *might* have done it, that's
all, and my mother hit me and pounded me in the
backseat of the car. I'm thirty-two years old,
Gus, and I know my mama loves me, but that
shows how great the denial is in our family."

"Your mother's a good woman, Terri. This
must have been a terrible ordeal for her."

"My parents don't have anything. They've
spent the last two years of their lives down here
away from their home, supporting Uncle O.J.,
being there for him, believing him. Do you have
any idea how much energy it takes to believe

something you don't believe? He's going to forget about us now. He doesn't need us anymore now that everything's over."

"Are you serious?"

"Oh, very serious. We were always in this strange position in our family, Gus, where we lived. We were related to this big famous celebrity, and that made us different from everyone, like we were special, but we never saw him, or hardly ever saw him. When he talked about family, it was Nicole's family he was close to, not our family. I'm sorry if I'm crying. Listen, Gus, is there any chance you're going to be out here? I know you're working on your book, but it's hard to talk on the phone. I need to make some money, Gus, some real money. If my parents have to move, I want to be able to buy them something."

"Are you talking about writing a book, Terri?"

"I'm afraid to even say it, Gus. This conversation can't get out. This has to be private. Something could happen to me."

"Don't worry. I've got tight lips. You've got to be prepared. They're going to ask you questions—what's it like nights in that house on Rockingham? What do you guys talk about at dinner? How much do Justin and Sydney know? What's the mood there now that Uncle O.J. is yesterday's news?"

"Jesus, Gus."

"That's what they're going to ask you if you want to get a deal somewhere. Could you handle that?"

"I don't know. I can't be disloyal to my family."

"If you're thinking about a pro-O.J. book, telling what a swell guy he is, forget it. No publisher would touch it. Your uncle's a hated man."

"Not pro-Uncle O.J., Gus. Not con either. Just what it's been like for us, being there, some of the things we saw, like the way Shapiro and Uncle O.J. were talking to Kato Kaelin at Rockingham on the night after the murders. Stuff like that."

"I heard about that from Grant Cramer."

"They had Kato in a corner and talked to him in low voices for the longest time."

"Setting up the old alibi. Actually, I am going to be out there soon for a couple of days. I'll call you, Terri."

There was the sound of two receivers hanging up. Then a second conversation started.

"Gus, you've been on television all day long."

"I was just saying to myself I've begun to sound like a nutcase, they've run that sound bite so many times."

"Why don't you come over tonight and watch your miniseries with us. We'll have dinner

485

on trays in front of the television. Just us. No party."

"Thanks, but I like to be alone when I watch my miniseries. I want to be near the telephone. I'm sure the boys will call when it's over."

"And some of your fans."

"Hardly. My luster is dimming. I was in the A and P today, and not one person came up to me to talk about O.J."

"Do you want company? I hate to think of you there all alone. Peter and I will come over, if you like."

"No, really, this is the way I always watch my shows. I get nervous when I'm with other people, wondering about their reactions rather than concentrating on the movie. Oh, God, I just realized I was taping this conversation. Let me turn this damn thing off."

"Why?"

"I had this amazing telephone call from O.J. Simpson's niece today, and I recorded it, like I sometimes do when I interview people over the phone. But I didn't tell Terri I taped it."

"O.J.'s niece? What did she want?"

"She called about the miniseries. She read the book during the trial. She's a very nice young woman. Then she told me that she told her mother she thought Uncle O.J. *might* have been guilty, and her mother hit her. She said, 'That's how great my mother's denial is.' It must be tough living like that, the whole family in denial.

Is your TV on? They've got another sound bite of me about the miniseries tonight."

"The miniseries is based on an actual unsolved murder in Greenwich, Connecticut, where a fifteen-year-old girl was savagely and brutally beaten to death by a wealthy young man whose powerful family has been able to hold off the police."

"I wonder if the Skakels are watching."

Berg listened again to the sound of two receivers hanging up. Then another voice came on:

"I can't imagine what show you're watching, Gus."

"What? Oh, my God! You terrified me. How did you get in this house?"

"I said to myself, Gus Bailey may go out to dinner every night of his life, but my money says that on the night his miniseries is on the air he's going to be sitting there all alone watching it in his media room. I'm a regular reader of *Architectural Digest*. That's how I know you call this your media room."

"What are you doing here? I can't remember your name."

"It'll come to you. I met you with Marcia Clark, remember? I met you with Bernard Lafferty, remember? You pretended you didn't know me at that party in New York for Princess Firyal of Jordan."

"Andrew Cunanan."

"I told you it would come to you."

"What the fuck are you doing in Prud'homme, Connecticut?"

The tape recorder stopped abruptly as the tape ran out. Berg rewound the tape to the beginning of the last conversation. He wrote down the name Andrew Cunanan. Then he picked up the telephone, thought for a moment before dialing, and replaced the receiver. For several minutes he sat there, perplexed.

Had Gus still been with us, he would have easily understood Scott Berg's dilemma. Should he pick up the telephone and call the home of State Trooper Conrad Winalski, whose number was in Gus's book, or should he save it for the final chapter of his biography of Gus Bailey?